Strengthening Social Solidarity through Group Work
Research and creative practice

I0124535

Proceedings of the XXXII International Symposium
on Social Work with Groups
Montréal, June 3 – 6, 2010

Strengthening Social Solidarity through Group Work

Research and creative practice

Edited by

**Valérie Roy, Ginette Berteau,
and Sacha Genest-Dufault**

w&b

MMXIV

© Whiting & Birch Ltd 2014
Published by Whiting & Birch Ltd,
Forest Hill, London SE23 3HZ

ISBN 9781861771261

Printed in England and the United States by Lightning Source

Contents

About the Editors

Valérie Roy Ph.D., Social Worker, is Professor at the School of Social Work at Université Laval (Quebec city, Canada). She teaches and specializes in group work and intimate partner violence.

Ginette Berteau A social worker and professor at the School of Social Work at the University of Quebec, Montreal (UQAM, Canada), Ginette Berteau has always been a passionate believer in group social work. That enthusiasm has led her to do group work, train and supervise social workers and students, earn a PhD in the skills specific to group work and publish a book on the subject.

Sacha Genest-Dufault , Social Worker, is Professor at the School of Social Work at Université du Quéebec à Rimouski (Rimouski, Canada). He teaches and specializes in gender studies and group work.

The Contributors

Allan E. Barsky, JD, MSW, PhD is Professor of Social Work at Florida Atlantic University in Boca Raton. He is also Chair of the National Ethics Committee of the National Association of Social Workers. Dr. Barsky's book authorships include *Conflict Resolution for the Helping Professions,, Ethics and Values in Social Work, Alcohol, Other Drugs, and Addictions,* and *Clinicians in Court.* Dr. Barsky may be reached at barsky@barsky.org.

Jean Bédard D.Ph. is a philosopher, a writer and a care worker. His area of interests is about women and men who made history, who live fully their spiritual experience, and who are at the same time people of intellect and lucidity, and politically engaged.

Catherine Coulthard, MSW, RSW is the social worker for the Inflammatory Bowel Disease (IBD) Program at Mount Sinai Hospital, Toronto, Canada. She facilitates a peer steering committee for a large IBD network, thereby utilizing small-group tools with large-group programs. She has presented her work at AASWG symposia and at Groupwork Camp.

Jean-Philippe É. Daoust, MAP, PhD is Professor of psychiatry at the University of Ottawa. He is also Psychologist and a Researcher at the Mental Health Program of the Hôpital Montfort in Ottawa, Canada. Dr. Daoust may be reached at jpdaoust@uottawa.ca.

Brenda L. Exum, MSW, ACSW is a Social Work Professor at Norfolk State University. For over 30 years she has been committed to empowerment and encouraging civic engagement with a focus on diversity. She has been active in leadership in NASW-VA, an International Trainer in the Art of Dialogue and is the founder of Hampton Roads Trust Building Taskforce. Her advanced training has included Public Peace Process Training at Kettering Foundation and Community Building Fellowships at Initiatives of Change.

Gilles Fleury, MD, FRCPC, is Professor of Psychiatry at the University of Ottawa. He is also Psychiatrist and Researcher at the Mental Health Program of the Hôpital Montfort in Ottawa, Canada. Dr. Fleury may be reached at gfleury@montfort.on.ca.

Martin Goyette Professor at the Ecole nationale d'administration publique (ENAP) since June 2007 and permanent professor since 2009. Martin Goyette has a doctorate (PhD) in Social Work from Laval University, and completed postdoctoral studies at the center for urban culture and society at INRS. His research focuses on the understanding of the experience and analysis of individuals and the forms of public interventions implemented to support them. He focuses specifically on the autonomy in transition to adulthood of young people, with youths at the end of their placement period, the dynamics of social inclusion / exclusion and the analysis of social networks. His work has been subjected to numerous publications. Since 2009, professor Goyette is chairholder of the Canada Research Chair in Evaluating Public Actions Related to Young People and Vulnerable Populations. In 2010, Professor Martin Goyette was nominated to the University of Québec Circle of Excellence and in 2012, Goyette win a Research Prize (2007-2012) of his institution.

Stéphane Grenier is Program Director of Social Work at the University of Quebec in Abitibi-Témiscamingue. He specializes in research partnership with Aboriginal communities. Stephane.Grenier@uqat.ca

Victor Hainsworth at the time of writing was at the Adelphi University School of Social Work

Alice Home, MSW, PhD, is professor emeritus of social work at University of Ottawa where her teaching focused on group work, research, community and preventive practice. Her practice interests centre on empowerment and mutual aid groups especially with women. Her current research examines parenting adopted children with special needs and groups for parents of children with invisible disabilities. She continues to publish extensively on these topics in a range of peer-reviewed journals and edited books.

Madhu Kushwaha, M.A. in Sociology and Ph.D. in Education, is Associate Professor, Faculty of Education, Banaras Hindu University,

Varanasi, India. Her area of specialization includes Sociology of Education and Gender Issues in Education. Her writings include Social Contexts of Women Education in India, Social Correlates of Educational Aspirations of Girls, School-Home Language Gap: Effects on First Generation Learners of Deprived Sections etc. She can be reached at: mts.kushwaha@gmail.com.

Dana Grossman Leeman, PhD, MSW, is Associate Professor of Practice at Simmons College School of Social Work in Boston, Massachusetts. She created, teaches, and coordinates multiple sections of a required social work with groups course and an advanced group work elective. Most recently she created an interdisciplinary post-Masters certificate in Advanced Group Work Practice, which will begin in Fall 2012. She provides ongoing group work consultation and training to several social service agencies in the Boston area, and provides writing mentoring to staff who wish to publish about their practice. She is the Massachusetts representative to the Board of AASWG, and serves on the executive committee as co-chair of symposia. She can be reached at dana.leeman@simmons.edu.

Diane Lavallée was the Director of the Mental Health Program of the Hôpital Montfort in Ottawa, Canada. Mrs. Lavallée may be reached at dlavallee@montfort.on.ca.

Andrée-Anne Lemay is a social worker. She works for the protection of youth in an Aboriginal community in northern Quebec.

Valérie Lemieux, BSc was a Research assistant at the Mental Health Program of the Hôpital Montfort in Ottawa, Canada. Mrs. Lemieux may be reached at vlemi081@uottawa.ca.

Kristy Macdonell, MSW RSW is a Clinical NICU Social Worker and Program Developer at Mount Sinai Hospital, Toronto, Canada, and an adjunct lecturer with the University of Toronto's Faculty of Social Work.

Mark J. Macgowan, PhD, LCSW, is Professor of Social Work at Florida International University in Miami, and recently served as Fulbright-Scotland Visiting Professor at the University of Edinburgh (2012-2013). He is Co-Chair, Commission on Social Work Education of the International Association for Social Work with Groups. Dr.

Macgowan's books include A Guide to Evidence-Based Group Work (Oxford University Press, OUP) and Evidence-Based Group Work in Community Settings (with David Pollio; Taylor & Francis). Dr. Macgowan may be reached at Macgowan@fiu.edu.

Amber Oke, MSW RSW was, at the time of writing, the social worker for Inpatient Gastrointestinal Oncology/General Surgery at Mount Sinai Hospital, Toronto, Canada. She is now the social worker for Slow Stream Rehabilitation and Complex Continuing Care, Credit Valley Hospital, Mississauga, Ontario.

Alexis Pearson was, at the time of writing, a graduate student at the University of Montréal

Danielle Perron-Roach, MSS, TSI is Social worker at the Mental Health Program of the Hôpital Montfort in Ottawa, Canada. She is also an accredited WRAP facilitator by the Copeland Center. Mrs. Perron-Roach may be reached at dperron@montfort.on.ca.

Michael Preston-Shoot, PhD, is Professor of Social Work and Dean of the Faculty of Health and Social Sciences at the University of Bedfordshire. He has specialised in teaching law to social workers and has recently published a series of articles in Social Work Education, Medical Education and the Journal of Medical Ethics on the outcomes of teaching and learning law in social work education and medical education. He has also researched how social workers have used legal rules in decision-making and in practice education, both papers published in the Journal of Social Work. He has recently completed research projects on adult protection in England and in Scotland, and has undertaken a systemic review of the effectiveness of governance arrangements for safeguarding children in England. He is a founding editor of the journal Ethics and Social Welfare and is the independent chair of a Local Safeguarding Children Board and a Local Safeguarding Adult Board in a local authority in England.

Sanjay, Ph. D. in social work, is Associate Professor of Social Work, M. G. Kashi Vidyapith Varanasi, India. He is a co-founder of MASVAW (Men's Action for Stopping Violence Against Women), FEM (Forum to Engage men) India and Masculinity and Society, Quebec, Canada. Dr. Sanjay's book authorships include Preventing the Culture of Violence: A Need for Positive Fatherhood, Ending Gender Based Violence:

Highlighting the Role of Men, Gender Sexuality and HIV/AIDS, Men's Sexual Practices and Policies, He can be reached at: sanjaysinghdr@sify.com.

Joanne Sulman, MSW, RSW is the research and group work consultant for Mount Sinai Hospital's Department of Social Work in Toronto, Canada, and an adjunct lecturer with the University of Toronto's Faculty of Social Work. Her groupwork interests include collectivity theory, single session groups and the use of groupwork skills in focus groups. Her clinical interests include the development and facilitation of a drop-in group for persons whose lives have been severely affected by IBD.

Lieve Verhaeghe, MSW, RSW is a social worker with the Mount Sinai Hospital Psychiatric Day Treatment Program, a 12 week group therapy program to help people who have received inpatient mental health care transition back to the community. Lieve was involved in the creation and development of the program and facilitates groups with her interdisciplinary colleagues.

Aviva Werek Sokolsky, Dip.S.S. RSSW is a social worker with Women's Unit and Out-patient Perinatology at Mount Sinai Hospital, Toronto, Canada. She is currently co-facilitating a group for single women who are electing to become mothers by choice.

Trisha Woodhead, MSW, RSW is the social worker for the Mount Sinai Hospital Breast Centre and Out-patient Oncology Unit. Trisha uses mutual aid in groups with women with early stage breast cancer to help them transition to post-treatment lives.

Kathleen M. Walsh, PhD, LCSW is an Assistant Professor and BSW Program Coordinator at Millersville University Department of Social Work, and a member of the Association for the Advancement of Social Work with Groups. She teaches a variety of policy and practice courses at both the undergraduate and graduate level and has vast generalist practice experience from micro, mezzo to macro practice. Her research includes predictors of salary in social work, workforce equity issues, social work professionalism, ethics and supervision.

Sue Worrod, MEd, MSW, RSW is the social worker for the Sarcoma Program at Mount Sinai Hospital in Toronto, Canada. She co-facilitates support groups for both sarcoma patients as well as caregivers of sarcoma patients. Sue also co-facilitates the annual Sarcoma Education Night.

Stephen J. Yanca, PhD, DIPLO, ACSW, LMSW, LMFT, was Professor of Social Work at Saginaw Valley State University. Prior to his recent passing, he was a productive university scholar and an active member of IASWG. He received an MSW from Wayne State University, and a Ph.D. from Michigan State University. He had experience in counseling, group work, child welfare, juvenile corrections, community mental health, supervision, and administration. He was the co-author of three social work texts, and his life and contributions are still cherished by his former students and colleagues.

Mary Yanisko, MSW , recently retired as an Assistant Professor in the School of Social Work at Norfolk State University. She continues to be active in the Hampton Roads community through volunteer activities, training, advocacy and hospice work.

Acknowledgements

Association for the Advancement of Social Work with Groups, Inc.

XXXII Annual International Symposium
Montreal, Quebec, Canada, June 3–6, 2010

Strengthening Social Solidarity Through Group Work:
Research and creative practices

The following people played a significant role in the success of the 32nd Symposium. We would like to thank them for their enthusiasm, their efforts and their high standards: Martine Beaulieu, Gaëlle Bonnet, Ghislaine Brosseau, Tom Caplan, Isabelle Côté, Nicole Dallaire, Sacha Genest-Dufault, Judith Goudreau, Étienne Guay, Alice Home, Marie Lacaille, Jocelyn Lindsay, Annie Pullen-Sansfaçon, Luc Trottier, and Daniel Turcotte. A special thank you also to Dominique Moyse Steinberg for her invaluable advice and support.

We would also like to thank all the institutions, organizations and other sponsors that provided financial support to the Symposium, especially the Fonds Simone-Paré [Simone Paré Fund] at the Université Laval School of Social Work, the Université du Québec à Montréal School of Social Work, and the Université Laval School of Social Work.

We would like to express our thanks to the following people for all their work on the Proceedings: Martine Beaulieu, Ève Bélanger, Éric Couto, Isabelle Côté, Jean-Martin Deslauriers, Marie-Hélène Morin, Julie Nadeau, Paule McNicoll, Annie Pullen-Sansfaçon, and Pierre Turcotte.

The Proceedings Committee
Valérie Roy, Ginette Berteau, and Sacha Genest-Dufault

Introduction

Strengthening social solidarity
through group work:
Research and creative practices

In 2010, the 32nd International Symposium on Social Work with Groups took place in Montreal. It was the fifth Symposium held in Canada and the third in Quebec. It drew close to 250 social workers, researchers, teachers, and students interested in group work from 11 countries, including India, Mali, Belgium, and Spain. Like their German colleagues in 2008 and Quebec colleagues in 1989 and 1997, the organizers felt it was important that the international dimension, as well as the diversity so important to group work, be reflected in the discussions among participants. Indeed, social work with groups has developed largely as a result of migration and international exchange (Andrews, 2001; Toseland & McClive-Reed, 2009). The 32nd Symposium therefore offered, in French and in English, keynote speeches, a panel of four international researchers, over 90 presentations, and 30 workshops, not to mention poster presentations, most of them by students from different countries. Although diversity presents challenges and demands innovation, it also contributes to openness, the forging of ties, and the development of knowledge. Those were the intentions behind the theme of the 32nd Symposium, Strengthening Social Solidarity Through Group Work: Research and Creative Practices.

The theme reflects not only the challenges facing group work today, but also its history. It was thanks to creativity and innovation that social work with groups was successfully developed as an intervention method to meet the needs of people and communities. Creativity is essential today, too. Group workers are seeing the social ties between people and communities undermined by an unstable economic situation and noninclusive social policies. Social problems are becoming more complex or being drained of their social content by an emphasis on the individual. Administrative logic increasingly interferes with practices and imposes constraints on social workers, whether in terms of group objectives, which are more individual than social, or in terms of the short duration of groups.

This picture may seem dark, but as history repeats itself, we can learn lessons on keeping groups focused on social solidarity. Innovations in group work research and practice are a very good way to maintain this focus. This book, a collection of papers presented at the 32nd Symposium, is a testament to group work's dynamic approach to taking up today's challenges. With more theoretical discussions of solidarity, experiences of collaboration with other social workers, descriptions of working with marginalized groups, concrete examples of research on group work practices and invitations to continue developing our knowledge, the authors, each in their own way, call on group workers to be proactive in their practice and research. We urge you to respond to their invitation by reading some of the talks and papers that made the 32nd Symposium memorable.

*

The first two papers are theoretical discussions of solidarity and two related concepts: mutual-aid and altruism. *Bédard* starts by underscoring the importance of solidarity. His original contribution is his approach to group solidarity from a dual point of view, ecological and power analysis, which provides a renewed understanding of collaboration and solidarity. Then *Hainsworth* sets out his thoughts on the relationship between altruism and mutual-aid groups, two concepts often dealt with in social work with groups but seldom explored in tandem.

Three papers bear witness to the solidarity among social workers who contribute to each other's professional development by sharing their knowledge and experiences. *Exum and Yanisko* outline an intervention model that uses group work to strengthen the relationships between social work schools and the community for the benefit of both students in training and people at risk. *Grossman Leeman* describes training facilitators for social work groups, with a focus on creating a meaningful learning environment using a mutual-aid system. In the next paper, *Walsh* describes the use of a group by and for social workers. The proposed peer supervision model is a promising alternative to traditional supervision methods, especially because of its accessibility and flexibility and the fact that social workers themselves take charge of their own continuing education.

Following on from these papers on the continuing education of group social workers, *Barsky* proposes a model for resolving ethical dilemmas experienced in groups. His paper will be of interest to practitioners and may be useful in training and supervision, especially in peer supervision groups. *Yanca* comments on the use of groups as a means of training students in cultural diversity. He makes it clear that cultural diversity has always been a central concern of group work.

The efforts in initial and ongoing training of group social workers documented in this collection are certainly worth pursuing. Four papers describe and analyze creative and supportive practices with various populations and in different organizational settings. *Sulman, Verhaeghe, Coulthard, MacDonell, Oke, Werek Sokolsky, Woodhead, and Worrod* present their thoughts on group work in hospitals, pointing out that social workers may sometimes feel unable to provide all the support patients need. In their view, group work skills can transform this perception by creating opportunities for inclusion, social support and solidarity. *Nisewaner and Abdi* discuss a group project conducted in a school setting with teenage Somali refugees. The issues in this type of group (interplay of cultural, clinical, and institutional aspects, cofacilitation by social workers of different cultural backgrounds, and adjustment of actions) are central to their discussion. Singh and Kushwaha recount their experience with a large group trying to prevent violence against women in India. *Grenier, Goyette, Lemay, and Pearson* describe their efforts to acknowledge the role and rights of Native peoples in Quebec. Using preliminary research data, the authors discuss the possibilities of using and adapting group social work to the reality of Aboriginal youths entering adulthood.

The last four papers encourage readers to do further research on group work practices. *Daoust, Lemieux, Fleury, Perron-Roach, and Lavallée* describe the results of their research on the effectiveness and efficiency of the Wellness Recovery Action Plan, a method of group work with mental health patients that sees peers as the primary agents of change. Home also presents an example of research on group work, but at the same time invites readers to consider research *with* groups. The description of the principles and challenges of research with and about groups will be of interest to researchers and practitioners alike. The paper provides a very good illustration of how researchers and practitioners need to work together to contribute to the development of knowledge of group social work. This same type of collaboration is dealt with by *Macgowan*, who discusses the importance of the production and use of evidence-based data by the community of researchers and social workers interested in group work. Although research is often perceived as removed from group work practice, the research described by Macgowan is an integral part of the intervention. Last, *Preston-Shoot* looks at legal and ethical issues, especially the underuse of research findings in practice. These examples of research and reflections on research should motivate group social workers to become more involved in the development of knowledge and practices.

We hope you enjoy reading this informative and thought-provoking collection.

Valérie Roy, Ginette Berteau, and Sacha Genest-Dufault

References

Andrews, J. (2001). Group work's place in social work: A historical analysis. *Journal of Sociology and Social Welfare, 18*(4), 45–65.

Toseland, R. W., & McClive-Reed, K. P. (2009). Social group work: International and global perspectives. *Social Work with Groups, 32*(1), 5–13.

1
Solidarity and universal democracy[1]

Jean Bédard

Abstract: *The originality of the phrase lies in the discovery of the following: whatever the size or nature of the human group, the power structure is similar. If we are to achieve a democracy, then it is this structure that we must change. We will, in this article, define democracy and solidarity, distinguish between power and strength and between power and authority, try to understand the progress of consciousness, and set forward the path to cooperation.*

It is likely that the survival of humanity depends on peace between humans and nature. Peace can only come from a conscious movement towards a global democracy based on:

1. The occupation of land. A country must be inhabited by people who love the land and the landscape;
2. The education of all of humanity, all humans, not merely the indoctrination of the masses;
3. The devolution and separation of powers (legislative, executive, judicial, religious and media);
4. The granting of authority by enlightened and informed consciences to competent and disinterested persons, rather than through dissuasion, retribution and manipulation of the richest people;
5. The inclusion of all people, not the exclusion of the poorest;
6. Social justice, not exploitation of man by man;
7. Respect for nature and not the abuse of its resources;
8. The disarmament of individuals and nations rather than a balance of terror.

Democracy is the opposite of the delegation of our civic responsibilities; it is about reclaiming those responsibilities. We know that democracy will be at the core of humanity the day that all people of the earth will have access to drinking water, three meals a day and a good education.

Such a global democracy is certainly a dream, but it is the only one that is sustainable. Currently, the way we live with power is no longer compatible with life itself. We must learn to cooperate. And this requires the development of small groups of life and action.

Many people do not want to live at the expense of overexploited workers (mostly women, fathers and children) and instead depend on the balance of nature. They drop out from society to save their morals. We could call them 'refugees of conscience.' It is through them that everything will start.

Introduction

Whether in a family, a large or small group, a village, a company, nation or the world, as soon as power is the way of rule, it takes a dedicated characteristic and identifiable structure,. We will try to outline this structure and why it is a structure and not a movement of intelligence, why it is mechanical, a 'machine' and not an act of freedom, and why this mechanism so naturally leads to unconsciousness, violence and destruction. No human organization escapes power and if power goes wrong, it brings about misfortune. The social worker dealing with groups or communities had better think about power, the power they exert over others and about the powers acting on them.

The objective of this communication is not be merely descriptive. This is not to recite the many dangers of power when it is carried away by the demons of possession, domination and exploitation. This is not to recap many millennia of history, or sound a further alarm by showing that in the hands of modern man, one that is highly armed, industrialized, computerized, the risks of yesterday are multiplied. The issue is not to add a sense of urgency. Yes! Perversion of power inevitably propels us toward tragedy. Yes! It causes wars, famines and deserts because it basically needs the sacrifice of many, and ecological destruction is the necessary fuel, but beyond these considerations, the interest of understanding the relationships involved in domination is that this structure offers its own paths of release. The more powerful the dominator, the more fragile is his Achilles tendon.

The aim is to agree with those who support the hypothesis that the current danger is not a patchwork of environmental, economic, social, political risks, etc.. It does not come from globalization, or technology, or a bad leader. All of these dangers have a common basis: power cannot be assumed as it has been for thousands of years, not by the rule of force, it must become the means of viable project for humanity.

Sometimes you have to stop 'covering' the limited areas of our specialties and look up above, embracing totalities. We cannot do this by the same methods. We must take the risk of caricature and terse sentences. This often leads more to suggestive formulas than stringent ones. However, we must do this. Because you cannot create a local drive without a global vision.

What is a universal democracy?

The Greeks had proposed aristocratic democracy (only male aristocrats were involved in government). France and the United States created a national bourgeois democracy (it takes a lot of wealth and media manipulation to gain power). Several countries have borrowed the French or American model. These national models are going nowhere, because they cannot prevent wars between nations or over-exploitation of man by trade and industry, nor the devastation of nature.

Humanity is invited to develop a universal democracy that is universally inclusive of all human beings.

The survival of humanity without doubt necessitates peace between humans and nature. Peace can only come from a movement of consciousness towards a global democracy based on:

1. Occupying territories. The country must be occupied by people who love the land and the landscape and who feel responsible for its beauty and fertility.
2. The education of all mankind, of all humans, not the indoctrination of the masses. Education, seeks the full development of all creative powers in order to achieve personal, economic and social autonomy.
3. The devolution and the separation of powers (legislative, executive, judicial, religious and media) and not the concentration of each among a few persons. This decentralization requires collective decisions;

4. The granting of authority by enlightened and informed consciences to competent and disinterested persons, rather than through dissuasion, retribution and manipulation of the richest people;
5. The inclusion of all people, not the exclusion of the poorest;
6. Social justice, not exploitation of man by man;
7. Respect for nature and not the abuse of its resources;
8. The disarmament of individuals and nations rather than a balance of terror.

Democracy is a moral imperative based on the inalienable human vocation to support their personal and collective freedom. It presupposes awareness of our interdependence on each other and our dependence vis-à-vis the environment.

A State, a government is not democratic. It is the individuals and populations that are or are not democratic. The essence of democracy is the rejection of subordination to those who manipulate the forces of violence, money and media.

Our freedom begins with the freedom of others. I am free only to the extent that others are too. Democracy is the opposite of the delegation of our civic responsibilities, it is the reclaiming of our civil responsibilities.

We know that democracy will be at the core of humanity the day that all people of the earth will have access to drinking water, three meals a day and a good education.

What is education?

Education, the first step to democracy is the opposite of indoctrination. Indoctrination is to snatch the child from their relationship with themself, animals, plants, and bring them into a world of representations and doctrines about things. To educate is to lead: lead oneself, others, nature, the great texts and great works.

Who should be educated? Everyone. For without education, we can not defend ourselves against poverty and injustice.

Education is not to convert people into gears. Children are not oil to be refined for industrial use. Education is the full development of all creative powers in order to achieve personal, economic and social autonomy.

Education is not a way to climb up the social ladder, but a means to bridge the social ladder by replacing competition with collaboration.

Education leads to peace because it places intelligence above force, and not in the service of power.

The human is not a monster of selfishness, which owes its salvation to subordination to the most dominant wolves. Adherence to such a belief necessarily leads to the vicious circle of violence.

Humans are good, but they do not know it. He does not know because he has not yet met himself. Today he is facing the consequences of this ignorance regarding himself. This will certainly benefit, because consciousness is inherent to living. If life has chosen the path of thought and conscience, it is because it is the best way to move towards a sustainable biosphere.

What is occupation?

Occupation allows democracy to have feet on the ground. A country must be occupied by people who love the land and landscape, and feel responsible for its beauty and fertility. The home of the country, its cities and its countryside requires maximum decentralization of responsibilities and authority consistent with these responsibilities to the communities living there. The country cannot be abandoned therefore to either the forces of industrial and commercial companies, or to the centralizing tendencies of states. The country must be taken over by those who actually live in it.

Democracy is certainly a dream, but in the present context, the only utopia that cannot function is to allow industrial and commercial forces to undermine the authority of human conscience and destroy the planet.

We can only move forward as a movement of people toward a real democracy through universal solidarity.

What is solidarity?

Solidarity is to be accountable to one another, be accountable to each other and know that our surroundings are no longer a quality conducive to collective happiness, but a necessity for the survival of the human species.

A key finding that we need to do make is that each link of domination breaks many ties of solidarity and collaboration, as the domination disempowers while collaboration empowers.

What is domination?

There is domination when violence, money or manipulation forces someone do something he would not do themselves.

It should be noted: every type of social tie pertains to power. Power, the ability to influence and be influenced, is a dimension of all human relationships. In the couple, family, work in group dynamics, power is everywhere. It is therefore very important to understand the workings of power.

When power turns sour, I mean when it becomes an attempt at domination, power becomes particularly destructive.

The findings

Power can no longer be regarded as it has been for a very long time, it cannot be the rule of force, it must be a means to a viable end for humanity. Said bluntly: Our way of life and use of power is no longer compatible with life. We must learn to cooperate.

Returning back about ten thousand years, two great evils have plagued humanity:

1. Wars motivated primarily by the military control of energy

resources;

2. Economic wars that cause large companies to embark on the over-exploitation of labor and nature, resulting in a kind of social war between the rich and the very poor and a kind of war against nature. Driven by over-exploitation of nature, we have seriously unbalanced our planet, we are destroying thousands of species of plants and animals, and we are eliminating large ecosystems.

These types of wars are well documented separately. I leave it to others to measure and demonstrate the seriousness of the situation.

For our part, we seek to understand the meaning of what is happening and more importantly, participate in the emergence of new bonds of solidarity as a management tool capable of taking care of life in the common interest of mankind and its environment.

This requires the development of small groups of life and action.

Extreme poverty, wars, ecological disasters are not separate phenomena, but manifestations of a single cause: our inability to view power by any means other than an attitude of domination.

Besides, no one doubts the cause. It is obvious that if human beings were not haunted by the need to rule, if they did not constantly try to use one another and nature to their advantage, we would not have reached this point. Imagine if the human being really sought justice, in fact it would give a value to everyone, including future generations, there would be constant adjustments, but there would be no global threat. This is not the case.

Why change now?

If power cannot be regarded as it was before, it's not because we are worse, but because the consequences of our injustices are multiplied by the overkill of our means. Our military industrial and information technology are so powerful that if we use them without control, we could destroy everything. In a class, when the children hit with fists, power games can last a long time, but if they kill each other with grenades, the game will not last long!

So everyone agrees on the cause: domination is not compatible with our technical overkill.

Is domination a law of nature or a group disease that has a cure?

Human beings have previously lived by the code of collaboration, what's more if they had not learned to cooperate, we would not be here to talk about it. However, from the Bronze Age civilizations based on domination invaded, assimilated or wiped out civilization based on collaboration. Today, almost every civilization based on cooperation has disappeared.

And now with the arrival of the military and industrial superpowers, history is going to prove to us that ruling by force is incompatible with life.

Power, domination and authority

However, collaboration is not just anything; it requires intelligence, consciousness and a particular type of organization.

In his *Res gestae*, the Roman Emperor Augustus said he won by *autoritas* what he could not win by *potestas*. Since the Romans, we have known that power can be imposed (*potestas*) by threat or violence, money or manipulation, which proves ultimately very costly for humans and the environment, but also the power can be exercise by *autoritas*, which itself requires a real and sincere pursuit of the common good. *Autoritas*, authority comes from the word auctor, meaning author. For example, we can say that Richard Desjardins is an authority on music, and a social authority by his commitment to it. An authority is a social group or a few people who have a means to facilitate collaboration through personal qualities such as sincerity, honesty, congruence, the ability to place the common interest over special interests, but above all, it is someone who has people skills such as listening and the ability to appreciate many views.

Imagine that we start to conquer Everest, if the group abides by the law of the jungle, we will not have much chance to reach the summit. In difficult situations, cooperation is a necessity. A group that lives by the law of the jungle is very fragile.

The law of the jungle was possible only after the Bronze Age and before the age of technological overkill: before the Bronze Age, the struggle for survival was too difficult, it was necessary to collaborate, now in the post-superpower age, our technological means are too dangerous, we must learn to cooperate once more.

That decisions are made under the 'one person, one vote' principle is not enough to guard against the law of the jungle.

A collective movement of consciences

In a civilization based on domination rather than work, humans are competing with each other. An example: the economy has long been based on competitive companies, not just any competition, but competition for dominance. This makes it almost impossible for a company to treat employees well and respect the environment. There is no competition to see which company is the fairest and most environmentally friendly. It is exactly the opposite. One day or another, a competitor will cut its prices by paying employees less and caring less about the environment. Shareholders will say we will put our money into the company involved in over-exploitation of labor and pollution because it makes more profit. As it is not enough to make a profit but to make more profit than the others, there is a premium for companies that over-exploit labor and pollute.

This kind of competition for dominance demands the sacrifice of the values of cooperation such as justice and respect for the environment. It is a destroyer of social relations, an 'individualization', it is to 'atomize' society.

Many of those that are not interested, that do not want to sacrifice their desire for justice and the environment, they do not want to destroy their aspirations by entering into such a competition. These people drop out, abandon. They drop out to save their values. We could call them 'refugees of conscience.' There are worldwide farm alternatives, cooperative houses, movement activists that are a kind of 'refugee camp of consciousness'.

At the same time, too many people give up their values. For example, they buy products without being faithful to their values, simply because the product is cheaper. They invest their money without regard for what the bank will use it for. They leave their health to doctors, education of their children to officials of the Ministry of Education ... They abandon their intelligence for television or playing computer games. Or they work for any company that pollutes, because one can earn a good living. They give up their power to exercise their values by their choice of work and in their purchases.

These abandoned powers are collected by others. The collectors of abandoned powers end up with a lot of power. This forms the division between the 'owners' of power (the rich) and those stripped of power (the poor). The more this division is polarized, the stronger the competition to attain the instruments of power. This forms a social gradient. This division is devoid of morals. Curiously, the one on top is said to have succeeded in life rather than having abused the powers that were abandoned. He that is underneath is said to have failed in his life rather than being exploited by others. One is much admired, the other rejected into poverty.

The poor become the pariahs of society, the scapegoats. They must bear the shame of society.

In addition to the people, who are rejected, also excluded are the values of collaboration and what is admired are the values of domination.

The media and advertising are the new priests who preach the possession of instruments of domination: money, weapons, beauty (in a defined format), the art of manipulating public opinion ... Commercial values are all in place. If there are some restrictions on the expression of certain religious values, there are no values for the expression of the dominant market.

In a society this polarized, only military or economic warfare can maintain social cohesion: united against the enemy.

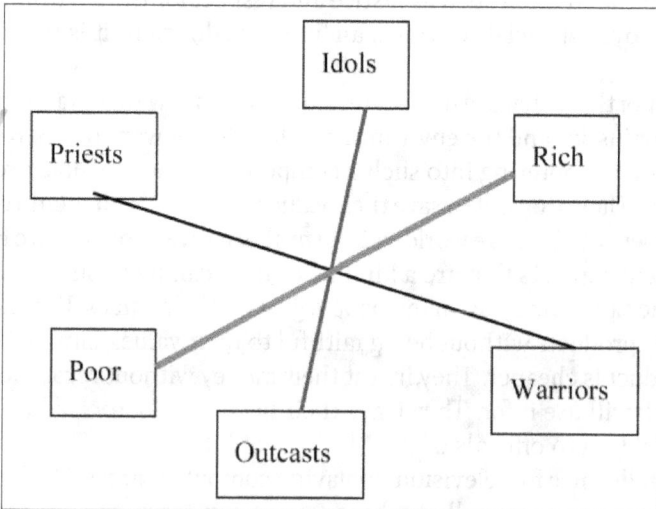

This structure is generalized and destroys us.

How to live by the way of collaboration?

It is entirely possible to live under the mode of collaboration. Living through collaboration is much more responsive to the needs of human beings. Why? Because the real needs of human beings are primarily relational.

The main need every human being has is to be recognized for what they are. A person wants to know whether they have a worth. How many people will make how much effort for them! They also want to know if they are fun. How many people take pleasure in their presence! They want to know if they are useful (utility value) and if someone is willing to pay for their skills (market value). They also want to influence their environment. They hope to be remembered (memory value). They feel the need for you to believe in them (potential value).

One could mention many other social ties. But above all, it is necessary that every person feels reassured that they be given the value of mere existence (dignity). If all the values given to human beings are conditional, the level of social anxiety is very high, because every human being knows that they can easily lose their conditional value (for example, a severely disabling injury).

Some range of values of social links:

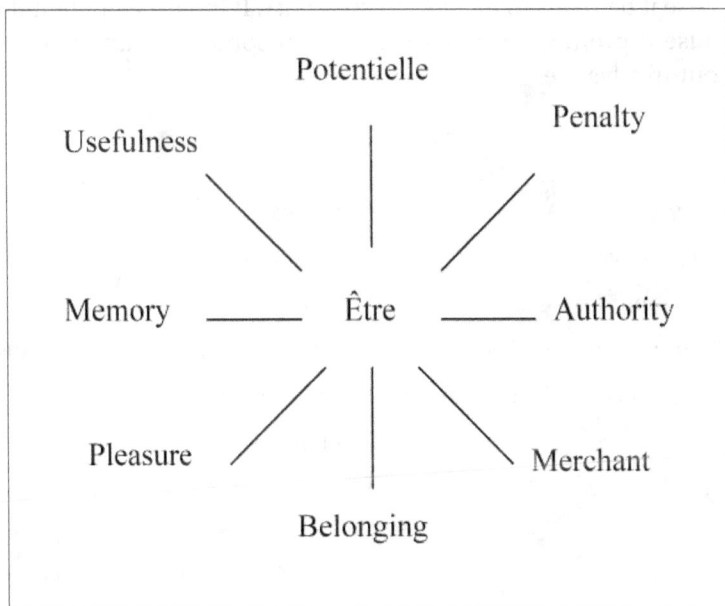

Back to the difference between '*potestas*' and '*autoritas*'. To dominate, is to bend something or someone into an exact form, a determined form. To dominate, the conductor must determine in advance what he wants. He knows in advance what he wants to hear and forces musicians to make music according to his expectations. He must have a clear idea of the future, he must have a goal in advance. For him, the future is not the result of a collective development, on the contrary, the future is clearly predetermined. This is a predefined value for exclusion. For example, one can define in advance a model of beauty, a beauty ideal. The closer you are to this ideal, the more beautiful you are. Those too far from this ideal are ugly. The idol of a society based on domination is an ideal defined in advance. It is from these ideals that a society defines who is successful and who should be excluded (the poor, the outcasts).

Authority cannot operate with predefined values of exclusion, it works by developmental values of inclusion. For example, the conductor will gain authority if he is competent enough to stimulate the creativity of each one and coordinating all these efforts to the most inspiring music. He does not know in advance the result, but he will search throughout the process, for a developmental beauty and harmony, something that he will recognize when the orchestra gets there, but is impossible to define in advance. It is a developmental value of inclusion because it happens to include all creativity. It is a developmental value because it promotes the development of something and not a result set out in advance.

In summary:

Potestas	*Autoritas*
1. Dissuasive, Retributive, Manipulative	1. Information, Reflection
2. Predefined exclusion values	2. Developmental values of inclusion
3. ~~Conscience Intelligence~~	3. Conscience Intelligence

What is a collaboration group?

These are people who come together around a project and are organized according to a model of collaboration. The values that mobilize them are developmental values capable of large inclusion. For example, ecology, since it retains its original meaning, is a developmental value of inclusion. Why? Because it is impossible to define in advance the form: you cannot lay out in advance, in our minds, a picture of what would be an ecological society. It can take many forms that are both different and valid at the same time.

What can an ecological society be? If anyone had a predefined template, we would no longer be in the world of ecology, but in the world of ideology. And in the world of ideology, there are plenty of people who know everything in advance. Certainly there are in the environmental movement, people who are fanatics of ecological ideology, but this is a deviation from the true meaning. Strictly speaking, ecology is a developmental value of inclusion and not exclusion of a predefined value.

A value of inclusion brings together people to develop an overall ecological life that can take many forms.

Social justice, too, is a developmental value of inclusion and should remain so. There is no predefined template for the 'democratic society'.

The dimensions of a collaborative group

To sum up: a collaborative group rallies around a developmental value of inclusion that is the purpose of the group. In relation to this purpose, the group will gradually 'elect' the authorities. Election is not *ad hoc* and strictly rational, it is a continuous act of consciousness and is also an emotional act, it is primarily an act that is constantly attentive. It should here be understood in a natural sense as when a lover says to his love: 'You are the chosen one of my heart'. In fact the election is the recognition of a trust that is built gradually, it is an inescapable dimension of social ties.

If an authority is real, its knows how to recognize its 'blind spots'. It is characteristic of an 'authority' to be able to recognize that which is not known. No one can mystify this authority; everyone will know that they will advance for as long as complementarities are created.

As an 'authority' is normally the person that is most skilled in the art of knowing and learning their limitations, they are well positioned to want and appreciate the skills that surround them.

The complementarity that is the most interesting and most constructive is to integrate people, especially the weakest, the least able, the least 'competent'. Usually, those 'losers', the 'rogues', people rejected or excluded, are not the lowest, but those who feel the more what does not work, and are those who suffer the most.

For example, when studying the history of madness, we realize that the crazy reflect more and better than the others, the collective madness in which they bathe. Similarly the socially 'inept' are those who feel the least able to adapt to a community reality. The 'deficient' intellectuals feel the loss of 'rationality' when dealing with human problems ...

In short, those that tend to be excluded are those most important to include because they are at sharp end of a community's sensitivity. These people are able to notice the blind spots of a given culture. In the early submarines rabbits were brought in because rabbits felt the pressure before anyone else and they showed, by their agitation, when it was necessary to raise the submarine. If we can integrate people, apparently, the most fragile, it is likely that we will develop the most effective complementarities that will bring us up when the pressure is too high.

To make the most exciting music, it takes three kinds of complementarity:

1. Everyone has a freedom and responsibility in which they can flourish to their maximum, be as creative as possible, the complementarity of talents. Here, the more the identity of each is unique, the better. The more each bears their own responsibility, the better things are. The greater the autonomy, the better.
2. Everyone should feel part of the whole form of the group. In short, everyone should feel like an authority, should feel responsible for the running of the community as a whole. Everyone should feel jointly responsible for common goals as if they were his or her own project while recognizing the authority of others and other authorities.
3. Everyone should feel beyond the group, the social context of the action that gives a precise purpose to the action. Each one sees

themselves as part of a common totality on a voyage in their planetary spacecraft. Otherwise, the group becomes a specific 'we' that risks losing an awareness of its meaning and openness.

These three forms of complementarity (the meeting of talents, responsibility regarding the project as a whole, the perception of the overall context in which the project develops) should never be absorbed by the obsessive effect of the action.

Life contains the project, but the project should not try to dominate life. A project resides in an environment that is larger and more vital than it.

In this environment, there are elements that seek to destroy the project by imposing ideology. One should know how to protect oneself from ideologies (closed systems with predefined values of exclusion).

However, life brings with it its own heterogeneous elements into the project, elements that apparently have nothing to do with the project, and are foreign to it. Action makes us easily obsessive. We must retain an openness to these heterogeneous elements. Agree to be stirred by the unexpected; something that is necessary for the health of a project. Knowing how to receive and integrate 'foreign' elements allows the project to proceed in harmony.

We can summarize the poles needed for a project based on collaboration:

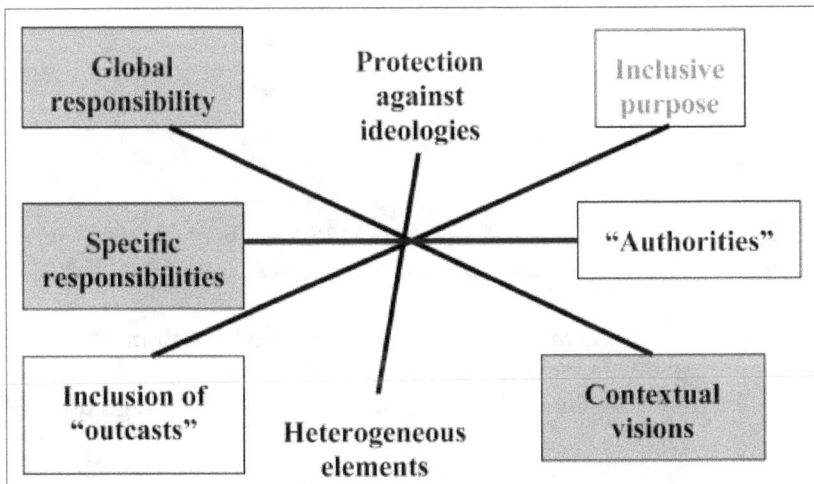

Conclusion

We need to get past the binary logic of dictatorship *vs* anarchy. We need to uncover the authority within ourselves and to exercise it in a responsible community.

Socially, we naturally seek to develop links that support us by giving us value. We will fight all forms of domination that destroy social bonds.

Well beyond the claim of our individual and collective rights, we will demand our responsibilities concerning our cities, our land and our homes because we want to take care of the country that we live in.

In everyday life, we will practice a collaboration based on *'autoritas'*, inclusion, complementarity, responsibility, vision, rejection of ideologies, openness to heterogeneity.

We will seek to develop a universal democracy by arousing awareness and educating minds on freedom.

Collaboration and universal democracy have become necessities. To arrive at collaboration, human beings have to discover new links for solidarity that cross interests, to reach all of humanity.

Notes

1. This manifesto summarizes the proposed ideas : Bédard, Jean (2008). *Le Pouvoir ou la vie*. Montréal: Fidès edition.

References

Abellio, R. (1962). *La fosse de Babel*. Paris: NRF, Gallimard.

Abellio, R. (1965). *La structure absolue, Essai de phénoménologie génétique*. Paris: NRF, Gallimard.

Aron, R. (1976). *Penser la guerre, Clausewitz*. Paris: NRF, Gallimard.

Bergson, H. (1997). *Les deux sources de la morale et de la religion*. Paris: PUF.

Broch, H. (2005). *Logique d'un monde en ruine*. Paris Tel-Aviv: Éditions de l'éclat.

Broch, H. (1990). *Les somnambules*. Paris: Gallimard.

Broch, H. (1961). *Les irresponsables*. Paris: Gallimard.

Clausewitz, Carl (1955). *De la guerre*. Paris: Les éditions de Minuit.

De Rougemont, Denis (1972). *Penser avec les mains*. Paris: Gallimard.

Girard, René (2001). *Les choses cachées depuis la fondation du monde*. Paris: Grasset.

Girard, René (2003). *Le sacrifice, Grandes conférences*. Paris: BNF.

Guyonvarc'h, C.J. & Le Roux, F. (2001). *La civilisation celtique*. Paris: Payot

Malherbe, Jean-François (1997). *La conscience en liberté*, Montréal: Fides.

Nicolescu, Basarab (1996). *La transdisciplinarité*. Paris: Éditions du Rocher.

Patocka, J. (1990). *Essais hérétiques sur la philosophie et l'histoire*. Trans: Erika Abrams. France: Verdier.

Patocka, J. (1990). *L'art et le temps*. Paris: POL, Presse Pocket.

Patocka, J. (1990). *Liberté et sacrifice, écrits politiques*. Grenoble: Jérome Millon.

Rivard, Yvon (2006). *Personne n'est une île*. Montréal: Boréal.

2

The importance of altruism for mutual aid group initiation and stainability

Victor Hainsworth

Abstract: Mutual aid cannot occur without altruism occurring first. This paper, by way of an analytical explanation, seeks to amplify the importance of altruism to both the initiation of a mutual aid group and the sustainability of the mutual aid group. Before that undertaking, a review of the seminal work of Peter Kropotkin (1902) provided an understanding of the importance of mutual aid in evolution. A review of Darwin (1872) added to understanding the interplay that natural selection has on the evolutionary process of mutual aid by natural selection. Adding an understanding of altruism according to Wakefield's (1993) definition that altruism is a motive only to help, it is theoretically argued that altruism would have evolved from violence in the environment (Tucker & Ferson, 2008) and resulted in a prosocial act based on suffering (Volhardt, 2009). A brief mutual aid literature review provided a glimpse of the possibilities of mutual aid group's utilization of altruism to sustain group coherence and provide group members a sense of accomplishment and self-esteem from helping a member in crisis or stress. Further research to gather evidence of altruism in mutual aid groups is, therefore, necessary. Much work is required to build evidence not only of the importance of altruism for social work with mutual aid groups but also of the application of altruism with mutual aid groups by way of interventions that help social workers achieve altruism within the group, and thus social justice for the group.

Introduction

In social work, social group work and mutual aid have been opposite sides of the same coin, bonded together by practice according to the described historical beginnings of each (Gitterman, 2004). An assumption of this paper is that mutual aid cannot achieve success without altruism occurring first. Since there is documented success of mutual aid group work (Cohen & Graybeal, 2007; Cameron & Birnie-Lefcovitch, 2000; Kelly, 1999), this paper will pertain to the primacy of altruism. This paper will ascertain, by way of an analytical explanation, the importance of altruism to both the initiation of a mutual aid group and the sustainability of the mutual aid group. Certain perquisite knowledge is needed to connect the theoretical underpinnings of this paper.

First, a review of the work of Kropotkin (1902) will provide background as to the evolutionary significance of mutual aid. However, prerequisite to Kropotkin is an understanding of Darwin's (1872) premise of evolution by natural selection as Kropotkin is in disagreement with the findings of Darwin (1872). With that background, a definition of altruism (Wakefield, 1993; Brosnahan, 1907) will provide an interpretive altruistic perspective to apply the concept for an analytic literature review. Finally, the literature review of mutual aid groups should provide information as to why it is that altruism is required before a mutual aid group can develop, and why altruism will be required to sustain the mutual aid group. A discussion of the synthesis of ideas will offer social work the evaluative importance of altruism for practice, especially as a conceptual tool to achieve positive client outcomes within social group work using the mutual aid model.

To amplify the assumption of altruism leading to mutual aid the following line of reasoning is offered, briefly: natural selection argues for individual benefits (Darwin, 1872) and 'nature favors none and offers no guidelines' (Gould, 1997, p.4), once secured the individual is ready to evolve to an altruistic motivation (Wakefield, 1993). Once altruistic motive has occurred, the individual is quickly ready to evolve to mutual aid cooperation (Kropotkin, 1903). Thus, the motive to help, altruism, must occur before the act of mutual aid, a type of prosocial behavior. Altruism is antecedent to mutual aid, not the other way around. If altruism is a motive and occurs first, then we avoid 'the altruism trap' (Glassman, 2000, p.404), the notion that sacrifice lessens survival. Moreover, Bester and Güth (1994) developed a mathematical expression of altruism demonstrating stable altruistic behavior when fitness is enhanced for a majority. Therefore, altruism as a motive only (Wakefield, 1993) is poised for mutual aid. Group members can act prosocial or not, the outcome of which can be effective or not.

It is this potential difference that sets apart mutual aid groups from support groups, groups that pertain to the primal attributes of altruism only. That is, the benefactor gives, and the recipient, in most cases, does not have the opportunity or is not encouraged to reciprocate immediately in some kind of way. Specifically, support group members are not deliberately encouraged to reciprocate to evolve to a state of mutual aid; therefore, seemingly the group does not recognize the importance of establishing altruism within the group to encourage mutual aid. The deliberate instruction of altruism is important to harness the full benefits of mutual aid, social justice (Steinberg, 2003) within a sense of community.

Kropotkin's mutual aid

Kropotkin's (1902) current influence on social work (Steinberg, 2002) is suggestive of the institutional social work core conditions dedicated to promoting 'mutual regard, respect and understanding, and appreciation' (p.33) so necessary to the evolution of civilized life. Kropotkin undertook to correct the inaccurate account of facts of nature perpetuated on the scholarship of Darwin (1872) by such distinguished scholars such as Huxley in his *Struggle for existence and it's bearing upon man* (Kropotkin, 1902, p.4). Traveling to Eastern Siberia and Northern Manchuria as a young man, Kropotkin was impressed with the struggle for life in extreme climatic conditions, the loss of life, because of natural occurrences, and the scarcity of life over a vast territory. To his surprise, where there was an abundance of life there was no struggle of life within species.

Kropotkin (1902) witnessed harsh conditions of weather and rugged land mass to which the struggle for existence took place. Such seemed to him to confirm the natural checks of over-multiplication according to Darwin (1872). Such natural occurrences lead to doubts of the struggle for life within species, and as the explanation for evolution. Where an abundance of life existed, mutual aid and mutual support seemed to be the evolutionary cause for within species existence. Such occurrences provided no support for a Darwinian law of nature within species by direct observation. Still to this day, scientific opinion of Darwin's view is seen, in some circles, as having a cultural influence when contrasted with the Russian experience of mutual aid (Borrello, 2004; Glassman, 2000; Gould, 1997), which produced scientific 'studies of the mutual aid among migrating fish to a Nobel prizewinning theory of inflammation and immunity' (Todes, 2009, p.36).

Before Kropotkin (1902) undertook his exploration, a substantial influence came from Kessler, Dean of the St. Petersburg University, on the law of mutual aid and the law of mutual struggle. Kessler's lecture suggested that the law of mutual aid is more significant than the law of mutual contest claimed by Darwin (1872). In the field, Kropotkin (1902) tested Kessler's theory or hypothesis and found much support and evidence of mutual aid among animals as well as among humans during his exploration. Mutual aid had developed overtime to allow animals and humans to live socially in mutual aid. From such observations, Kropotkin interpreted mutual aid as a law, a law having evidence that showed mutual aid progressing both animals and humans.

Amending Darwin

Social work needs to take a fresh look (Strohman, 2003) at the body of work and thoughts (Colp, 1986) of Charles Darwin (1872) to find an application and perspective. To begin such a journey an analysis of Darwin's (1972) knowledge claim should be conducted (Toulmin, 1964). For example, no tautology exists in the knowledge claim by Charles Darwin as well as in an operational definition according to Gould (1976). The knowledge claim of natural selection made by Darwin is as follows:

> ...geometrical powers of increase.... This is the doctrine of Malthus, applied to the whole animal and vegetable kingdoms. As many more individuals of each species are born than can possibly survive; and as,

consequently, there is a frequently recurring struggle for existence, it follows that *any being, if it vary* however *slightly in any manner profitable to itself,* under the complex and sometimes varying conditions of life, *will have a better chance of surviving,* and thus be naturally selected. From the strong principle of inheritance, any selected variety will tend to propagate its new and modified form. (Darwin, 1872, p.3) (*Emphasis my own*)

Gould (1976) explains that natural selection is actually an analogy to 'artificial selection,' a slippery slope indeed. However, natural selection does have an independent criterion providing a testable operational definition: namely, if A is superior to B, then A's superiority is determined to be different based on survival (Gould, 1976). In other words, those things that make A different from B, explains the theory of A's survival relative to A's environment, not superiority. If A defined by superiority, then Darwin's theory of natural selection will be refuted. Darwin's clear contribution therefore is that evolution occurs by way of natural selection.

Therefore, although this is a cursory review of Darwin (1872), natural selection should have a voice in social work, as humans are free from genetic determinism (Strohman, 2003). We need each other in so many important ways by way of mutual aid (Kropotkin, 1908), if humanity is to adapt, then evolve as necessary, relative to the immediate and dominant environment, the varying and diverse traits of humanity for survival.

The exact mechanism of how evolution is achieved by natural selection is becoming clear (Strohman, 2003) and is not limited to within species competition but rather to natural environmental controls of over-multiplication. It is the dominance of natural environmental controls that force species to survive by the law of mutual aid or decay, and become extinct (Kropotkin, 1902). In short, both genetics and the environment are significant to evolution 'but the one may not be predicted by, or reduced to, the other.' (Strohman, 2003, p.191.)

To restate, Kropotkin (1902) made clear the law of mutual aid has evidence that counters the law of mutual contest. Therefore, an amendment to Darwin by adding the phase '*or profitable to another*' where 'profitable to itself' ends the theoretical statement, we therefore can understand how mutual aid, and indeed the environment cannot predict genetics (Strohman, 2003). Better still, in paraphrase: *if a being changes profitable to itself or another, the species will have a better chance of survival.* Perhaps as a result of chaos (Hudson, 2000) or suffering or adverse conditions, altruism (Volhardt, 2009) became more significant to evolution allowing mutual aid to develop. Altruism here considered, is a necessary evolved trait in humans, coming about as a result of extreme environmental conditions threatening or putting the species, not in mutual aid, at risk (Tucker & Ferson, 2008).

Altruism as a necessary trait of evolution for a species, not in mutual aid, would have evolved to activation – based on actual violence from the environment and then evolved to the more advanced perception of violence from the environment (Tucker & Ferson, 2008) for a motive to help. Such perceived violence would motivate a passive or aggressive altruism, live or die – the ultimate sacrifice for others, as the environmental condition required. In the extreme case: the species will not reproduce if it does not live to reproduce; the act of altruistic behavior benefits survival of the species (Wilson, 2005). Also supporting, altruism is suggestive in a model of natural selection across species (Frank, 1994). Thus, this assumption to modify Darwin (1872) based on Comte's altruism (Brosnahan, 1907) has some support, and with that support altruism attains the suggested primacy in importance as a motivation to help (Wakefield, 1993).

Comte's altruism: Then and now

Auguste Comte, the French founder of sociology, introduced the concept of altruism in 1851 to support his religion of humanity (Brosnahan, 1907). The concept of altruism, 'live for others' has changed in meaning (Simon, 1993) to suggest 'behavior that reduces the actor's fitness while enhancing the fitness of others' (p.156). That definition is an evolutionary or biological understanding of altruism since it expresses altruism in terms of fitness. Other definitions pertain to psychological and ethical altruism (Piliavin & Charng, 1990). Psychological altruism refers to the motives to help others despite a potential or actual loss, whereas ethical altruism refers to morals or values to help others despite a potential or actual loss because it is the right thing to do. To date the most parsimonious definition is from social work by Wakefield (1993), who defines altruism as *a motive only to help;* no outcome is required, not even the act of helping.

Current altruistic study

Volhardt (2009) amplifies the concept of 'altruism born of suffering' supported by research (Shakespeare-Finch & Copping, 2006; Brown, Brown, House & Smith, 2008) and various theories of the social sciences such as negative state relief (Cialdini, Schaller, Houlihan & Arps, 1987) and empathy (Eisenberg & Miller, 1987). Long established thinking has prosocial behavior linked to positive experiences, and antisocial behavior linked to negative experiences. Volhardt thesis is that there are times when negative experiences will produce positive experiences or 'altruism born of suffering.' Volhardt developed a motivational process model inclusive of a typology or types of factors that produce altruism born of suffering. Synthesized are clinical (i.e. helping as a coping mechanism) and social psychological theories (i.e. required helpfulness) that explained the underlying process for altruism born of suffering to occur. Volhardt also suggested mediators and moderators that facilitate altruism born of suffering to occur.

From a mutual aid perspective (Kropotkin, 1908), groups tend to establish because of events in the environment negative or positive. Volhardt's work has many implications (practice, intervention and research) for mutual aid groups that may have started because of group experiences of violence and adversity and their motivation to help (Wakefield, 1993) or specific 'altruism born of suffering' may activate group prosocial behavior. Volhardt is instructive for the study of mutual aid groups in two important ways: providing understanding of prosocial behavior stemming from adverse experiences, and understanding that negative behavior based on adverse experiences is not absolute and can be turned into prosocial behavior.

Factors that foster 'altruism born of suffering' come from violence and adversity stemming from individual or group acts such as abuse and neglect, physical or sexual abuse, and from societal effects such as persecution, and genocide. Attenuating factors after such an experience by victims are empathy for other victims, and prosocial behavior to prevent the violence and adversity, the suffering from happening again.

However, from an evolutionary perspective (Darwin, 1872), in order to get to mutual aid behavior, altruistic motive is necessary first, as mutual aid behavior does not happen simultaneously. That altruism requires the perception of a need for help be it from suffering or a benevolent gesture, results more from the motive only to help (Wakefield, 1993). Much overlap occurs before a synchronization of mutual aid behavior becomes apparent. Thus, this paper suggests a primacy of altruism to achieve mutual aid. Simply put, altruism enables mutual aid.

Thus, Darwin (1872) and Kropotkin (1902) are both right when altruism (Wakefield, 1993) is a factor.

Review of mutual aid

Currently, there is very little mutual aid group literature relating or discussing altruism and mutual aid groups as a significant factor of mutual aid group interaction. Altruism has standing in other modalities. For example, Yalom (1995) suggested altruism to be a 'therapeutic factor' (p.1), number four on his list of eleven therapeutic factors, and defined altruism as the act of 'giving not only as part of the reciprocal giving-receiving sequence but also from the intrinsic act of giving' (p.12). The reason why other modalities recognize altruism may have more to do with the theoretical underpinnings from Yalom's (1995) seminal work in group psychotherapy as it relates to altruism, whereas mutual aid group work theoretical lineage is attributed to the seminal work of Kropotkin (1902), which did not amplify altruism. Therefore, where other modalities such as support groups are *deliberate* to exploit, for example, the instance of altruism in therapeutic sessions (Magen & Glajchen, 1999), and the success of clients becoming altruistic to achieve heightened self esteem (Bonhote, Romano-Egan & Cornwell, 1999), mutual aid group work is *silent* as to, for example, group methods to achieve altruism (Schulman, 2005), and best practices (Steinberg, 2010) for client altruism.

Specifically, research into support groups as opposed to mutual aid groups had important contributions regarding altruism. Here, it is important to clarify the distinction between support groups, self-help and mutual aid groups (Katz, 1981; Gitterman, 2004; Shulman, 2005; Steinberg, 2010). Support groups and self-help groups are aware of altruism as a factor but do not instruct it; whereas, serendipity explains more the instance of altruism in mutual aid groups. Magen and Glajchen (1999) found altruism to be important to support group members as indicated by the high ranking altruism held among therapeutic factors. Moreover, a study of a long-term support group

(Bonhote, Romano-Egan & Cornwell, 1999) concluded that altruism allowed members to interact 'with a heightened sense of integrity' (p.614) and developed group members' sense of success from generosity of the shared experience stemming from altruism. Indeed, helping behavior such as prosocial behavior was suggested to result from altruism (Volhardt, 2009).

Within mutual aid group study, hardly any direct connection to altruism is mentioned within the literature ranging from the history of mutual aid to the current empirical research program. For example, Katz (1981) reviewed the state of mutual aid and provided an overview of mutual aid that can help us understand where the research interest for mutual aid has predominated in the past. The phenomenon of mutual aid groups received little systematic study (Katz, 1981) during its early inception. However, mutual aid groups had increased in number and organizational startup in Western countries. By the late 1980s to the 1990s, mutual aid had received distinguished attention from 'mainstream academic and medical journal such *as Journal of the American Medical Association* and *New England Journal of Medicine*' (Archibald, 2007, p.599). As a result, social service agencies made numerous referrals, and mutual aid groups became diverse in groupings and utilized by just about any group interested in its particular organizational structure.

Formal study of mutual aid did not start earnestly until the beginnings of the 1970s. Most early studies of mutual aid by social scientist to include social workers did not reference or paid 'little attention' (Katz, 1981, p.132) to Kropotkin's (1908) theoretical foundation let alone altruism. The focus of research seemed to be very scattered or spread out like it was just taking snapshots from different angles of a camera and could not make sense of the different views or findings, and made superficial conclusions like mutual aid is 'an important social movement' (Sagarin, 1969 as cited by Katz, 1981, p.133). Groundbreaking research into the dynamics of mutual aid organization seems an important step in understanding mutual aid groups (Archibald, 2007).

Founding rates discussed by Archibald (2007) are interesting but still lacking is by what mechanism do mutual aid groups become existent? What in the environment (chaos, suffering or adverse conditions) motivates founding a mutual aid group? This paper supposes an answer is by way of altruism of an individual or group to help an unorganized collective become a group. The rational for disbanding rates (Archibald,

2007) would conversely be because of the lack of sustained altruism within the group. Therefore, a question to follow-up with the Archibald (2007) study is, where social, political, or economic unrest exists, will there be more startups of mutual aid groups?

Perhaps a content analysis of the mutual aid group literature may answer the genesis and sustainability questions, and provide clues for discovery. Four mutual aid articles (Steinberg, 2003; Jagendorf & Malekoff, 2005; Chien, Norman & Thompson, 2006; Ngai, Cheung & Ngai, 2009) inform this very limited review of the relationship between altruism and mutual aid groups.

Mutual aid groups experiencing altruism

We should see within this limited mutual aid literature (Steinberg, 2003; Jagendorf & Malekoff, 2005; Chien, Norman & Thompson, 2006; Ngai, Cheung & Ngai, 2009) the startup and sustainability of mutual aid groups as a result of altruism 'however slightly' (Darwin, 1872, p.3).

Examples of mutual aid impress Steinberg's (2003) chapter, and one particular example personifies altruism. The story of the social work intern that provided tea settings for her group because they never ate from plates before is symptomatic of altruistic sustainability of a group (p.95). Analysis of this segment of the chapter suggests that the environment made members suffer (Volhardt, 2009), as perceived by the intern, for lack of proper tea settings as establish by custom from the dominant culture. Tea settings appropriate for the occasion gave the British-style High Tea Group social justice, an outcome of the altruism of the intern.

Steinberg (2003) makes the case for social justice resulting from mutual aid in that when people stop talking to each other the process of understanding common ground to enable social justice shuts it down and is not advanced. To practice social work with groups is to recognize that something in the environment is wrong or went wrong, and the goal of social work is to advance social justice. There is no excuse not to introduce mutual aid in social work practice so that it contributes to the social work process and thus gains social justice for clients and groups members.

To be effectively unified is synonymous with being holistic (Smuts, 1926), and as Steinberg (2003) notes, 'every system needs to have some degree of common ground between or among its parts, and it needs to recognize that common ground' (p.14). Ultimately, when mutual aid is realized, needs are realized from actual social work advancing social justice. Moreover, Ngai, Cheung and Ngai (2009) provided discussion of social worker effectiveness to actualize mutual aid in groups having emotional and behavioral problem (EBP) youth.

Social work input is crucial to the sustainability of mutual aid youth groups based on altruism (Ngai, Cheung & Ngai, 2009). In their qualitative study to discover how to maximize the benefits of the mutual aid group, Ngai, Cheung and Ngai (2009) asked fifteen experienced mutual aid group social workers to relate their experience with EBP youth. Focus group members unanimously encouraged mutual aid within youth groups. Focus group results also suggested that social workers helped group members build a sense of oneness by establishing reciprocity in transactions (Ngai, Cheung & Ngai, 2009). Augmenting is the establishment of the expectation of returning aid to the 'immediate helper' (p.450) without conditions. The input of helping in mutual aid groups with EBP youth received consensus in the establishment of prosocial behavior reinforced by the social worker's recognition of the act.

Although not initiated without prompting, altruism in a mutual aid youth group on-the-go (Jagendorf & Malekoff, 2005) was likewise recognized by the social worker. From that example, a mutual aid group of teens in a high school spontaneously formed as a result of environmental conditions that made it necessary: namely, staff members attended a conference, which left one social worker to cover caseloads (Jagendorf & Malekoff, 2005). Empowerment of the on-the-go mutual aid group resulted from altruism of the teenagers to give help to a fellow teen without compensation. The social worker requested the teens to help another teen in distress, without warning or preparation. The authors, to explain the process of other teens to help a distressed teen, used an analogy of a car needing a jump-start from a fully charged car. Teens realized that by helping another teen, they helped that teen not just with a substantive need but also with a more normative need of dancing, which the teen required for the sweet sixteen-birthday party. A residual outcome was that the altruistic teens helped themselves in terms of self-esteem development by helping the teen to dance.

A teen boy Jay was depressed and related that he did not want to attend a sweet sixteen party because he did not know how to dance. Interrupted during the one-on-one meeting with the youth by another teen, the social worker enlisted the other teen to help with the permission of the distressed teen Jay, and soon another teen, then another teen joined the group in mutual aid to help the distressed teen to learn how to dance. One teen Jerold was an acknowledged great dancer and with prompting from the social worker offered his services to teach Jay to dance, the other teens, females, were excited to participate even though they needed help with dancing as well.

The altruism of Jerold, although encouraged, provided the energy and direction for the group to help Jay become somewhat of a dancer to attend the sweet sixteen-birthday party and ultimately empowered the group to realize that with the help of all attending this group-on-the-go, they can achieve despite their socially ascribed limitations. Conventional mutual aid groups have also experienced altruism sporadically (Chien, Norman & Thompson, 2006).

In their qualitative exploration of participants' views on the benefits and difficulties in a mutual aid group, Chien, Norman and Thompson (2006) discovered three main themes from interviews of thirty family caregivers and ten patients. Positive personal changes from mutual aid group participation, positive characteristics of mutual support from the group, and major inhibitors of group development gave Chien, Norman and Thompson (2006) an enhanced understanding of mutual aid support groups for Chinese family caregivers of patients who have schizophrenia. Within positive characteristics of mutual support, a caregiver provided an example of altruism of family caregivers.

Of the thirty family caregivers, 13 suggested that they experienced a dedication to the group and to each other. One caregiver indicated that other members had helped him outside of group with housework and family issues, which he did not expect. Chien, Norman and Thompson (2006) concluded that altruism was an important attribute that helped the group sustain to resolve substantive needs of group members to care for their family member with schizophrenia.

Discussion and conclusion

Altruism is an important concept for mutual aid groups and needs the development of intervention methods to enhance practice by social workers. Positive individual and group outcomes can occur from the exercise of altruism within the group (Jagendorf & Malekoff, 2005). A sense of accomplishment, self-worth and self-esteem can occur when a group exercises altruism externally to the community at large (Bonhote, Romano-Egan & Cornwell, 1999). Social justice resulting from mutual aid groups practice has significant outcomes for clients (Steinberg, 2003; 2010). Such factors can become sustainable; it is surmised here, with a sense of community to which mutual aid supplies in abundance if altruism is deliberately taught within the group.

Specifically in terms of initiation and sustainability, a determination of the extent altruism had an influence on the successful outcomes of mutual aid group members was a primary goal of this paper. The importance for altruistic intervention as a practice method is, therefore, clear and its importance cannot be understated although more empirical study of mutual aid groups would provide support for this claim, empirical support like that from psychotherapy (Magen & Glajchen, 1999; Bonhote, Romano-Egan & Cornwell, 1999).

Until such time, the gap in knowledge as to the mechanics of mutual aid group initiation and sustainability of altruistic behavior requires a research program to filter out the altruism embedded in mutual aid groups, and develop intervention to initiate altruism deliberately within the mutual aid group. Further research to gather evidence of altruism in mutual aid groups is; therefore, necessary to understanding how to keep it going deliberately.

For example, qualitative research could explore, by way of in depth interviewing, the experience of group members and determine the circumstance which allowed them to become altruistic. A probing question could also determine if the altruistic behavior was voluntary or encouraged by the social worker facilitator. Content analysis could focus on the context of initiation and sustainability of the group, as to when the concept altruism was also demonstrated as a motivation or behavior. A focus group discussion could augment the in depth interviews by asking group members their consensus opinion of how, when and why altruism occurred. Finally, an interview with the social worker facilitator would provide triangulation to the above qualitative efforts. Gathering such data would provide an evidence-based understanding of altruism from qualitative methodology.

In addition, asking the question to what extent does the environment effect altruism would be a supportive follow-up to Archibald (2007). That is to say, is there a relationship between environmental conditions that exacerbate social existence and the founding of mutual aid groups, and altruism (Volhardt, 2009)? Conversely, with the improvement of environmental conditions, individually and collectively, do mutual aid groups disband?

A quantitative study would require development of a survey asking quantity questions that parallel the qualitative interview above. Overall, quantitative studies should be mindful that current altruistic scales seem, on the surface, outdated (Sawyer, 1966; Rushton, Chrisjohn & Fekken, 1981). Such instruments should be assessed as to the current best thinking regarding altruism. For example, it is suggested that altruism is only a motivation (Wakefield, 1993), that the prosocial behavior inspired by suffering (Volhardt, 2009) is not required to be altruistic. Asking agreement to suffering questions may measure agreement with prosocial behavior, and asking motivation questions may measure the antecedent motivation for altruism.

The implications of altruism from this paper and further research are considerable as discussed above. Further research is required to build evidence of not only the importance of altruism for social work with mutual aid groups but also the application of altruism with mutual aid groups by way of interventions that help social workers achieve altruism within the group, and social justice for the group.

References

Archibald, M.E. (2007). An organizational ecology of national self-help/ mutual-aid organizations. *Nonprofit and Voluntary Sector Quarterly, 36*, 598-621.

Bester, H. & Güth, W. (1994). *Is altruism evolutionarily stable?* Retrieved March 2, 2011, from http://arno.uvt.nl/show.cgi?fid=3026

Bonhote, K., Romano-Egan, J. & Cornwell, C. (1999). Altruism and creative expression in a long-term older adult psychotherapy group. *Issues in Mental Health Nursing, 20*, 603-617.

Borrello, M.E. (2004). 'Mutual aid' and 'animal dispersion': an historical analysis of alternative to Darwin. *Perspectives in Biology and Medicine, 47*(1), pp.15-31.

Brown, S., Brown, M., House, J. & Smith, D. (2008). Coping with spousal loss: Potential buffering effects of self-reported helping behavior. *Personality and Social Psychology Bulletin, 34*, 849-061.

Brosnahan, T. (1907). Altruism. In *The Catholic Encyclopedia*. New York: Robert Appleton Company. Retrieved October 10, 2008, from http// www.newadvent.org/cathen/01369a.html

Budd, L.J. (1951). Altruism arrives in America. *American Quarterly, 8*(1), 40-52.

Cameron, G. & Birnie-Lefcovitch, S. (2000). Parent mutual aid organizations in child welfare demonstration project: A report of outcomes. *Children and Youth Services Review, 22*(6), 421-440.

Cheon, T. (2003). Altruistic duality in evolutionary game theory. *Physics Letters A, 318*(4-5), 327-331.

Chien, W., Norman, I. & Thompson, D.R. (2006). Perceived benefits and difficulties experienced in a mutual support group for family carers of people with schizophrenia. *Qualitative Health Research, 16*, 962-981.

Cialdini, R., Schaller, M., Houlihan, D. & Arps, K. (1987). Empathy-based helping: Is it selflessly or selfishly motivated? *Journal of Personality and Social Psychology, 52*, 749-758.

Colp, R. (1986). 'Confessing a murder': Darwin's first revelations about transmutation. *Isis, 77*(1), 8-32.

Darwin, C. (1872). *The origin of species by means of natural selection* (6ᵗʰ edn.). London: John Murray. Retrieved September 21, 2006, from *The writings of Charles Darwin on the web* (J. van Wyhe, Ed.): http://darwin-online.org

Eisenberg, N. & Miller, P. (1987). The relation of empathy to prosocial and related behaviors. *Psychological Bulletin, 101*, 91-119.

Frank, S.A. (1994). Genetics of mutualism: The evolution of altruism between species. *Journal of Theoretical Biology, 170*, 393-400.

Gitterman, A. (2004). The mutual aid model. In C.D. Garvin, L.M. Gutierrez, M.J. Galinsky, C.D. Garvin, L.M. Gutierrez & M.J. Galinsky (Eds.), *Handbook of social work with groups* (pp.93-110). New York, NY: The Guilford Press.

Glassman, M. (2000). Mutual aid theory and human development: Sociability as primary. *Journal for the Theory of Social Behavior, 30*(4), 391-412.

Gould, S.J. (1976). *Darwin's untimely burial.* Retrieved on October 8, 2006, from http://www.stephenjaygould.org/ctrl/gould_tautology.html

Gould, S.J. (1997). Kropotkin was no crackpot. *Natural History, 106*, 12-21.

Jagendorf, J. & Malekoff, A. (2005). Groups-on-the-go: Spontaneously formed mutual aid groups for adolescents in distress. In A. Malekoff & R. Kurland (Eds.), *A quarter century of classics (1978-2004): Capturing the theory, practice, and spirit of social work with groups.* The Haworth Press, Inc. Retrieved on October 26, 2009, from http://www.harworthpress.com/web/SWG

Katz, A.H. (1981). Self-help and mutual aid: An emerging social movement? *Annual Review of Sociology, 7*, 129-155.

Kelly, T.B. (1999). Mutual aid groups with mentally ill older adults. *Social Work with Groups, 21*(4), 63-80.

Kropotkin, P. (1902). *Mutual aid: A factor of evolution.* Retrieved October 27, 2009, from Anarchy Archives: An online research center on the history and theory of anarchism: http://dwardmac.pitzer.edu/Anarchist_Archives/kropotkin/mutaidintro.html

Magen, R.H. & Glajchen, G. (1999). Cancer support groups: Client outcome and the context of group process. *Research on Social Work Practice, 9*(5), 541-554.

Ngai, S.S., Cheung, C. & Ngai, N. (2009). Building mutual aid among young people with emotional and behavioral problem: The experiences of Hong Kong social workers. *Adolescence, 44*(174), 447- 463.

Piliavin, J.A. & Charng, H. (1990). Altruism: A review of recent theory and research. *Annual Review of Sociology, 16,* 27-65

Rushton, J.P., Chrisjohn, R.D. & Fekken, G.C. (1981). The altruistic personality and the self-report altruism scale. *Personality and Individual Differences, 2,* 293-302.

Sawyer, J. (1966). The altruism scale: a measure of co-operative, individualistic, and competitive interpersonal orientation. *The American Journal of Sociology, 71*(4), 407-416.

Shakespeare-Finch, J. & Copping, A. (2006). A grounded theory approach to understanding cultural differences in posttraumatic growth. *Journal of Loss and Trauma, 11,* 355-371.

Shulman, L. (2005). Group work method. In G. Herman & L. Shulman (Eds.), *Mutual aid groups Vulnerable populations & the life cycle* (pp.38-72). NY: Columbia University Press.

Simon, H.A. (1993). Altruism and economics. *The American Economic Review, 83*(2), 156-161.

Smuts, J.C. (1926). *Holism and evolution.* New York: MacMillan Company.

Steinberg, D.M. (2002). The magic of mutual aid. *Social Work with Groups, 25*(1/2), 31-38.

Steinberg, D.M. (2003). Social work with groups, mutual aid, and social justice. In D. Goodman, D. (Eds.), *Social work with groups: Social justice through personal, community, and societal change* (pp.91-102). Binghamton, NY: Haworth Press.

Steinberg, D.M. (2010). Mutual Aid: A contribution to best-practice social work. *Social Work With Groups, 33*(1), 53-68.

Strohman, R.C. (2003). Genetic determinism as a failing paradigm in biology and medicine: Implications for health and wellness. *Journal of Social Work Education, 39*(2), 169-191.

Todes, D. (2009). Global Darwin: Contempt for competition. *Nature, 462*(5), 36-37.

Toulmin, S.E. (1964). *The uses of argument.* New York: Cambridge University

Press.

Tucker, W.T. & Ferson, S. (2008). Evolved altruism, strong reciprocity, and perception of risk. *Annuals of the New York Academy of Sciences, 1128*, 111-120.

Volhardt, J.R. (2009). Altruism born of suffering and prosocial behavior following adverse life events: a review and conceptualization. *Social Justice Research, 22*, 53-97.

Wakefield, J.C. (1993). Is altruism part of human nature? Toward a theoretical foundation for the helping professions. *Social Service Review, 67*(3), 406-458.

Wilson, E.O. (2005). Kin selection as the key to altruism: Its rise and fall. *Social Research, 72*(1), 159-166.

Yalom, D. (1995). *The theory and practice of group psychological theory* (3rd edn.). NY: Basic Books.

3

The model, a continuum of connecting the classroom and community: Utilizing group work

Brenda Exum and Mary Yanisko

Abstract: This paper describes a sequential model for educating social work undergraduate students on group process, emphasizing the importance of task groups, integrating group work practice and cultural competence across three semesters. The model will demonstrate an empowerment partnership between the School of Social Work and the community to facilitate the strengthening of these partnerships to benefit students, communities and the populations at risk.

Key words: group work, task groups, cultural competence, community partnerships, experiential learning

Introduction

After many years of clinical practice experience, their involvement in professional activities such as organizational boards and community task forces and from implementing classroom instruction, the authors realized that optimal learning occurred when students were able to experience in multiple modalities the content that is taught in the classroom. 'The model, a continuum of connecting the classroom and community: Utilizing group work' was created to address this need and also in response to the emergence of such arenas as evidenced based social work practice.

The model developers were also conscious that task groups are one of the most widely used forms of group work in social work practice. Yet, it continues to be an overlooked consideration in human service agencies (Toseland & Rivas, 2005). The authors realized early in their careers the significance of students being participants in task groups to create the change process in the community. Franklin and Hobson (2007) assert:

> ...the time has come for universities to take a greater responsibility for resolving the issues of implementation of evidenced based practice by making community agencies a part of the educational research enterprise (p.397).

There is a rich tradition in the field of social work that knowledge, skills and values focused experiences for multi level service delivery, be provided for students who are in CSWE accredited programs. In response to the challenge of strengthening the learning experience, this model is a continuum of instruction in the area of group work practice on the BSW undergraduate level. It links goals for students, community partners, and community clients in a three component educational approach. The model also incorporates the thread of cultural competence throughout.

This article will describe the model, outline the goals of each tier/semester, demonstrate how each is operationalized and provide examples of the results of the task group experiences in impacting the community.

Group work as the modality of choice

Group work is the modality of choice for these model developers who are concerned about preparing students for the delivery of interventions for clients with consideration of the complexities related to funding and staffing organization. The purpose of using group work for this model is to provide students with experiential opportunities in and outside of the classroom. This modality fosters the opportunity to use Bandura's (1986) Modeling and Coaching techniques for students to replicate in the community practice arena. In addition, Soliman (1999), suggests that working in small groups can increase student motivation. The size of the groups changes each semester with the students experiencing smaller task groups as they develop increased competencies in leadership and membership participation. The learning experience is structured throughout the tiers for each student to have responsibility to increase their competencies. This prepares them for effective group leadership post graduation.

Model

To initiate the model, the approach included the development of the structure of the relationships between the faculty and the community partners. The goal is to provide formal reciprocal volunteer consultation services with the community professionals. This facilitates input into student learning activities that would result in a positive impact for the partners' client communities. Community partners are contacted at the beginning of each semester to explain the students' learning assignments, to give the names of the student group members, to establish a meeting with the groups and to develop a feedback mode for the agency partners, students and faculty members.

The model develops students' competencies over three tiers/ semesters that begin in the junior year and conclude in the capstone course, which is offered concurrently in the first semester of the field experience. The overarching goal is to increase student capacity building in understanding the dynamics of multi cultural task group work, the nature of community intervention, and the functions of organizations in the community (Warren & Warren, 1984). This model increases social workers' abilities to commit to the poor and underserved in a multi cultural context (Mulroy, 2010). Generalist practice learning objectives focus on, prior to the field experience, the integration of classroom study content, opportunities for observation of best practices and the special challenges in the community of clients. The reciprocal experience is critical for schools of social work because the training of students and practitioners is closely related and results in mutual gain for all participants (Franklin & Hobson, 2007).

The goals of the model are:

1. To formally introduce differential approaches of group work by exposing students to the benefits of task groups;
2. To decrease student anxiety related to participation and leadership in groups;
3. To involve students in experiential learning in the community in order to observe social work models;
4. To develop networking skills to encourage a vision for the student to see themselves as the future task group leaders and members of community organization task groups;
5. To facilitate the integration of community partnerships as a resource in the classroom;
6. To challenge students to value community partnerships in providing community services, and
7. To increase cultural competencies through authentic interactions with diverse populations.

Tier one/first semester

The goal of this tier is to introduce students to a formal task group experience beginning in the introductory practice course. This is operationalized through the incorporation of a university required service learning component. Students are assigned to teams of 5-8 students, based on their interest, for a one semester exposure experience in addressing a community need. The faculty and community partner introduces the learning activity as an unmet need that requires the intervention of restoring, enhancing or creating a resource. The students meet in their first formal classroom task group to brainstorm to create a project that will impact resource for the community. They meet with the partner to develop a timeline and to observe the partner as a change agent. The project is completed by the last month of the semester and students participate in a poster presentation display at the university service learning showcase for a university wide audience.

Example of learning experience

The community agency referred to in this example is a long term care facility that borders the university campus. The students' task group provided a one time event that enhanced the well being of the residents. The literature warns of the danger of service learning in higher education becoming 'charity work' (Ward & Wolf-Wendal, 2000). Social work students are challenged to operationalize the core value of respecting the dignity and worth of persons served. The community partner, as a mentor, facilitated the learning objectives and ensured inclusion of the clients' perspectives.

Working under the creative supervision of the community partner, the students in this example provided an event called the 'Wall of Fame'. This event provided residents an opportunity to celebrate and honor their significant life events. The students created the Wall of Fame by exhibiting posters of residents with their pictures and stories in the facility and at the university.

Tier two/semester two

The goal of this tier is to have students develop skills in participating in a task group, while studying human behavior and families, and to understand treatment group approaches that impact diverse family groups in communities. The faculty and community partners meet to discuss the resources of the community organization. The goal is to facilitate student exposure to the family multicultural context and to learn about culturally sensitive social work practice. The community partners commit to accommodating observational experiences in the community and to support the classroom learning with presentations about the experiences of the population in their environment. A strong focus is on the ecological systems perspective to help students develop knowledge and values related to how families impact the environment and how the environment is impacted by families (Iatridis,1995).

The students are assigned to task groups of 4-6 persons that meet formally each week. In the first week of the course, the groups are given guidelines to use in the development of a formal presentation, for the class. The research findings and the learning outcomes from community partner coaching are shared in the final presentation. The partners assist the classroom learning by providing opportunities for students to learn/observe about ongoing treatment groups, social action and social reform initiatives and empowerment activities in their communities. In addition, students research diverse protective factors for various ethnic groups and share how they strengthen family units. The semester provides students with opportunities to experience shared traditions, rituals, customs, and celebrations that help to sustain families of different ethnic groups in the global society. The emphasis for the task groups in this tier is to recognize the responsibilities we all share in fulfilling the commitment to ensure social and economic justice thrives for all families.

Example of learning experience

The second tier semester involved 5 different task groups, in one class, with each group focusing on a different ethnic group. Throughout the semester each group researched ethnic strengths, patterns of family organization, core values, and coping philosophies. The learning included a study of contemporary issues related to immigration as it relates to ethnic family and community wellbeing. The task groups deliberated on the content to share with the total class to prepare them for a closing event. The teams collaborated to coordinate a 'Celebrating Families Forum', a closing class event, which was open to the university campus. The combined task groups provided a panel of individuals from different ethnic/cultural groups to speak on their challenges and strengths in an effort to preserve their ethnic heritage and wellbeing. It included a major showcase exhibit of memorabilia, religious objects, art, clothing, and food. A sweet potato pie throw down contest for the African American community was to demonstrate how families use preparation of food to facilitate family solidarity.

Tier three/semester three

The goal of this tier, which takes place in the capstone course, social work with groups, communities and organization, is to use task groups to implement a program for an unmet need in the community. Students work in formal task groups of 3-5 members (approximately 4 groups per class), based on their passion for addressing a gap in services in the local community for populations at risk. The focus of purposeful task group work is highlighted in the major assignment that requires each student task group to develop a new grassroots organization that will partner with an existing community service provider to address a barrier that creates an obstacle for clients in meeting their basic needs (Maslow, 1970).

The students work in partnership with the community partners and the network of key informants that they develop through attending staff meetings and/or focus groups for clients, etc. The partners assist the faculty with concrete, real life, experiential learning in the areas of membership in task groups, developing professional networking relationships, team building, fundraising, conducting needs assessments, and exposure to the current use of task and treatment groups in agencies.

The classroom learning involves instruction on how to do program development. In addition, budgeting, resource development, fundraising and marketing techniques and program evaluation are covered. Students use this knowledge and skill base to develop a new resource to implement for the partner's clients, prior to the end of the semester. The evaluation of the semester experience is done by the students in assessing if the goals stated by each student grassroots organization were met. The final presentations are conducted as mock proposal review panels to determine which task group project is worthy of funding for future replication. The community partners also give feedback to the groups.

Example of learning experience

One grassroots task group project was a Women's Wellness Forum for public housing residents. Students partnered with the local housing and redevelopment authority and case managers and collaborated with major health organizations who provided speakers, health screenings, and displays. Students developed directories to link residents to local services. The task groups with additional coaching from the community partners learned techniques to solicit in kind donations to provide a healthy dinner and gifts for the 100 residents who attended. In addition, a children's group was conducted concurrently by students and volunteer professional social workers for the participants' children.

The evaluation of this program, by the resident participants and the administrative teams from the housing authority and the health organizations, was so favorable that this has developed into an ongoing event each semester.

Each tier provided increasing levels of competency in group work practice. This increases the students' skill level and knowledge of group work modalities as an effective planned change process.

Outcomes

The outcomes for the students in this three tier model of connecting the classroom and the community were that each student successfully completing this model is able to actively participate as a member of a task group, assume leadership for a task group, develop a needs assessment with a community partner, and broker resources to support interventions using developmental group models. In addition they can apply macro skills such as collaboration, negotiation, team building, budgeting, marketing, and conduct evaluation of their interventions.

The outcomes for the community partners were the opportunity to assist the faculty with classroom learning based on the current/ contemporary needs of their clients, to have the resource of formal volunteer consultation by the faculty to plan intervention for their clients, to utilize the faculty member as a trainer for staff and community leaders, to utilize the energies and creativity of students in facilitating change in their communities.

Finally, the outcomes for the client community were access to new resources created by the students, access to empowerment opportunities, opportunities to serve as resources and consultants to students and faculty, and opportunities to be valued as major participants, in sharing their perspectives, in the education of future social workers. An unexpected benefit for the clients was the exposure and opportunity to explore their future personal, educational and career goals. Students served as models for clients and their children.

Discussion

This model has evolved over a five year period and the developers have had opportunities to receive formal and informal feedback from students in the three courses, other faculty, community partners and community clients. It was intentional to have the task group sizes decrease with each tier to increase the level of responsibility for each task group member. The task groups organized as committees and evolved in the third tier to using a board or taskforce format. The size was also tied to the number of community partners depending on the variance in class sizes. It was fortunate that the developers were able to sustain the commitment of a core group of community partners to facilitate the mutual advantage for continuity in the classroom and the community. Throughout the years the developers continued with high visibility in the partners' organizations.

This model has been evaluated from four perspectives. They include the formal university evaluation instrument that is implemented at the end of each semester/tier with students evaluating the course and the professor. The rating system includes a rating scale of very effective, effective, moderately effective, somewhat effective and ineffective. In 2009, for the category of faculty student interaction, students reported a 100% rating in the very effective to effective range in tier one and two and a 96% rating in that range for tier three. In the category of helpfulness of assignment in understanding course material, there was a 94% rating in the range of very effective to effective and 6% in the moderately effective for tier one and two and a 93% rating in the very effective and effective range and 7% in the somewhat effective category for tier three. Faculty, in each class, also have students complete an evaluation of the experience at the conclusion of their presentations in class (written analysis, verbal analysis and video tapings) in which 100% of the students in all three tiers rated their experience with the community partners in the very effective to effective range.

A second method of evaluation is to have students incorporate the learning from their research classes in the development of an instrument used to assess client satisfaction with the programs implemented in the community. This is required for tier two and three. In 2009, students developed a satisfaction survey, distributed it to clients who received services in the programs and 91% of the clients assessed the programs as very effective.

A third method is students, in the third tier, complete peer evaluations of the effective use of mezzo and macro skills in their grass roots organization.

A fourth method is the formal meetings between faculty and community partners throughout the semester and at the conclusion of the semester to evaluate the students and the outcomes of the learning activities in order to modify on going activities and to plan for future classes. These sessions have provided very positive feedback about the students and their contributions as well as thoughtful insights into additional activities that could be utilized in the future. Of the community agencies, 100% have continued their commitment to be community partners. Focus groups are also conducted to obtain the voice of client leadership groups and employees of the agencies served. Feedback from both of these populations was very positive and the client leadership expressed the hope that the students would provide even more educational groups for them in the future.

Future plans include the development of evaluative tools to measure benchmarks and final outcomes of the model, to develop procedures and instruments to assess changes in the service environment in order to provide competent practitioners to respond to community needs.

The developers would like to follow up with future research in the development of a model on sustaining the relationship with community partners in social work education.

Overall, there were many advantages to utilizing this model. It provided a win-win situation, as it contributed to the development of students to be effective generalist social work practitioners and group workers, it strengthened university relationships with community agencies and social work professionals, and increased community residents' involvement in providing positive interaction with social work professionals.

References

Bandura, A. (1986). *Social foundation of thought and action: A social cognitive theory.* Englewood Cliffs, NJ: Prentice-Hall.

Bloom, B.S. (1956). *Taxonomy of educational objectives. Handbook 1: The cognitive domain.* New York: David McKay Co., Inc.

Butin, D.W. (2006). Special Issue: Introduction. Future directions for service learning in higher education. *International Journal of Teaching and Learning in Higher Education, 18*(1), 1-4.

Franklin, C. & Hopson, L.M. (2007). Facilitating the issue of evidence-based practice in community organizations. *Journal of Social Work Education 43*(3), 377-404.

Iatridis, D.S.(1995). Policy practice. In R.L. Edwards (Ed.-in-chief), *Encyclopedia of social work* (19th edn., vol 3, pp.1855-1866). Washington, D.C.: NASW Press.

Krumer-Nevo, M. & Lev-Wiesel (2005). Attitudes of social work students toward clients with basic needs. *Journal of Social Work Education 41*(3), 545-556.

Maslow, A.H. (1970). *Motivation and personality.* New York: Harper & Row.

Mulroy, E.A. (2005). Group work in context: Organizational and community factors. In G.L. Greif & P.H. Ephross (Eds.), *Group work with populations at risk* (2nd edn., pp.446-456). New York: Oxford University Press.

Rothman, J. (2008). *Cultural competence in process and practice.* Boston, MA: Pearson Education, Inc.

Soliman, I. (1999). *Teaching small groups.* Biddeford, ME: University of New England.

Toseland, R.W. & Rivas, R.F. (2005). *An introduction to group work practice.* Boston: Pearson Education, Inc.

Troparon, J.E., Enlich, J.L. & Rothman, J. (2001). *Tactics and techniques of community intervention.* Itasca, IL: Peacock Publishers.

Ward, K. & Wolf-Wendel, L. (2000). Community centered service learning: Moving from doing for to doing with. *American Behavioural Scientist 43*(5), 767-780.

Warren, R.B. & Warren, D.E. (1984) How to diagnose a neighbourhood. In F. Cox, J.P.L. Erlich, J. Rothman & J.E. Tropman (Eds.), *Tactics and techniques of community practice* (2nd edn., pp.27-40). Itasca, IL: Peacock.

4

Pedagogy without pretense: Preparing non-social workers to facilitate social work groups

Dana Grossman Leeman

Abstract: This paper discusses the experiences of a group work instructor who is engaged to provide consultation and training to a group of non-social workers facilitating groups in a public health agency during the height of the economic recession in the United States. Differences in values and practice approaches clinical disciplines are explored. Tensions between academic institutions and agency settings in their approaches to supervision and practitioner training are elucidated. The author also considers the ways in wh ich effective group work skills were used to promote a collaborative and creative classroom environment that catalyzed and nurtured adult learning, and her own development as a social work educator.

Keywords: Group work, pedagogical method, interdisciplinary collaboration, co-occurring substance use disorders and mental illness, at-risk clients.

Introduction: 'The Early Recovery Four'

Eighteen months ago I got a call from a former student who is now the chief of mental health and substance abuse recovery programs for a public health agency located in Boston. She told me that because of changes in funding sources and funding cuts, her agency's treatment program for men in recovery from co-occurring mental illness and substance abuse disorders, traditionally an individualized treatment program, was undergoing some radical restructuring and would become a group program. 'None of the staff know how to run a group', she told me, 'This is a huge change for them.' So, I asked the consultant's $64,000 question. 'What can I do to help?' It seemed that my help was needed in a variety of ways. After speaking with the assistant director of the program, I was asked to help the staff develop a compendium of reliable and effective group activities and interventions, known in the states as 'manualized curricula,' as well as teach the staff some of the 'how-tos' of group work. Treatment had to be based on evidenced informed protocols; failure to do so might further jeopardize funding sources. It seemed pretty clear. I knew what was being required of me and how to prepare. Or so I thought.

Providing group work training and consultation to four adult learners in an urban public health agency in Boston was an important experience for me. Principally because it reinforced how good group work skills are synonymous with good teaching skills. And when one creates a mutual aid system in any group, whether it is in a formal classroom, or in a consultation and supervision group, everyone – the facilitator and participants – comes out of the encounter a little bit changed.

All group workers are teachers. As group workers we teach group members how to use groups. As practitioners we teach each other through conversation and consultation. We teach our interns and students how to do group work through supervision and in the formal classroom. We have many ways of transmitting our profession, but it is essentially accomplished through pedagogy and reflective practice.

Pedagogy is defined as the theories and skills that guide all teaching (Brookfield, 1986). The word derives from Greek, and means to 'lead a child.' In ancient Greece, the pedagogue was a slave who was selected by the master to literally lead his son to and from school each day. Pedagogy is more broadly conceptualized as the network of theories that guide our thinking about the process of learning and the practice of teaching. We all have our own pedagogical methods: some are explicit, purposeful and executed with careful intentionality. Explicit methods may include lectures, presentations, written scholarship, or the use of role-play, for example, as a way of elucidating and imparting theoretical concepts to our students. Other methods may be more implicit. They are intuitive, and not always fully known to us. Implicit methods tend to be instinctive or based on 'feel.' For example, one can see and sense when a class is disengaged from the content of a lecture. Even the most novice teacher can feel in her gut when she and the class are on different wavelengths. The way in which a teacher responds to this sense may be based on implicit methods. Sometimes, as teachers, we react in the moment. We do not always know why but we know that we must. The willingness to shift from a lecture to a more experiential activity is just one example of an implicit teaching method. Instinct, or what I think of as a kind of internalized radar of sorts, enables me as a teacher to tune-in to and respond to my students' curiosity or their disengagement, and make 'in the moment' shifts in order to increase the energy level in the room and deliver information in a way that is more interesting, accessible, or exciting for them. I would argue that my ability to read the affect in the classroom and then draw from implicit and explicit teaching methods is very much reflective of my years as a group worker.

Context

The story of my work with the staff of the early recovery program is situated in the political, cultural and practical. I will begin with the political context.

The political context

The landscape of social services in the United States is always changing. Fueled by ever diminishing resources, many agencies were forced to change the ways in which they provided care long before the economic recession. Fiscally conservative elected officials at the state level, and particularly at the federal level during the Bush Administration cut costs by limiting the scope of services provided by many health care and social service programs, or eliminating them entirely. In 2010, the Department of Mental Health in Massachusetts threatened to shut down many group support and treatment programs for homeless persons, including group programs housed in shelters, because of proposed legislation from republican members of the state senate. Publicly funded programs that serve chronic and persistent mental illness, the homeless, and clients with chronic substance use disorders are the most vulnerable programs, and many have been dismantled or significantly altered offering limited services. Social day programs for chronically mentally ill have closed. Residential treatment programs have closed or have had to reduce staff and admit fewer residents. Many community programs subcontract physicians, licensed psychologists and social workers. In addition, the necessity of having to provide services for less money has contributed to the preponderance of paraprofessionals and licensed clinicians from other disciplines providing care and services that have traditionally been performed by social workers. As a profession, this undoubtedly feels threatening to us, but *it is an undeniable market reality.* Licensed Mental Health Counselors, Licensed Alcohol and Drug Counselors and Licensed Alcohol and Drug Assistants, as they are known in Massachusetts, are treating more of our clients. Unlike licensed Bachelor level social workers, and Licensed Mental Health Counselors (LMHCs), who have master's degrees in psychology or counseling, a high school diploma or passing a high school equivalency exam administered by the state are required for pursuit of these certifications. I am not suggesting that only degrees from institutions of higher education qualify one to perform direct service with clients, but many are being entrusted with the care of some of the most challenging, at risk, and needful clients that we see. Most of their training is on the job, and they receive minimal formal training and often little clinical supervision. Does this affect the quality of treatment? I believe that it can. I worry that these folk are undertrained. I worry that they lack the guidance and supervision that clinicians who have graduated with Bachelor and Master degrees receive during their formal schooling. Do I make assumptions about the quality and nature of the practical training that licensed clinical staff receive? Yes. Are my assumptions elitist? Perhaps. Probably. Indeed.

The cultural context

The second context involves the impact of two very strong cultures: the academy and the agency. The academy directly influences social work practice and our collective professional identity. We do this in the ways that we inculcate our students with a worldview that considers diversity, oppression, social justice, and an attention to client strengths and empowerment (Saleeby, 2009). We do this with language. We have an established professional lexicon. We do this when we choose the network of theories that become the conceptual scaffolding for our students' clinical practice (Saleeby, 2009). These are the 'trappings' of the academy: the values, assumptions, language, theories, and various scholarly tools that we use to indoctrinate and 'grow' social workers. These tools have power and influence; they are the chosen ingredients by the educational arm of the profession. I admit that as a citizen of the academy, I have become quite reliant, perhaps too comfortably, on these trappings. And to be candid, I never thought much about the status and power they afforded me until I began my work with 'the early recovery four' and found myself straddling the cultures of the academy and the agency, which led me to more closely scrutinize the culture of the academy, in which I have always felt at home.

The academy and the agency: A complex cultural dance

In the world of professional social work the academy trains the professionals who ultimately occupy positions in agencies. Despite our best attempts to remain current and sensitive to market realities, agencies do not always feel that the academy makes good on its promise to thoroughly prepare social work students to take their place in the trenches. And, conversely, those of us in the academy sometimes feel that in the day-to-day struggles to provide quality services to demanding clients with less than adequate resources, our colleagues in the field do not always make good on their promises to provide our students with a more intellectual and conceptual orientation to practice. The nurturing of the whole social worker through the supervisory relationship is often diminished by time constraints and the need to focus intern instruction on practical and concrete tasks. Although the academy and the agency depend upon one another in many respects, there are tensions between them.

In addition to the differences between academic and agency cultures, there are cultural disparities between disciplines. With that in mind, permit me to state the obvious: the assumptions and values that are central to our profession are not necessarily the same for other disciplines. And some of the values and ethics social workers hold most dear are of little or no importance to other disciplines, and are absent from their professional discourse. Despite years of working on multi-disciplinary teams, fully cognizant of the different lenses that we all brought to our work, I have always felt that our ethics and values were the 'right' ones and I secretly judged other disciplines that did not imbue their professionals with an awareness of the impact of racism and oppression, the client's right to self-determination, and a dedication to the creation of an inter-subjective, mutually respectful, strengths-based, collaborative partnership with our clients (Saleeby, 2009).

Another important cultural distinction that can be seen across agency contexts and disciplines is that clinical supervision holds different currency. In the United States, social workers are required to receive a proscribed number of supervision hours until they achieve advanced licensure. Historically, our profession has been nurtured, sustained and transmitted as much through supervision and interpersonal dialogue as it has been through written scholarship and formal instruction. In the early recovery program, staff received very little supervision. Their director received monthly supervision, and he was charged with supervising his staff. This happened infrequently and informally, and as capable as he was, he was often perplexed and at a loss as how to best support his colleagues. I soon realized that while I may belong to a profession that tends to place a very high premium on supervision in the developmental trajectory of a clinician. I in many agency settings. Supervision is not a right. It is a privilege.

The practical context

The practical context refers to the 'how's and the 'why's of my teaching, and the process by which the 'Early Recover Four' and I discussed theories and concepts and applied them to practice.

My approach to teaching is based on the idea that the classroom needs to be a safe, dynamic and intersubjective space. To me, the best classes are those when students debate, grapple, challenge me and each other, and strive to make meaning of new and often abstract concepts. Students need to be encouraged to question and make meaning for themselves. I have accumulated practice wisdom that they do not yet have, and I have knowledge of theory that they have yet to develop. I am not interested in transmuting absolute truths. Rather, I am committed to being in a place of intellectual and emotional transition with my students. A place where their world views and conceptions about life, relationships and themselves are unsettled. This is an often uncomfortable place, but it is always replete with possibility and discovery. This cannot happen if the classroom is rigid, and the learners are passive participants. Freire (1970) refers to this as praxis: a subject-to-subject interactive and dialogic process. Dee Fink (2003) refers to this as the creation of a significant learning environment. Gitterman and Shulman (2005) contend that this is the core of any mutual aid system. Irving and Moffat (2002) refer to this as the carnival classroom. Combined, these paradigms gird my explicit and implicit pedagogical methods.

When one teaches graduate students or is asked to consult to a professional staff, one is engaged as an expert. I am not and will never consider myself an expert. I take this stance as a group worker and as a teacher. While I may possess certain competencies and knowledge, my social work training has taught me to embrace living in a place of perpetual 'not knowing.' In other words, I accept that there is always more to learn, and I am transparent about this with every student, and in every consultation. I assume this positionality because my most meaningful learning experiences were those where the teacher created space for me to continually wonder and muse, and where I was urged to be intellectually questful, even if I felt lost at times. This environment stimulated me, and this is when I learned the most. Irving and Moffatt (2002) contend that:

> ...classrooms can provide places/spaces for intellectual tumult that can be facilitated by conversations, confessions and carnival. We argue for an approach that values permanent unresolve...the posture of the professor is of 'not knowing' (p.1).

Moreover, the authors suggest that the 'event' of the classroom – the dialogue and the evolving relational dynamics – are as important, if not more important, than the content:

Explicitly, I am trying to encourage critical thinking. Implicitly, I hope to de-emphasize my alleged expertise, and put my students' curiosities front and center of the learning encounter. I do this by asking them a litany of questions, such as: 'What do you think?' 'What does this mean to you?' 'How does this resonate with you?' 'How do you imagine putting this idea into practice with a client or group?' This method demands that the instructor respond to students' latent and manifest content – what is spoken, non-verbal, and sensed as present in the room, but not yet named. Group workers do this in groups. We sit in, and explore silences, and any other form of affective expression. We support and encourage group members to ascribe meaning to group process, rather than imposing our construction of meaning on their experiences and feelings. These are the rudiments of a mutual aid group, and evident in the alchemy of a classroom.

Merging contexts

For me, the political merged with the practical when I accepted this consulting job at the early recovery program. A colleague of mine said, 'Why are you sleeping with the enemy?' When I asked her what she meant and who the enemy was, she said, 'the agency and the staff. They are taking our jobs, and now you are going to help them.' I was very taken aback. I had not considered the possibility that training paraprofessionals and licensed staff to do group work would effectively render social group workers obsolete.

My decision to work with this staff reflects the political and cultural contexts in which I live. I am a passionate group work advocate and educator. I teach and write about group work. I am devoted to the promulgation and survival of group work. My decision to work with the early recovery program staff is simple: they needed my help. I am a group worker, but I am also a teacher. If I am in a position to train providers to serve their clients well, I am fulfilling my ethical responsibility as a social work educator. Furthermore, I think that social group workers are uniquely suited to provide this kind of training. We have the knowledge. We have the skills. This creates a place for us where we may serve the profession, advance group work, support our colleagues, and ensure that our clients get their needs met. And, at the end of the day, this matters to me most.

The agency in which these four men were working is complex. It provides care and support to some of the most problem saturated, under served, and marginalized clients. They are very poor. They are predominantly of color. Many struggle with chronic and persistent mental illness, substance use disorders, and homelessness. Many of their lives regularly intersect with the criminal justice system, child protection systems, and youth services. The philosophy behind the treatment involves engaging very difficult clients to remain clean and sober and in treatment. Concepts like empowerment, shared decision making, collaborative treatment planning, and process versus content responsiveness, and acknowledging the impact of power, status, and difference on the group-as-a whole (Gitterman & Shulman, 2005) are not widely known or practiced, and essentially foreign to this particular culture.

This is also an agency that lives and dies by public funding. It is affected on an almost daily basis by decisions made on Beacon Hill (the seat of government in Massachusetts) and Capitol Hill, Washington, D.C. The budget, the work that this agency does, and the work force who provide services are largely decided by policymakers unconnected to the clients and the agency. Because of these market forces, this program was forced to transform its service delivery model, a by-product of the overarching political context, which evoked a great deal of apprehension and created an anxious overlay to the agency culture. All of these contextual exigencies walked in the door of the consultation room, and were embodied by each of the staff.

Creating a significant learning environment within a mutual aid system

Before my first consultation with the staff, I met with the chief of mental health and substance abuse programs and the director of the early recovery program. During that two-hour session, I sought to find out more about the staff, but most of our time was spent reviewing volume after volume of curriculum. I was very impressed by the recovery program's clinical director, an extremely bright young man. He was full of energy, curiosity and very self-reflective. He was in his late 20s, had a Masters in Psychology, and was a man of color. I will call him Jaio. He was also extremely over worked, and in addition to managing a hefty caseload of his own, had to manage the anxieties and needs of his staff. He mentioned to me that he was overdue for a vacation, but felt he could not take time off when there was so much work to be done, and aware that the staff needed him during the transition.

The other four staff members were comprised of Licensed Alcohol and Drug Counselors or of those training to become Licensed Alcohol and Drug Counseling Assistants. Although not technically paraprofessionals because of their licensure, one was college educated, and at least two of them had passed their General Education Development (GED) exam, and thus had a high school equivalency diploma. They were all of color, in various stages of recovery, and between the ages of 25 and 55. Three had been in jail for crimes related to their addictions, and two of them disclosed that they had earned their GEDs while serving time.

My initial sense of what I was there to do and what I 'should' teach, which had been suggested to me by the administration, ended up being quite different from what the group articulated and enacted needing from me. It became clear early on in our work together that what the administration might have wanted the staff to get from our sessions together was not going to actually meet the learning needs of the staff, so I had to shift my focus and readjust my functional clarity (my clarity of purpose and use of self) (Gitterman & Shulman, 2005) on a dime – a facility I owe to my group work training.

The work began on a blustery day in January when I walked into a small conference room. There was no chalkboard, so I requested that they provide a flip chart. I arrived that day with a fully realized lesson plan. I brought some snacks, a number of handouts, and mindfully avoided sitting at the head of the table in an attempt to lessen the power differential. As they came in, they were very quiet. They introduced themselves and took their seats. One of the counselors, whom I will call Gary, the most experienced counselor on staff, and a favorite among the clients, came in first and was very friendly and chatty. Of the group, he was the most curious and engaged member. They addressed me as 'ma'am,' 'professor,' or 'doctor.' I asked them to call me by my first name, but they were insistent. I asked them if they preferred to be addressed as 'Mr,' and they laughed. Gary claimed that someone who had worked hard enough to 'become a doctor should be called a doctor.' I told them that I really preferred to be called 'Dana.' And then, seizing a teachable moment, told them that group workers value minimizing the power difference between the worker and the group members. Silence. They looked at me. They looked at each other. More silence. 'Fantastic!' I thought, 'Their first demand for work and my first misstep!'

I began this first meeting like I begin every group, with introductions, but then launched right into a theoretical riff. I invoked Bion, the primacy of the collective, the importance of consistent structural elements like contracting, starting and ending on time, and pluralistic use of group time. They looked at me skeptically and were silent. Normally, I would sit in the silence a bit, but I was unsure at first what the silence was about, and this made me nervous. 'Thoughts or questions?' I asked. More silence. I broke the silence by telling them what administration had asked me to focus on with them, and asked them if this made sense to them. They nodded in unison followed by more silence.

The nausea in my stomach told me that I was totally missing the boat, and that the way I was talking at them with theory, and the very terminology I was using, so common to the classroom, was a different language. They did not seem to understand me. They were not engaged. They were not interested. I had already lost them. In that instant I realized how presumptuous I was and have been as a teacher. I have been speaking a language that I have expected my students to quickly learn. And I know that I am not always as vigilant as I need to be; I have not always been careful to stop and check-in with them to see if we were on the same page. I imposed a thought system and a language on my students and never questioned whether or not it fit, or if they really understood it. I expected them to learn it, to use it, and make it fit. More evidence of my power in the classroom.

In his work, Dee Fink (2003) describes interactive, energized, evolved learning environments, which he refers to as significant learning experiences. Significant learning experiences contain both process and outcome where adult learners are encouraged to be actively engaged agents in their own learning, and where the 'classroom' is charged with energy. Most notably, the outcome of this experience is that both teacher and student grow and change, personally and professionally, with lasting effect (pp.6-8).

In traditional educational settings, even progressive ones, there is a fair amount of lecture and presentation, even when integrated with discussion and experiential learning. Friere (1970) referred to this pedagogical method as the banking system, a subject-to-object exchange where educators transmit information to passive learners, and which leads to the perpetuation of oppression. This idea greatly resonates with that first consultation session. There I was, a white, privileged woman with a degree from a prestigious institution making 'deposits' into the learning banks of four adult men of color, who undoubtedly had already experienced their fair share of institutional racism and oppression. Recalling this makes me want to kick myself.

Sensing that things were not going well, and trusting my group work instincts, I asked if we could stop, switch gears, and start again. They nodded and looked at me quizzically. I then asked them to share what they hoped to get out of our work together and any concerns or worries they had about moving to a group treatment program. Jaio began to talk about having met individually with clients for years, and that the agency culture allowed clients to show up at any time, whether scheduled or not, and be seen by staff. 'So, what if you are meeting with another client and one of your clients shows up unannounced?' I asked. 'We see him,' he said. 'What if you have other things scheduled or are with another client?' I probed further. 'If they are in crisis, we drop what we're doing or put it off until later in order to see a client,' Gary added. 'Do you ever say 'no' to a client? Do you ever tell clients that they need to make an appointment or see emergency services if they are in crisis?' I asked. They shook their heads in unison. A quiet staff member, whom I will call John, mouthed, 'no way.' 'Wow,' I exclaimed. 'That is amazing. You are always there to take care of them?' I asked. I scanned the room. I made eye contact with the fourth staff member, whom I will refer to as Edwin. 'If we're not there for them. No one is. If we're not there, they'll pick up.' I slowly scanned the room again, making it a point to make eye contact with each of them. I sat in silence for a few minutes, exhaled and said, 'I am not sure I have ever met such devoted clinicians. You take their well being so seriously. What a tremendous responsibility. Does that ever feel burdensome or scary?' Gary shook his head, but John and Jaio agreed. Edwin seemed pensive. "Tell me everything about moving to a group program that troubles you, and also, what about it may be interesting or exciting to you as well?' We sat in silence for about five minutes. 'Groups are really hard work.' I said. 'I have been doing them for twenty years, and sometimes I go into a group and just get nervous. Sometimes I worry that nothing I say or do is helpful or right. Any of you ever feel that way?' I scanned the room again. One by one, they began to disclose. They admitted that they did not always know 'the right things' to say in group. Jaio worried that group treatment would not give the clients enough airtime, and that they were too needy to benefit from group. They feared that the clients would stop coming. They worried that their clients would feel abandoned. They talked about feeling tremendously responsible for their clients' sobriety, and burned out. They admitted coming to work anxious, and sometimes feeling lost. I tried to validate their concerns by describing clinical work as being 'the burden of the privilege of the responsibility of working with people who need our help.' This was a concept that had been taught to me by one of my teachers during my doctoral training. Jaio smiled and said that he had not heard that before, but that it made a lot of sense to him.

I then asked them to ask me any question they wanted to about group. The questions varied in nature. How do you handle group members who came late to group, or left group early? They asked about members who fell asleep during group, and whether or not swearing should be permitted during group time. They asked me about group members who had erratic attendance. They asked about group members who came to group intoxicated or psychoactive. Question after question. And after each question, I asked them to consider how setting limits, boundaries, contracts with consequences, and a predictable and consistent group schedule might impact the clients? Jaio, John, Gary and Edwin agreed that many of the clients would struggle to adjust to the new program. I predicted for them that a few of their clients would not come back, as they would not be able or willing to 'get with the new program.' This pronouncement was followed by what felt to be a sad silence. Jaio broke the silence by admitting that it was hard for him not to feel responsibility for their clients' health and sobriety. I smiled and nodded. 'That is so wonderfully put, Jaio. That makes such sense to me. Not working harder than our clients is our life's work as clinicians.'

Just before it was time to end I said, 'It seems to me that you have been a really worried bunch, which, given all the program changes, and your concerns about your clients getting taken care of, makes a lot of sense to me. As I sit here, I am thinking about *our* contract, and I am wondering if it makes any sense to you at all. And I am wondering if we should focus our work together on all of your worries and questions, rather than on writing a manual. Perhaps we should leave that to someone else for now, or work on it another time. I can advocate for our work with your supervisors. We can work on whatever you want and need to work on. This is your time. I am here to help you as best I can. Tell me what you need from me, and what you want to know about groups so that you worry a little less about your clients, and feel more confident about yourselves, and better about group work.'

Friedman (2008) maintains that an effective teacher always involves the learner in the learning process. This includes identifying learning goals and objectives, and relates the subject matter to the learner's goals so that content is relevant and useful. Furthermore, a skillful teacher endeavors to actively engage learners in problem solving to further their own learning, is flexible, and incorporates varied approaches. These include lectures, discussion, and experiential activities to meet diverse learning needs (pp.10-11).

With this in mind, I effectively stopped the group, assessed the experience with the group, re-contracted, and began again. The need to do this was instinctive – an implicit pedagogical method, directly informed by group work practice wisdom. From their laundry list of worries, we devised a group purpose and contract. We also decided that before each meeting, Jaio would email a list of 'wishes and wants' from the staff, and I would make a brief presentation of some foundational content to them, integrating case examples from their groups. For example, during our third session together, Gary brought up a moment from a group during which a client began to cry after telling a very painful story. Gary shared that he normally would have extended some form of compassionate touch when a group member became visibly upset, which was normative to the program's culture, but did not because this client was an out gay male. I asked Gary to talk about why his client's sexual orientation informed his decision not to reach out in the way that he customarily did, and Gary expressed the concern that any kind of touch might be misperceived as a sexual gesture. This led to a conversation about biases and assumptions, and homophobia. It also led to a conversation about what it means to have self-awareness in our clinical work, and the ways in which we communicate messages and values through our behaviors.

By listening, tuning-in, and being curious, the essentials of mutual aid *and* significant learning experiences, our sessions together became lively conversations, and 'the early recovery four' were attentive and invested students. Upon further reflection, they were some of the best I have ever taught. Each of them participated, and together we created a vibrant and fun learning community. Through them, I gained a mindfulness and honesty about my teaching, which Brookfield (2006) refers to as 'the truth of teaching' (p.12).

> By growing into the truth of teaching I mean developing a trust, a sense of intuitive confidence, in the accuracy and validity of one's judgments and insights...All I can do is try to remove whatever organizational, psychological, cultural, interpersonal or pedagogic barriers are getting in the way of them learning, provide whatever modeling I can, build the best possible case for learning, and then cross my fingers and hope for the best (p.12).

Coda

If the outcome of a significant learning experience is that teacher and student are changed in lasting ways, I can speak to the ways in which my teaching was and continues to be transformed by the 'early recovery four.' I recently began a new semester teaching a foundation course in group work with first year MSW students. Before I launched into the content, assuming that they would have some familiarity with it, as I had assigned a selection of articles that would supplement my presentation, I began by putting a list of words on the chalk board. I said, 'let's begin by defining some terms so that we can create a common lexicon. I want to make sure that we develop a common language and understanding.' Not only had I learned not to take what my students do and do not know for granted, but I was also inviting them to co-create the class with me.

I do not know if the effects of having spent time together continue to resonate with 'the early recovery four' or their group work. My teaching, and the way that I think about it, however, attests to the lasting impression that they made on me.

References

Brookfield, S.D. (2006). *The skillful teacher: On technique, trust, and Responsiveness in the classroom, second edition.* San Francisco, CA: Jossey-Bass.

Brookfield, S.D. (1986). *Understanding and facilitating adult learning.* San Francisco, CA: Jossey-Bass.

Dee Fink, L. (2003). *Creating significant learning experiences: An integrated approach to designing college courses.* San Francisco, CA: Jossey-Bass.

Friedman, B.D. (2008). *How to teach effectively: A brief guide.* Chicago, Ill: Lyceum Books, Inc.

Freire, P. (1970). *Pedagogy of the oppressed: Thirtieth anniversary edition.* New York/London: Continuum Press.

Gitterman, A. & Shulman, L. (Eds.) (2005). *Mutual aid groups, vulnerable and resilient populations, and the life cycle.* New York: Columbia University Press.

Irving, A. & Moffatt, K. *Intoxicated midnight and carnival classrooms: The professor as poet.* http://radicalpedagogy.icaap.org/content/issue4_1/05_irving-moffat.html. Retrieved 1/11/11.

Saleeby, D. (2009). *The strengths perspective in social work practice.* Boston, MA: Allyn and Bacon.

5

Introduction of a model of social work peer consultation groups

Kathleen M. Walsh

Abstract: Supervision is an important element of professional development that frequently leads to enhanced client outcomes (Munson, 2002). Three common formats for supervision include one on one supervision, group supervision, and peer consultation (Bogo & McKnight, 2005). Peer consultation groups are cohorts of professional social workers voluntarily seeking input and guidance outside of an agency framework (Munson, 2002). Typically, there is no formally designated leader, members share equally in responsibility for learning, and a case consultation format is employed (Berger & Mizrahi, 2001). In settings/areas where clinical supervision is scarce or inaccessible, peer consultation groups are an alternative to the more common one on one and group supervisory models. This paper describes a model for establishing peer consultation groups.

Background

Introduction

The purpose of this manuscript is to propose a model for establishing peer consultation groups as an alternative to more traditional approaches to clinical supervision, and to address limited access to clinical supervision. This manuscript arose as a response to community concerns regarding limited access to clinical supervision among Masters social work practitioners situated in the Eastern United States with a mixed geographic community and large rural population. Following is a description of clinical social work and supervision, including a discussion regarding barriers to supervision, a justification of need for peer consultation, a review of the literature related to supervision, and the introduction of a model for peer consultation groups. The literature review will address the definition of supervision including the various functions, distinguish clinical and administrative supervision, as well as provide an overview of the traditional models for supervision. Exploratory research examining social worker access to and supervision in a rural geographic region will also be discussed.

Clinical social work supervision

The American Board of Examiners in Clinical Social Work (n.d.) defines clinical social work as:

> [a] mental-health profession whose practitioners, educated in social-work graduate schools and trained under supervision, master a distinctive body of knowledge and skill in order to assess, diagnose, and ameliorate problems, disorders, and conditions that interfere with healthy bio-psychosocial functioning of people – individuals, couples, families, groups – of all ages and backgrounds (ABECSW, n.d., para. 1).

Thus, clinical social work supervision is conducted by experienced and skilled workers for the purpose of assisting in the development of knowledge and skills in direct practice, continued learning, job management, and treatment collaboration (Munson, 2002; Tsui & Ho, 1997). Clinical supervision is an integral component of professional learning and development (Munson, 2002). It is essential to ethical and competent practice, and it serves as the foundation for enhanced client outcomes (Kadushin & Harkness, 2002). Supervisors serve in a consumer protection role to guard against sub-standard and incompetent practice. According to the American Board of Examiners in Clinical Social Work (ABECSW, 2004), the importance of clinical supervision is acknowledged by the laws of every state and province in the United States and Canada, which require that clinical social workers be supervised for specified periods of time prior to autonomous practice. Further accountability is assured by many states and provinces where clinical supervisors are required to provide licensing boards with objective evaluations of each supervisee's functioning and ability to function without risk of public harm (ABECSW, 2004).

The National Association of Social Workers Code of Ethics (NASW, 2008) asserts that 'Social workers continually strive to increase their professional knowledge and skills and to apply them in practice' (NASW, 2008, p.6). One strategy for enhancing competence and professional development is supervision. It is widely held that agencies should make efforts to provide, and workers to actively seek supervision (Munson, 2002). Almost thirty years ago, Schreiber and Frank (1983) suggested that many independent social workers lacked the means and opportunity for further clinical advancements due to the absence of agency-based systems for supervision and limited available methods for skill refinement. As suggested by Berger and Mizrahi (2001), this tendency has continued and traditional supervision formats including one on one supervision and group supervision have been threatened. They attribute this to several trends in the service delivery system including cost containment strategies (managed care) that have lead to the elimination of many management and supervisory positions (Berger & Mizrahi, 2001). One result of cost containment strategies is that social workers lack clinical supervision completely, or receive supervision from professionals in other disciplines (Gibelman & Schervish, 1997; Berger & Mizrahi, 2001).

Access to clinical supervision; exploratory research

The author is a licensed clinical social worker in a rural area, and has observed that social workers experience challenges in obtaining employment that includes clinical supervision. Through discussions at continuing education workshops, it became evident to this writer that there was a gap in access to clinical supervision especially for those who are already licensed.

In discussions with this writer, some participants in the workshops speculated that this is due to a low value placed on clinical supervision and clinical licensure in their geographic region. Burkemper (2005) asserts that there may be additional barriers to supervision in rural communities where frequently less attention and resources are dedicated to clinical supervision especially when it cannot be immediately obtained within an agency setting.

To further examine access to clinical supervision a convenience sample of 19 school social workers at a continued education workshop in January 2010 were surveyed as to their current supervision experiences and their satisfaction with the supervision they currently received. The purpose of this exploratory research is to assess the need for clinical supervision and propose a model of peer consultation to address unmet community needs.

An anonymous, self administered questionnaire with 26 closed ended questions was distributed to participants upon completion of a continuing education workshop. Participants were asked questions related to their experiences with clinical supervision, educational background of their supervisor, and their agency model of supervision. Of the 19 respondents, none indicated that their supervisor was a social worker and only four indicated that they were receiving clinical supervision. Among those receiving clinical supervision (4), only 2 were receiving supervision from their employer. Respondents were asked to identify all of the types of clinical supervision they were receiving. The types reported were one on one (1), group (1), peer consultation (3), and other (1).

With respect to the educational background of each supervisor, among the 19 respondents, only one (1) supervisor had any social work education at all (a BSW). The majority (8) had a background in special education. Seven (7) had a background in education.

These findings, although exploratory in nature, appear to be consistent with Berger and Mizrahi's (2001) research. Changing trends in clinical social work practice including cost containment strategies, practice in host settings, as well as rural practice barriers, suggest the need to pursue alternative models to enhance competence and promote ethical social work practice. One such approach is peer consultation.

To address the barriers to accessible supervision and limited availability of professional consultation, clinical social workers may seek out supervision privately or via peer consultation (Berger & Mizrahi, 2001). Peer consultation groups are cohorts of professional social workers voluntarily seeking input and guidance outside of an agency framework (Munson, 2002). Typically, there is no formally designated leader, members share equally in responsibility for learning, and a case consultation format is employed (Berger & Mizrahi, 2001).

Literature review

To best understand the structure, advantages, and challenges of the proposed peer consultation model, it is necessary to briefly review the literature that frames supervision generally, distinguishes clinical versus administrative supervision, as well as provides an overview of the traditional models for supervision including casework, group, peer, team service delivery, and autonomous modes (Tsui & Ho, 1997). The proposed peer consultation model will be described in greatest detail. The review will demonstrate how this model may be used as an adjunct and compliment to other models or as the sole source of consultation in its own right.

Supervision

While there is no one unifying definition of social work supervision, it is commonly held that supervision is the primary mechanism for promoting agency accountability and delivering services in an efficient and effective manner (Kadusin & Harkness, 2002). In most cases, the supervisor and the supervisee are employed within the same agency or the supervisor has a contractual arrangement with the supervisee's employing agency (Munson, 2002).

The relationship between the supervisor and the practitioner is the primary medium through which human service professionals learn, and are evaluated for, how they perform her/his job. The quality of this relationship in turn, has impact on accountability and achievement of goal of competent service to clients. Further, supervisors are most directly responsible for insuring ethical, competent practice, and are ethically obligated to ensure that supervisee's do not harm and are successful. (Kaiser, 2004). Increasingly, supervisors are held vicariously liable for the actions (or inactions) of supervisees (Reamer, 1989). Consequently, supervision and consultation are important ethical considerations for both practitioner and supervisor. To this end, major considerations regarding supervisory relationships include power and authority, shared meaning and trust (Brashears, 1995). These considerations are equally important when considering the varied administrative, educational, and supportive supervisory functions.

The administrative conceptualization of the supervisory function typically involves a direct agency link and typically includes task and time management, record keeping, legal issues and risk management, as well as practice protocols (Munson, 2002). Administrative supervision is the primary vehicle for worker performance evaluations and decision making regarding salary and career advancement (Gibelman & Schervish, 1997). Some of the related skills associated with administrative supervision include resource development, management, planning, budgeting, evaluation, organizing, and developing human resources (Munson, 2002).

Education and support are another two commonly referenced and related functions of supervision (Kadusin & Harkness, 2002; Munson, 2002; Shulman, 1993). The responsibilities of clinical supervisors, who assist supervisees explore their interactions with clients, are most closely associated with educational and supportive functions (Gibelman & Schervish, 1997). The education function of supervision is related to professional development and enhancement of knowledge, skills, and self awareness. This typically includes direct activities associated with social work practice (Bogo & McKnight, 2005). Supportive supervision is primarily concerned with worker morale, job satisfaction, and stress management. This is typically achieved through encouragement, reassurances, and levels of autonomy (Kadushin & Harkness, 2002).

Clinical versus administrative supervision

While clinical supervision may include administrative and supportive elements, it is critical that clinical supervision be conducted by an experienced and skilled clinical social worker to fulfill the requisite educational functions (ABECSW, 2004). Among the most significant responsibilities of the supervisor are public protections from sub-standard, incompetent, or unethical practice. Accordingly, the ABECSW (2004) asserts that every state and province in the United States and Canada require that clinical social workers be supervised for specified periods (usually two years) prior to applying for a license to practice autonomously.

According to the American Board of Examiners in Clinical Social Work, clinical supervision embodies four major domains including direct practice, treatment team collaboration, continued learning and job management (2004). Direct practice includes assessment, treatment/intervention, identification and resolution of ethical issues and evaluation of client interventions. Treatment team collaboration refers to interactions with other professionals in the service environment. This includes political systems when the policies impact treatment or interventions as well as the capacity to influence policy making and procedures in a professional environment. Continued learning includes activities associated with education and skill development during the lifetime of the clinical social worker, whereas job management refers to work related issues that frame the clinical work. This includes record keeping, fees, missed appointments and caseload management (ABECSW, 2004.).

Traditional models of supervision

Five models of supervision have been identified by Tsui and Ho (1997) including casework, group, peer, team service delivery, and autonomous models. The casework model is the most common and utilizes one on one supervision. Group supervision typically involves one supervisor leading a group of supervisees (Bogo & McKnight, 2005), and is often used in conjunction with individual models (Tsui & Ho, 1997). In Tsui and Ho's conceptualization, peer supervision includes no formally designated leader and uses a case consultation format where members share equally. Bogo and McKnight (2005) assert that use of the terminology 'peer consultation' as opposed to 'peer supervision' is a better characterization of this approach because it is distinguished from traditional 'supervision' where there are power imbalances between supervisor and supervisee. In peer consultation, participants occupy similar positions in an agency hierarchy, and there is an absence of an authority figure. The team service delivery model combines the leader's role as educator and coordinator for the team activities and serves as a facilitator. In the autonomous practice model the practitioners choose the approach that works best and may draw on a variety (Tsui & Ho, 1997). Traditionally, the most common formats for supervision include one on one supervision, and group supervision (Bogo & McKnight, 2005).

Peer consultation model

The following proposal of a model for peer consultation is derived from a review of the literature, and the experiences of this author. For the purpose of this paper, consultation refers to social workers voluntarily seeking professional input and guidance outside an agency framework (Munson, 2002). Peer consultation groups may include members who occupy similar positions, but participation occurs voluntarily and outside of any agency hierarchy and free of performance appraisals/ evaluation. Group members may be employed in the same agency, but this is not a prerequisite. In a peer consultation model, mutual aid may flourish as a result of the reduced power and control issues that may occur with the presence of an authority figure or supervisor (Brashears, 1995; Berger & Mizrahi, 2001; Bogo & McKnight, 2005). The interdependence and non-competiveness of a mutual aid group or peer consultation better fits within the constructs of social work and empowers group members in the decision making process and in acknowledging the experience and skills they bring to the group (Brashears, 1995).

Establishing a peer consultation group has rewards and challenges. To minimize challenges and optimize potential for professional development and enhanced client outcomes, screening potential group members is a critical element of group preparation. It is essential to all participants, that group members share similar expectations regarding the group itself and have similar ideas about the function of supervision. While there is no one idea that is paramount, it is important to have clarity of role, purpose and expectations for the overall experience. Ideally, members will have similar or complimentary scopes/areas of practice to promote consistency, competence and sharing of expertise. Wiker (2001) reports participating in peer groups with as few as three and as many as six members. The number of members for peer consultation groups should be negotiated and considered during the preparatory phases and reevaluated during discussions regarding the consultation process itself. To promote cohesion, Schreiber and Frank (1983) suggest that, initially, commonalities such as comparable experience, length of training and background are beneficial. They also suggested, however, that group members with varied approaches and skills brought a diversity that furthered members' professional development.

Another important preparatory activity for peer consultation is to consider the inclusion of issues of confidentiality, privacy, and consent to share information (Wiker, 2001), and relationships with employing agencies or other entities. Depending on the group composition, the geographical area, and clientele, it may be necessary to obtain releases of information and consent to discuss client issues in the peer consultation group or for group members to take additional precautions and effort to disguise case presentations (Wiker, 2001).

Supervisory and practice skills, knowledge, values and expertise are other important considerations for group preparation and execution. Berger and Mizrahi (2001) assert that members in groups 'need to develop skills in the area of leadership, conflict management, effective communication of feedback, and group behavior if the group is to be successful in promoting professional development' (p.53). Skill development for peer consultation is especially challenging in that it requires the requisite practice, group work, team building and supervisory skills. Members must also have the ability to interpret and decipher the group needs when balancing essential skills. Among some of the most important group knowledge essential for peer consultation is mutual aid, the role of group process, and group dynamics. Supervisory skills related to the education and supportive functions are most critical with respect to peer consultation. Supportive skills such as coping with stress, time management, ethical dilemmas, along with educational skills related to training, practice expertise and competence, may be beneficial.

Once group members have been identified, it is necessary to address issues related to group process. As Brashears (1995) suggests, peer consultation groups allow the opportunity for reduced power and control issues more common in agency hierarchical settings. It is still necessary to negotiate leadership responsibilities, group dynamics, levels of intimacy and trust, interpersonal dynamics and the handling of group challenges such as tardiness (Wiker, 2001). Based on member experiences, expectations, and needs, some groups may opt to designate a leader or facilitator, or to rotate this role between members. The group structure itself should also be negotiated and agreed upon. Schreiber and Frank (1983) suggest that the level of commitment to the group may vary and that accepting and understanding differences is a challenge for group members. In light of the limited research in the area, the following questions should be considered during the establishment of a peer consultation group and as part of the ongoing process of the group itself.

1. What will our leadership/facilitation look like?
2. How many group members will we have?
3. How will new membership be handled?
4. What will be the frequency and duration of our meetings?
5. Where will we meet and does the location meet ethical mandates/ obligations (i.e. to promote privacy and confidentiality for clients)?
6. What (if any) will contractual obligations be?
7. How will we handle issues of intimacy and trust?
8. How will we handle group challenges such as lateness/frequent absences?
9. How will we handle issues of interpersonal dynamics and conflicts?

There is agreement in the scant professional literature on peer consultation (supervision) that the prevailing method be case consultation (Schreiber & Frank, 1983; Berger & Mizrahi, 2001; Wiker, 2001). Wiker (2001) and Schreiber and Frank (1983) suggest that meetings begin with open ended conversation, followed by prior session follow up, then movement into current case presentations with discussions afterward. Flexibility in structure and routine is also an important consideration so that group members are able to address more urgent issues such as ethical or legal dilemmas.

Implications

Limitations and areas of development

It is important to identify some of the limitations and areas for development with respect to the establishment of peer consultation groups. As Wiker (2001) so aptly observes: 'the process of creating successful leaderless supervision groups can be long and painstaking. But the rewards are well worth the efforts' (p.84). The limitations include challenges associated with the administration and continuity of the groups, including such issues involving group dynamics, recruitment, retention, and general sustainability. Additionally, administrative and personal factors related to group membership such as sub-standard or incompetent practice by a member of the group may create additional ethical, legal, and personal obligations for the group as a whole, and individual members.

Some of the notable areas for development include the need for further research related to the prevalence, creation, evaluation, and sustainability of such groups. Further, it is not as widely practiced as the more traditional models of one on one and group supervision (Bogo & McKnight, 2005), therefore, both research and guidance on administration of such groups are relatively scarce. It is also important to acknowledge that within both the United States and Canada, only one on one supervision, and group supervision experiences meet the requirements for licensure qualification at the advanced clinical social work level (Association of Social Work Boards, 2008).

Strengths

Professional development, enhanced client outcomes, and increased levels of practitioner competence are among some of the benefits of peer consultation. Agencies and social work professional boards may benefit from helping social workers to establish and participate in peer consultation. Incentives for participation, such as continuing education and work-released time, are some cost effective strategies to promote such professional development and ethical practice.

While there is some debate regarding the desirability and efficacy of peer supervision, the current environmental trends highlight the need for alternative approaches to traditional methods of individual and group supervision. Peer consultation groups are an alternative format for promoting professional development in the absence of a supervisor in an authority role (Bogo & McKnight, 2005) or when the supervisor lacks social work training. Peer groups present an opportunity for those working in host settings, rural communities, or in environments where supervisors are not social workers. Other strengths include reduced power and control issues, and increased opportunities for mutual aid. Supervision is an important element of professional development that frequently leads to enhanced client outcomes. In settings/areas where clinical supervision is scarce, peer consultation groups are an alternative model to promote these ends.

References

American Board of Examiners in Clinical Social Work (n.d). *Clinical social work defined.* Retrieved 2010-05-23 from http://www.abecsw.org/about-definitions-csw.html

American Board of Examiners in Clinical Social Work (2004). *Clinical supervision: A practice specialty of clinical social work, position statement of the American Board of Examiners of Social Work.* Retrieved 2010-05-23 from http://www.abecsw.org/images/ABESUPERV2205ed406.pdf

Association of Social Work Boards (2008, June). *Social work laws & regulations database.* Retrieved 2010-06-28 from https://www.datapathdesign.com/ASWB/Laws/Prod/cgi-bin/LawWebRpts2DLL.dll/EXEC/1/05ytsvn1461 7o6194kpwn0q3mxkx

Berger, C. & Mizrahi, T. (2001). An evolving paradigm of supervision within a changing health care environment. *Social Work in Health Care, 32*(4), 1-18.

Bogo, M. & McKnight, K. (2005). Clinical supervision in social work: A review of the research literature. *The Clinical Supervisor, 24*(1/2), 49-67.

Brashears, F. (1995). Supervision as social work practice: A reconceptualization. *Social Work, 40*(5), 692-699.

Burkemper, E. (2005). *Ethical mental health social work practice in the community.* In L.H. Ginsberg (Ed.), *Social work in rural communities* (chap. 10, pp.175-188). Alexandria, VA: Council on Social Work Education.

Daley, M.R., & Doughty, M.O. (2006). Ethics complaints in social work practice: A rural-urban comparison. *Journal of Social Work Values and Ethics, 3*(1), 28-44. Retrieved 2010-06-28 from: http://www.socialworker.com/jswve/content/view/28/44/

Gibelman, M. & Schervish, P.H. (1997). Supervision in social work: Characteristics and trends in a changing environment. *The Clinical Supervisor, 16*(2), 1-15.

Kadushin, A. & Harkness, D. (2002). *Supervision in social work* (4th edn.). New York, NY: Columbia University Press.

Kaiser, T. (2004). Supervisory relationships. In M. Austin & K. Hopkins (Ed.), *Supervision as collaboration in the human services* (pp.21-34). Thousand Oaks, CA: Sage Publications, Inc.

Munson, C.E. (2002). *Clinical social work supervision* (3rd edn.). Binghamton, NY: The Haworth Press, Inc.

National Association of Social Workers (2008). *Code of Ethics.* Washington, DC: NASW.

Reamer, F.G. (1989). Liability issues in social work supervision. *Social Work,*

34, 445-448.

Schreiber, P. & Frank, E. (1983). The use of a peer supervision group by social work clinicians. *The Clinical Supervisor, 1*(1), 29-36.

Shulman, L. (1993). *Interactional supervision.* Washington, DC: NASW Press.

Tsui, M. & Ho, W. (1997). In search of a comprehensive model of social work supervision. *The Clinical Supervisor, 16*(2), 181-205.

Wiker, M. (2001). Sustaining ourselves: An interdisciplinary peer supervision group for Orthodox Jewish therapists treating Orthodox Jewish patients. *Journal of Psychotherapy in Independent Practice, 2*(1), 79-86.

6
Managing ethical issues in social work with groups

Allan E. Barsky

Abstract: Social work with groups presents many ethical challenges, as well as unique opportunities for managing ethical issues. This article illustrates how to apply a Framework for Managing Ethical Issues in Group Work that incorporates multiple theories of ethics with an interest-based approach to ethical conflict resolution between group members.

Keywords: Group, social work, ethics, conflict resolution

Introduction

Traditional frameworks for analyzing ethical issues provide social workers with a series of steps that individual workers can use to determine the best way to respond to a particular ethical problem (Reamer, 2006; Dolgoff, Loewenberg, & Harrington, 2009). Although these frameworks offer workers concrete strategies for thinking through ethical issues on their own, in practice, ethical decision making should be a joint, interactive process. For instance, a social worker who is concerned about whether she is competent to provide a particular type of family counseling should consult with her supervisor. A worker who wonders whether he should initiate involuntary committal of a suicidal client should discuss the concerns with the client and strive to develop a mutually acceptable solution rather than simply impose a solution on the client. In group work, the focus of this paper, ethical issues often arise between group members and should be managed between group members. These issues may pertain to confidentiality, self-determination, informed consent, boundary crossings, respect, cultural competence, and conflicting values, worldviews, wishes, and interests of the members (NASW, 2008). This article provides a framework for managing ethical issues that includes methods of critical thinking, but also includes strategies for helping social workers and clients work through their issues within the group process. By using this framework, social workers can engage group members early in the process, using collaboration and consensus building to empower the group to participate fully in how the issues are managed. The following sections describe the framework, illustrate its application to social work with groups, and discuss the implications of using an interest-based approach to resolving ethics within social work groups.

The framework

The general Framework for Managing Ethical Issues consists of six steps, as outlined in Figure 1. This Framework provides social workers with a strategic approach to analyzing and dealing with various ethical issues that may arise in practice. Steps 1, 2, and 3 provide social workers with a basic structure for analyzing ethical issues, taking values, ethical duties, professional virtues, social context, and the consequences of options into account. Step 4 guides workers on how to engage clients, co-workers, administrators, and others in a conflict resolution process so they can work through the issues on a collaborative and consensual basis. Steps 5 and 6 provide guidance on how to plan, implement, evaluate, and ensure proper follow-up for the implementation of the plan. Workers should not use this model as if it is a rigid series of linear steps. Rather than following the steps in a bureaucratic manner, they should use the framework as a general guide, reflecting on the relative merits of each step as they go through the process. In practice, workers may need to cycle back to earlier steps as they work through the processes in order to deal with new information, new insights, and reactions of relevant stakeholders. In some cases, ethical issues may be resolved without having to go through all the stages in sequence. Given the dynamic nature of group work, flexibility is particularly important

Figure 1
Framework for Managing Ethical Issues

1. Identify Ethical Issues
   - Learn relevant laws, agency policies, ethical standards, and professional values
   - Recognize ethical questions or problems as early as possible
   - Articulate the specific issues that require attention

2. Determine Appropriate Help
   - Identify which types of help may be most useful (ethical or legal advice, clinical expertise, moral or financial support, conflict resolution, risk management, implementation)
   - Determine which sources of support are appropriate (supervisor, attorney, ethics expert, professional association, insurer, colleague, individual client, group members, friend, or others)

3. Think Critically
   - Reflect on one's values, virtues, attitudes, beliefs, motivations, emotions, capacities, challenges, and context
   - Consider multiple perspectives
   - Define goals for the ethical management process
   - Identify and weigh obligations
   - Brainstorm options and assess consequences

4. Manage Conflict
   - Analyze the nature of the conflict (rights, interests, power, miscommunication)
   - Define goals for conflict resolution
   - Determine appropriate strategies for engaging relevant parties in a constructive process (negotiation, mediation, advocacy, arbitration)

5. Plan and Implement Decisions
   - Determine who is responsible for performing which tasks, and when
   - Develop strategies to avert problems and to raise the likelihood of success
   - Monitor implementation to enable early response to problems that may arise

6. Evaluate and Follow Up
   - Evaluate the extent to which the goals were achieved and determine what types of follow-up (if any) are needed
   - Evaluate the effectiveness of the ethical management process and determine recommendations for change

*Loop back to earlier stages as needed.

(Source: Barsky, 2010)

when dealing with ethical dilemmas in group work. Consider, for instance, the possibility that different group members may be operating at different stages of the process One group member is still trying to define the issue, while another is reflecting on her values or problem-solving. The social worker may need to attend to both their needs, as well as giving the group some structure for working together.

I developed this framework by combining my expertise in ethics with my knowledge and experience with mediation and conflict resolution (Barsky, 2007). I originally published this framework in a textbook on social work values and ethics that covers not only practice with groups, but also with individuals, families, organizations, and communities (Barsky, 2010). The advantage of using an ethical decision-making model that cuts across all systems levels and contexts of practice is that social workers can use the same framework for all situations, rather than have to shift from one model to another when they are doing different types of work, or when working through ethical issues with social workers from other contexts of practice.

The framework views social work as one profession by providing all social workers with the same model for approaching ethical issues. Still, the framework has flexibility to take the context and type of social work practice into account. For example, the third step of the framework incorporates critical thinking from the three primary approaches to ethical analysis: deontology, utilitarianism, and virtue ethics. Deontology highlights the importance of a person's moral obligations: accordingly, all social workers should act in accordance with their fundamental ethical duties (Kant, 1964/Orig.1785). The duties of a social worker working with groups are similar in many ways to those of a social worker working with other client-systems: for instance, the duties to *respect clients*, the duty to *be honest*, and the duty to *practice within one's area of competence*. However, duties may also be specific to a social worker's roles; for instance, when working with groups, social workers should *act fairly* as between group members. This duty does not arise when working with individuals. Applying a deontological approach may be relatively straightforward when there are clear ethical duties that everyone agrees upon. Deontological analysis becomes more complex when there the ethical duties are not so clear, when ethical duties (such as honesty and safety) come into conflict, or when reasonable, prudent people disagree about which duties are more important (Reamer, 2006).[1]

The second approach to ethics, utilitarianism, suggests that social workers should focus not on their acts, but the consequences of their acts (Bentham, 1823; Markóczy, 2007). Utilitarianism encourages a social worker to consider a broad range of options to resolving an ethical issue and to choose the option with the most beneficial (or least detrimental) results. Utilitarianism permits social workers to take the context of their work into account, so social workers can easily translate this model from working with groups to working with other client systems. Consider an individual client who asks a social worker for a hug. Standard 1.10 of the NASW Code of Ethics suggests that social workers should maintain culturally appropriate boundaries and should not engage in physical contact with a client when there is "a possibility of psychological harm to the client." If the social worker is working with an individual client, the worker should assess potential for harm with just that client; for instance, what is the risk that hugging a client will mislead a client into thinking that the worker is romantically interested in the client (Gutheil and Brodsky, 2008)? If the client is part of a social work group, the worker should assess not only for risks to the individual client, but for potential psychological harm among all the group members; for example, will other group members feel offended or resentful if the worker hugs the client? Utilitarianism suggests that worker ask what are the potential risks and benefits of hugging, for group members individually and as a whole. Utilitarianism also suggests considering a broad range of options. By evaluating the potential consequences of many options, one has a greater opportunity to maximize happiness (benefit) and minimize harm (costs or risks). Just as a deontological analysis can become quite complex when there are conflicting moral duties, utilitarian analysis can become complex when there are many options to consider, when the risks and benefits of each option are uncertain, or when there is disagreement about whose benefit should we be considering (e.g., the benefit of all, the benefit of a particular client or group, the benefit of the social worker, or the benefit of the most vulnerable people in society)

The third approach to ethics, virtue ethics, focuses on moral character. Rather than focusing what duties to follow or which course of action will lead to the best consequences, virtue ethics suggests that social workers should simply *be moral.* Virtues are enduring character traits such as integrity, moral courage, moderation, respect, and caring (Walker & Ivanhoe, 2007). Thus, virtuous social workers respect a client's right to self-determination, not because the NASW Code of Ethics tells them to, but because that is how social workers live the virtues of respect and caring. The virtues that apply to social work with individuals also apply to social work with groups and other client-systems. Similar to utilitarianism, a virtues approach to ethics encourages the person to take the context into account, including the type of social work practice. Managing ethical issues from a virtues perspective is relatively straightforward when people are aware of their virtues and when the context calls them to respond in a definitive manner. "I am an honest person, and an honest person discloses conflicts of interest to clients." Applying virtue ethics becomes more challenging when people do not have strong awareness of their virtues, or when their virtues do not provide them with clear direction on how to live their virtues in a particular situation. "I am a caring social worker, as well as a law-abiding social worker. I am not sure how to live these virtues when a group of undocumented migrants needs my services, but the law says that it is illegal to provide them with such services." When challenging ethical dilemmas arise, having a structure for analyzing the issues and working through the conflicts is particularly important. Exploring one's virtues within a group context may be particularly helpful, as the group can act as a mirror to help each person raise self-awareness and focus on what attributes are particularly salient to the ethical issues at stake.

A case example

To illustrate application of the Framework for Managing Ethical Issues, consider the following scenario:

> A social worker named Sharon is facilitating a trauma support group for marines returning from service in Afghanistan and Iraq. During the initial session, Sharon advises members, "What goes on in the group is confidential, meaning that what people say in the group stays in the group." During the third session, one member, Mona, suggests that another member, Greg, has been gossiping about her outside the group. Greg claims that the only person he's told about the group is his wife, Wilma, and he needs to be able to talk with her. Mona claims that Wilma has been talking about her with other marines and their spouses. Group members raise concerns about trust within the group

and demand that Greg be evicted from the group for breaking its rules about confidentiality. Sharon hears the group's concerns, validates them, and asks if they can continue the discussion in the next session, after everyone has a chance to think about what has happened and what to do going forward.

In Step 1 of the Framework for Managing Ethical Issues, Sharon needs to identify the ethical issue raised by this scenario. To identify an issue, the Sharon first needs to be aware that there is an ethical question to consider (Barsky, 2010). Ideally, Sharon has a high sense of self-awareness and reflects on her interactions with clients as they are occurring, as well as afterward. In this case, the existence of an ethical issue was obvious to Sharon given that one client breached confidentiality and the rest of the group was demanding eviction. Sharon has asked the group to put the discussion on hold until the next session, which gives her time to think about the issue before responding.[2] Once the social worker is aware of the ethical issue, she needs to articulate the specific nature of the ethical issue. To define the issue, Sharon explores the relevant values, ethical standards, agency policies, and public laws. Sharon values the privacy of her clients and knows that client confidentiality is central principle in the NASW Code of Ethics (2008). When she reads Standard 1.07 of the Code she notes that while subsection (a) advises social workers to respect client confidentiality, subsection (f) is not so clear about the obligations of clients. This subsection advises workers to seek agreement about confidentiality among group members and to advise members that the worker cannot guarantee that members will abide by this agreement. In retrospect, Sharon realizes that she told members that the group was confidential rather than processing the issue and trying to build agreement among members. She also realizes that she should have ensured that group members knew that she could not control everything that every member said outside of group. Sharon knows she cannot go back in time and correct these deficiencies, so she looks forward and articulates the primary ethical issue as follows: "The group was intended to be confidential. Greg has shared confidential information outside the group and some group members believe that trust cannot be restored unless Greg leaves the group. Greg wants to remain in the group to continue to work on his trauma issues. Given these circumstances, what consequences or corrective actions are appropriate?"

In Step 2, Sharon considers who to consult for help with the ethical issue. She decides to speak with her clinical supervisor, Claudia, who has greater experience and familiarity with agency policies. Claudia helps Sharon reconsider the circumstances and how she has formulated the question. In particular, Claudia helps Sharon realize that confidentiality is not the only ethical issue at stake. Both the NASW Code of Ethics and agency policy suggest that Sharon has a duty to ensure access to services. In particular, Standard 1.16(b) of the Code suggests social workers should not abandon their clients; thus, if the group asks Greg to leave the group, Sharon is responsible for ensuring Greg has ongoing access to needed trauma support services. Claudia helps Sharon reframe the ethical issue as, "How should the group balance Greg's interest in remaining in the group with other members' concerns about maintaining trust and confidentiality in the group?"

Claudia wonders whether Sharon or the agency may be liable for malpractice, given that Sharon's discussion of confidentiality was less than perfect and some clients have raised concerns about breach of confidentiality. Claudia seeks advice from the agency attorney, Alex. Sharon describes what transpired in the group and asks for a legal opinion regarding the potential breach of confidentiality. Alex explains that in order for a claim of malpractice to be successful, a client must prove the worker had a duty of care (e.g., to maintain client confidentiality), the worker breached the duty, and the breach resulted in specific, direct damages to the client (Houston-Vega & Nuerhing, 1997). After gathering information and assessing the situation, Alex suggests that a lawsuit for malpractice seems unlikely at this time. Although Sharon may not have lived up to Standard 1.07(f) in terms of gaining agreement from the group and explaining the limits of confidentiality, group members have not identified specific damages caused by the possible breach. The breach was relatively minor and can likely be handled within the group and the agency. Alex suggests that Sharon and Claudia should develop a risk management plan (Falvey, 2002) that includes documenting the confidentiality concerns raised by group members, developing a plan to address their concerns, engaging group members in a collaborative manner, and monitoring implementation of the plan so that any new concerns can be addressed as efficiently and effectively as possible. Specifically, Alex suggests that Sharon should ask group members about what specific risks concern them if there are any further breaches of confidentiality within the group. This will enable the group to develop plans to address each risk. Sharon asks if she should apologize to the group for not discussing these risks earlier. Alex notes that, from a legal perspective, issuing an apology might be tantamount to admitting malpractice (Robbennolt, 2003); he suggests that Sharon should focus on plans for the future rather than apologizing for what happened in the past. Finally, Alex notes that because Sharon is licensed as a clinical social worker, state laws require her to maintain confidentiality of information shared in her group. Thus, Alex encourages Sharon to continue to discuss group issues with Claudia and himself, but warns her not to share group information with people outside the agency.

In Step 3, Claudia and Sharon use critical thinking strategies and explore the issues from various ethical perspectives. From a utilitarian perspective, for instance, they consider what course of action will lead to the greatest good for the greatest number (Dolgoff, Loewenberg, & Harrington, 2009; Markóczy, 2007). If they ask Greg to leave the group, his recovery from trauma may suffer; however, the other group members may benefit because they will feel safer in the group, thus making them more likely to stay in the group and benefit from their participation. From a deontological perspective, social workers should identify their core duties and act in a manner that fits with these duties: acting in an ethical manner is more important than the particular consequences of the action (Kant, 1964; Reamer, 2006). Sharon might note her professional mandate to protect the interests of the most vulnerable in society and ensure they have access to services. In this case, one could query whether Greg is particularly vulnerable because of the trauma he has suffered and how he is being singled out by the group for expulsion. On the other hand, one could argue that all group members have suffered trauma, so all are vulnerable. Another core ethical principle for social workers is self-determination: Greg wants to remain in the group, so respecting his right to self-determination could mean encouraging other members to allow Greg to remain; other group members want Greg to leave, so respecting their self-determination could mean encouraging Greg to leave. If both Greg and the group stay adamant about their positions, Sharon faces an ethical dilemma – whose self-determination does she prioritize, Greg's or the group's (Association for Advancement of Social Work with Groups, 2010)?

At this point, Sharon cannot resolve all the ethical issues. She will need to engage the clients in further discussion and conflict resolution. She identifies the following ethical goals, knowing that these goals are conflicting and she may ultimately need to prioritize some goals over others:

1. To respect Greg's right to self-determination regarding his participation in the group.
2. To respect the group's right to self-determination regarding group guidelines and the consequences for group members if the breach such guidelines.
3. To ensure a safe place for group members to process their trauma issues.
4. To ensure that all clients, including Greg, have access to appropriate services for their trauma issues.

In Step 4, Sharon plans to engage the group in a conflict resolution process to help them work through their concerns about confidentiality and Greg's participation in the group. Sharon considers a range of conflict resolution approaches, including transformative, settlement focused, and narrative.[3] She decides on an interest-based approach (Barsky, 2007). According to an interest-based approach, Sharon will help group members focus on their core, underlying interests and use creative brainstorming to develop solutions that may resolve their joint and individual concerns (Fisher, Ury, & Patton, 1997).

At the beginning of the meeting, Sharon invites members to discuss their concerns about confidentiality within the group. Mona says, "Greg is a pathological gossip so he can't be trusted and needs to be evicted from the group." Sharon helps Mona separate the person from the problem by reframing, "So, you believe that trust is vital for the group and that people need to keep what's shared in the group within the group." Mona resists this reframe, contending, "Actually, I believe that Greg broke our trust so he needs to leave the group." Sharon reflects Mona's position, "So you think Greg should not participate in this group," and then refocuses her on the underlying interests, "What purpose would it serve to have Greg leave the group?" Mona responds, "It would make the group a safer place to talk." Sharon engages the rest of the group in a discussion of why *confidentiality* and *having a safe place to talk* are important interests. Various members discuss feeling embarrassed about coming to a group, not wanting their colleagues in the marines to know about their mental health issues, and fearing that information from the group could be used to make life more difficult in the marines. They discuss the importance of being strong and mentally stable, and the worst-case scenario of being discharged because superiors doubted their ability to serve. The group, including Greg, agrees that having a safe place to talk is a vital interest.

Sharon re-focuses the discussion to elicit Greg's other underlying interests. "Greg, you agree that it is important for the group to be a safe place to talk, yet you shared information about the group with your wife and you seem to feel that it would be appropriate to do so in the future. Can you help us understand why it is important for you to be able to speak about the group to your wife?" Greg explains how the trauma of war has not only affected him, but also his wife. He says his wife's support is important to him, and he also wants to provide support to her. He said that he only shared information with his wife about the group to show her that they were not the only ones struggling with post-traumatic stress. He apologizes for breaking the group's trust and says he wants to do what he can in order to be able to continue participating in the group. Sharon invites others in the group to paraphrase Greg's interests and concerns. Initially, they want to contradict him and argue their points, but with Sharon's assistance, Mona is able to state, "I suppose that Greg understands the importance of confidentiality to the rest of us, but he also wants his wife to benefit from what goes on in the group."

Now that group members have a better understanding of their key interests, Sharon engages group members in brainstorming. "Let's make a big list of all the different ways that we could move forward with this group. What types of group rules could we develop in order to ensure the group is a safe place to talk, but also one where group members can take what they are learning in the group to help close family and friends?" Initially, the group is silent, not knowing what types of rules might be appropriate. Sharon encourages members to be creative, possibly suggesting crazy ideas and whatever pops into their heads. She reassures the group that they won't evaluate any of the options until they have a big list (Fisher, Ury, and Patton, 1997). She notes that even silly ideas can stimulate creativity and promote more effective solutions. Group members come up with the following suggestions:

- Evict Greg from the group and refer him to individual counseling.
- Evict everyone else from the group and refer them to individual counseling.
- Make the group absolutely confidential so that nobody can say anything to anyone about the group, ever, upon penalty of capital punishment.
- Make the group absolutely open, so that everyone can share anything to anyone, and even post the group sessions on YouTube. com.

• Have group wear paper bags over their heads to make the group completely anonymous.

The extreme and silly suggestions start to give way to more serious ones. Group members recognize that both confidentiality and family support are important, so they think about ways to achieve both. Eventually, they settle on the following agreement:

> Closed group sessions will be confidential, meaning that group members will not share any personal information that they learn from the group with other people, including family members. Group members may share general information from the group, provided that they do not talk about the thoughts, experiences, or concerns of particular group members. The group will also offer family-group sessions that family members and friends may attend. The group will ask family members not to share personal group information to anyone outside the circle of group members and family.

Sharon does some reality testing with the group to ensure that the agreement will work in practice. For instance, she asks what will happen if a group member or relative does disclose information. They discuss having certain penalties for sharing information, but eventually conclude that the agreement will only work by trust and commitment of all.

During Step 5, planning and implementation, Sharon discusses who will be responsible for which tasks. Some group members agree to write and distribute a list of group rules. Sharon agrees to interview each family member who expresses interest in attending the family meetings. Sharon will discuss confidentiality concerns with each relative in order to obtain their trust and commitment. Claudia agrees to take responsibility for monitoring implementation of the plan by inviting verbal feedback from group members and relatives in one month, and again in six months.

In Step 6, evaluation and follow-up, Claudia conducts a more formal evaluation, using written anonymous feedback. The survey includes questions about trust, confidentiality, self-determination, and the effectiveness of the family support sessions, ensuring that at least one question pertains to each ethics goal that Sharon identified in Step 3. Claudia meets with Sharon and the group to discuss her findings and determine what follow-up, if any, is needed. For instance, although some members felt the family support sessions were useful, others did not want their relatives involved in groups. The group concludes that the families group should continue to operate, but as a distinct group rather than an add-on to the group specifically for marines. By having separate groups, self-determination is maximized and nobody feels they have to participate in the family group if they only want to participate in the marine group.

Conclusion

The foregoing case illustrates how a process-oriented framework can be used to manage ethical issues that may arise in group work. The results illustrated in the case may appear fairly simple and straightforward, but imagine what might have happened if the group facilitator applied a traditional ethical decision-making model to determine the best course of action. Upon weighing her ethical duties, Sharon might have decided that she had an obligation to provide services for all marines in need and thus informed the group that Greg could not be evicted. While this solution is ethically justified, the process may be more important than the outcome. Had Sharon informed the group of her decision, they might have rebelled, demanded that Greg be evicted, or threatened action against Sharon for failure to properly manage confidentiality within the group. By involving the group in an interest-based discussion, she was able to help them develop and implement ethical solutions in an ethical manner.

A process-oriented approach to managing ethical issues fits well with the foundations and premises of group process. Empower the group rather than make and impose decisions. Trust the group rather than fear it. Build on the strengths of the group rather than belabor past ethical failings or vulnerabilities. Foster a group culture that values participation, mutual decision making, respect, dignity, understanding, and empowerment (Toseland & Rivas, 2009).

In the case example, the social worker (Sharon) assumed primary responsibility for guiding the process of managing the ethical issue. She was the one who initially decided how the ethical issue would be framed and who to consult for help with the decision making process. The advantage of this approach is that Sharon gave herself time to think through the issues and consult with others before re-engaging the group members. One critique of this approach is that she took ownership of the process away from the group members. She could have enabled the group to share ownership of the process by engaging them in all six steps of the framework, perhaps even inviting them to help facilitate the discussion. Philosophically, sharing ownership of the process fits well with the notion of group empowerment. In practice, however, sharing ownership of the process can be very challenging: in the case study, there was a high level of conflict and Sharon needed time to reflect and consult before engaging the group in a fuller discussion of the issues. Time to reflect and consult may be particularly important for students and novice social workers. Still, seasoned workers may also need time and space to think through complex ethical issues before bringing them back to the group. Ultimately, the framework does provide group members with decision-making power, with the social worker acting as a facilitator to help members reach consensus about how to manage the ethical issues.

Whereas most frameworks for ethical decision making encourage the social workers to reflect on their feelings, attitudes, and values, this model also encourages the social worker to engage the entire group in a process of self-reflection. Consider a group for teenaged girls who are dealing with unplanned pregnancies. Group members are split over how much say their parents should have over how they raise their babies. Rather than impose certain beliefs on the group, the facilitator engages members in a process of reflection, helping them explore feelings, values, and attitudes related to their *strengths and need to express their personal will* versus their *vulnerabilities and need for assistance from others.* Although the social worker might be inclined to focus on client strengths and their ability to parent by themselves, Hegel suggests that people need to be able to reflect and recognize both vulnerabilities and strengths (Bransford, 2011). Group members, individually and as a group, can use this reflective process to make ethically important decisions.

There may be times when group facilitators need to impose decisions, but imposing solutions to ethical issues should be viewed as a last resort – after collaborative attempts have failed and after consultations with supervisors or other experts determine that collaborative solutions are not feasible. Consider a group for teens at risk of dropping out of high school. The facilitator learns that group members are planning to have a sleepover at the home of a group member, Gina. The facilitator knows that Gina's father has a history of physical violence and does not think a sleepover would be safe. Group members do not know that child protection services placed Gina in foster care because of these concerns, but recently allowed her to return home. When the facilitator tries to resolve the safety issues privately with Gina, she insists that the sleepover will go ahead as planned. She instructs the facilitator not to disclose anything about her father with the group. Ideally, the facilitator would try to work through the issues collaboratively. In this case, the facilitator and supervisor decide that the issue of safety is paramount and they cannot ensure safety unless they act against Gina's stated wishes. The facilitator meets with Gina's father and asks him to cancel the sleepover. To help Gina save face, the facilitator advises the group that they have made plans for a group camping experience to replace the sleepover. Although the plan ensures safety and saves face for Gina, the process was unable to maximize Gina's self-determination. Still, the facilitator made a good faith attempt to empower Gina and develop a mutually acceptable solution to the ethical issues.

A process-oriented approach to managing ethical issues does not guarantee that ethical dilemmas will be resolved smoothly and collaboratively. Still, this approach fits with the tenets of group work by blending the critical thinking required for analyzing ethical issues with conflict resolution processes that can be used to resolve issues by consensus and collaboration. This article focused on the use of interest-based conflict resolution to resolve ethical issues in groups. Further theory and research could be used to compare and contrast the use of other conflict resolution approaches within groups.

Notes

1   Entire textbooks could be devoted to a single approach to ethical analysis. The relatively brief descriptions of deontology and utilitarianism provide a general description of these approaches. A comprehensive analysis by either of these approaches would require greater depth and complexity than can be offered here.

2   Note that there is no single, correct process for responding to an ethical issue. In the case example, Sharon takes extra time to think about the ethical issues and how to frame them. Alternatively, she could have processed the issues with the group, empowering them to frame the ethical issue and move through the other steps of the decision-making process.

3   A transformative conflict resolution approach helps people deal with conflict more effectively, encouraging each person to pay attention others' experiences rather than being self-absorbed in their own views, helping each person listen to and validate each other's concerns, and empowering each person by fostering self-determination, choice, and autonomy (Bush & Folger, 2005). A settlement-focused approach encourages parties to resolve disputes quickly and efficiently, sometimes through compromise or dealing with surface issues rather than resolving underlying issues, emotions, and ongoing conflict in relationships (Barsky, 2007). A narrative approach helps people deconstruct the current story of their conflict and reconstruct a more productive narrative (or story) that may focus on common ground, strengths, and opportunities for the future (Winslade & Monk, 2000).

References

Association for Advancement of Social Work with Groups (2010). *Standards for social work practice with groups* (2nd edn., copyedited revision). Retrieved April 6, 2011 from http://www.aaswg.org/files/AASWG_Standards_for_Social_Work_Practice_with_Groups.pdf.

Barsky, A.E. (2010). *Ethics and values in social work: An integrated approach for a comprehensive curriculum.* New York: Oxford University Press.

Barsky, A.E. (2007). *Conflict resolution for the helping professions* (2nd edn.). Belmont, CA: Brooks/Cole.

Bentham, J. (1823). *An introduction to the principles of morals and legislation.* Retrieved April 6, 2011 from http://www.econlib.org/library/Bentham/bnthPML.html.

Bransford, C.L. (2011). Reconciling paternalism and empowerment in clinical practice: An intersubjective perspective. *Social Work, 56*(1), 33-41.

Bush, R.A.B. & Folger, J.P. (2005). *The promise of mediation: The transformative approach to conflict* (2nd edn.). San Francisco: Jossey-Bass.

Dolgoff, R., Loewenberg, F.M. & Harrington, D. (2009). *Ethical issues for social work practice* (8th edn.). Belmont, CA: Brooks/Cole - Cengage.

Falvey, J.E. (2002). *Managing clinical supervision: Ethical practice and legal risk management.* Belmont, CA: Brooks/Cole.

Fisher, R., Ury, W. & Patton, B. (1997). *Getting to yes: Negotiating agreement without giving in* (3rd edn.). New York: Penguin.

Gutheil, T.G. & Brodsky, A. (2008). *Preventing boundary violations in clinical practice.* New York: Guilford.

Houston-Vega, M.K. & Nuerhing, E.M. (1997). *Prudent practice: A guide for managing malpractice risk.* Washington, DC: NASW Press.

Kant, I. (1964/Orig.1785). *Groundwork of the metaphysic of morals.* New York: Harper-Collins.

Markóczy, M. (2007). Utilitarians are not always fair and the fair are not always utilitarian: Distinct motives for cooperation. *Journal of Applied Social Psychology, 37*(9), 1931–1955.

National Association of Social Workers (NASW) (2008). *Code of ethics.* Washington, DC: Author. Retrieved April 6, 2011 from http://www.socialworkers.org/pubs/code/default.asp.

Reamer, F.G. (2006). *Social work values and ethics* (3rd edn.). New York: Columbia University Press.

Robbennolt, J.K. (2003). Apologies and legal settlement: An empirical examination. *Michigan Law Review, 102,* 460-517.

Toseland, R.W. & Rivas, R.F. (2009). *An introduction to group work practice* (6th edn.). Boston: Allyn &Bacon.

Walker, R.L. & Ivanhoe, P.J. (2007). *Working virtue: Virtue ethics and contemporary moral problems.* New York: Oxford University Press.

Winslade, J. & Monk, G. (2000). *Narrative mediation: A new approach to dispute resolution.* San Francisco: Jossey-Bass. (summarized online at http://v3.crinfo.org/narrative_mediation).

7

Increasing diversity: Competence in social work students through group research projects

Stephen J. Yanca

Abstract: The paper accompanied a workshop that was given at the 32nd International Symposium. It describes how social work students can develop diversity competence through an experience with groups conducting research and presenting their findings. The author first explains how values, attitudes and beliefs are developed through collective experiences. Social work with groups is discussed in terms of its history with a focus on how settlement workers may have dealt with diversity. We learn that settlers may have sought to live and work collectively in order to receive reinforcement for attitudes and beliefs about the immigrants they served that were different from those held by the majority of American society. Despite this strength, the structure and philosophy of settlement houses were not adequate to fight discrimination. Then the author describes the teaching method used in a practice course that helps social work students become more aware of oppression, cultural differences, and diversity competent practice by using research groups. Teamwork and discussion groups are the preferred methods. The paper closes with excerpts from students' work by way of illustration.

Introduction

The U.S. is experiencing major demographic changes that will inevitably lead to all races becoming a minority some time around the middle of this century. These changes are evident in the election of Barak Obama as the first African American President. His election represents a watershed moment that marks the power of people of color in the American electorate. However, while some have hailed this event as signaling the beginning of the post-racial era, the rise in racial hatred and hate groups and hate crimes indicate otherwise. The fact is that a majority of white voters did not vote for President Obama, but this was overcome by a huge majority of nonwhite voters.

By the middle of this century, projections indicate that more than half of American high school graduates will be children of color, as well as half of working-age adults. In the U.S., the majority of social workers are white middle and working class females. However, significant numbers of social work clients are not members of this demographic group. There is a great likelihood that social workers and other human service providers will be working cross-racially, cross-culturally, cross-gender, or cross-diversity. Thus, it is imperative that professional social workers become competent in working with clients from diverse backgrounds.

This paper will discuss the concept of diversity competence, the use of groups to increase diversity competence, a model for doing so, and examples of student papers that demonstrate the results of using research groups to study diverse populations.

Diversity competence

At one time, diversity was seen as a barrier to be overcome. During the 1960s when the Civil Rights Movement was at its peak, there was a belief that one should be 'color blind.' However, it is not enough to be 'color-blind' or 'culture blind' or 'diversity blind.' Professing tolerance for diversity can easily be interpreted as being insensitive. Assertions of tolerance may not lead to developing trust in clients who are diverse. In fact, it is more likely to lead to mistrust. Clients may interpret this as diversity does not matter when they know that it does (Johnson & Yanca, 2010). Obviously it should not, but reality is that members of diverse populations have continued to face prejudice, discrimination, and oppression despite the fact that it is now against the law.

Next came the development of ethnic sensitive practice in which the worker respected and valued the ethnicity and culture of the client. However, being sensitive does not mean that the worker would make substantial changes to the way in which services were delivered. Typically it meant that the worker would continue to deliver services in a manner with which he felt comfortable, but he would be sensitive to the differences between himself and his client.

The next step in this evolution has been to develop the concept of cultural competence. This calls for the worker to practice in ways that are consistent with expectations for giving and receiving services or help within the client's culture. This is a very significant and qualitative change in working with diverse cultural groups. In a sense, it calls on the worker to be the one who is likely to feel uncomfortable, not the client. Of course this is really how it should be since the worker is the professional and should be more capable of handling the discomfort involved with the situation. In many respects this approach can serve as the great equalizer in balancing the relationship between helper and the person receiving help.

In the last three editions of *Social work practice: A generalist approach* (8th, 2003; 9th, 2007; and 10th, 2010) and in two other texts that form a trilogy that covers the entire generalist practice curriculum [*Generalist social work practice with families* (2008) and *Generalist social work practice with groups* (2009a)], Louise C. Johnson and this author take this evolution a step further by developing what is called diversity competent practice. This takes the concept of cultural competence and extends it to all forms of diversity. The term diversity may include differences related to age, class, gender, color, culture, disability, ethnicity, marital status, family structure, race, national origin, religion, sex, sexual orientation, or any other distinctive feature or trait. Diversity competent practice is a more descriptive term than cultural competence. The list of populations extends well beyond culture and recognizes that people can be different from each other in many ways, and in multiple ways, as well.

Often students have difficulty in identifying their own diversity. Nichols (unpublished paper cited in Dewees, 2001) found that

...many students from White, dominant, middle-class status, particularly in geographical areas with limited racial diversity, regard themselves as having no culture or ethnicity.

This is consistent with the author's experiences teaching BSW students. Some of the lack of cultural identity may be a consequence of the mixing of cultures and ethnic groups in the U.S. Unfortunately, the inability to identify one's own culture or ethnicity does not mean that cultural or ethnic influences do not exist. It merely means that one is not aware of these influences. The author has frequently observed that many young female students have difficulty in recognizing discrimination toward women. This tends to change when the discussion shifts to male privilege especially who did what around the house when they were growing up or in their current living situations (Johnson & Yanca, 2010).

The problem is that the social worker is not likely to recognize or be open to the effects of diversity on his relationships with his diverse clients and will not be prepared to deal with issues his clients' experience related to their diversity. The competent professional social worker must include being 'diversity competent,' or competent in working with diverse clients, especially those who are different from him. Diversity competence begins with becoming aware of one's own diversity, experiences with diversity (direct and vicarious), and the effect that diversity has in one's personal life. Leigh (1998) proposed that knowing one's own cultural influences is critical to developing cultural competence and that everyone has unconscious cultural influences that either are directly prejudicial toward certain other cultures or that lead in that direction. Okum, Fried and Okum (1999) discussed the need to develop self-awareness regarding diversity before being able to develop an awareness of the diversity of others. Lum (1999) cited sources that reinforce the need for self-awareness. According to Diller (1999), one cannot appreciate the effects of culture on others, especially clients, if one is not aware of one's own cultural background. Lu, Lum and Chen (2001) developed a conceptual framework for cultural competence that begins with becoming aware of cultural and ethnic experiences, both personal and professional. They included racism, sexism, homophobia, and other forms of prejudice/discrimination. Two out of four steps proposed by Dewees (2001) for cultural competence with families are related to the need to identify one's own cultural influences (Johnson & Yanca, 2010).

Thus, to become diversity competent, the social worker must begin with an examination of her own diversity, along with examining how her experiences have shaped her attitudes toward her own diversity and the diversity of others. Cultural influences play a major role in this process. The authors cited above indicate that the social worker needs to obtain knowledge about the culture of the client and skills in working within the client's cultural system (Johnson & Yanca, 2010).

Using groups to increase diversity competence

The author was not able to find much research on the effects of using groups to develop diversity or cultural competence. In particular, it appears that little is known about the effects of working together in a research group on the attitudes and beliefs of group members toward diversity. It is suspected that this method may be much more widely used than would be indicated by the paucity of literature. Educators may be using groups to enhance diversity competence, but there does not seem to be actual research or publication regarding the effectiveness of this method.

The research that was found on group work and diversity was focused on the direct interaction among diverse group members. DeLois and Cohen (2000) developed an educational support group in a seminar format to share experiences and study topics by and about people who are GLBT. The article included research activities, but it was clear that the authors saw the interactions among group members as the most salient features of this experience. Nagda, Kim and Truelove (2004) looked at combining classroom learning and intergroup learning to teach about diversity. Teasley, Gourdine and Canfield (2010) found that school social workers identified collaborative practice and increasing knowledge as major facilitators in developing culturally competent practice. In each of these, the concept of collective learning was used, but not with a focus on using research groups. Instead, it was the interaction with diverse members that facilitated the development of diversity competence and not the research activities by the group.

All modern group work texts include a consideration of diversity, but this is focused on diversity within the group as opposed to the use of groups to research and increase diversity competence. However, some potential for the latter is implied by Toseland and Rivas (2005, p.8) when they identify one of four key values: '... We value the ability of groups to help enrich members by acquainting them to people from other backgrounds...' While this refers to direct interaction with those from diverse backgrounds, it could also be applied to group experiences in which members develop an appreciation for diversity by studying diverse groups.

Considering the development of group work in the early settlement houses can lead one to surmise that attitudes and beliefs among group members can at least be reinforced if not changed by the group experience. The people who were served in the early settlements were immigrants, mainly from Europe. In the larger society, these immigrant groups were looked down on and their status in American society was quite low. This led to prejudice and discrimination. Many of these groups were portrayed in very derogatory ways by the media and others. Most were from countries where autocratic rule and the use of the police and authority against them were the norm. These immigrants were easily exploited by employers, landlords, businessmen, and the like. They needed assistance in making the adjustments necessary to be successful in America. They needed advocacy and the ability to organize to overcome exploitation.

Settlement workers devoted their time and energy to this cause in ways that established what would later become the core of professional social work practice. That is, they were caring, empathetic, genuine, and accepting. In many ways they were the prototypes for modern diversity competent social workers. One might assume that this was planned, but it may not have been. In reality, the settlers had little choice if they were going to be successful in helping the populations they sought to serve. Without these traits, they would have had difficulty in attracting the immigrants to the settlements. After all, their clients were voluntary and the settlers had no real hold on them. On the other hand, caseworkers from charity organization societies (COS) were focused on establishing eligibility for charity. They frequently went out on home visits in doing this. Clients could refuse to let them in, but then that would mean a loss of any benefits. The truth is that COS workers did not need to be caring, empathetic, and accepting. That is not to say that they were not, but there is something coercive and judgmental about establishing eligibility for assistance or for services. In the settlement movement there was a considerable focus on the democratic way of functioning. Jane Addams saw groups as epitomizing the democratic way and allowing group members to experience democracy as part of life and not just a concept or a distant political process (Yanca &

Johnson, 2009b).

Gertrude Wilson (1976) made an interesting observation on the development of group work. She indicated that the settlers did not set out to use group work as a means of delivering services. They did so because people frequently came to the settlement with friends, neighbors, and family members (pp.3-4). They might come alone but often they came in groups. Settlement social workers served people in whatever way they presented themselves. As groups were formed, others joined in and social work with groups began. What is particularly important is that groups were generated by the participants. The settlement workers' response represented an early version of 'starting where the client is,' a fundamental principle of social work practice. Allowing the situation to dictate the type of client system (individual, group, family, organization, or community) is a basic principle of generalist social work practice which began with settlement social workers. Of course the principle 'starting where the client is' is also fundamental to diversity competent practice (Yanca & Johnson, 2009b).

The author was not able to uncover any research or consideration of the extent to which settlement workers developed anything resembling diversity competent practice as such. It would seem that at some level, they were cognizant of the need to accept participants as they were before offering them opportunities to learn how to survive and prosper in their new environment. It would seem that developing a culture of caring and acceptance within the settlement house was essential for success. Some settlers lived in the settlement house. Others lived in the community, but would spend time at the settlement house. It would seem that working together collectively was probably some of the attraction for this kind of work. There is also the sense of being part of a movement. However, as accepting as settlers were, early settlements were segregated by race. It is questionable whether settlements could have survived if they were integrated given the intense racism that existed in the U.S. at the time. It is unlikely that whites and blacks would have been comfortable mixing when the larger society was invested in maintaining separation between the races.

The larger society looked down on immigrants who were served by settlers and some looked down on settlers themselves as well, along with their work. To counteract the effects of these negative attitudes, the settlers created a haven from it. They created what might be called a counterculture. Indeed, later counterculture groups formed communes and communities where they lived collectively. It would seem that collective identity and commitment are necessary ingredients to developing and maintaining a counterculture. This serves as part of the rationale for using groups to increase diversity competence. The ability of groups and group behavior to influence individual attitudes and beliefs can be applied to efforts to establish alternative attitudes and beliefs that are different from those that society at large might hold.

Another aspect to consider is the source of negative attitudes and beliefs about various populations that are or might be the objects of prejudice and discrimination. It is proposed that much of this is born out of messages from members of one's family and later from peers and others who hold negative attitudes and beliefs. As a result, it makes sense that some form of collective experience may be necessary to overcome negative attitudes and stereotypes.

In addition to the collective nature of the establishment of negative attitudes, beliefs, and stereotypes, most people who hold these typically have little if any contact with the populations that are the objects of them. Thus, there are few if any opportunities to examine or refute misperceptions. In the absence of support for changing erroneous perceptions, most people will hold on to what they know, especially when those perceptions are supported by both their nurturing and their sustaining environments (Norton, 1978).

Thus, overcoming negative attitudes and stereotypes requires exposure to and information about the objects of these attitudes and stereotypes. To some extent it would seem that this needs to be done in an environment that supports change. It is proposed that such an environment needs to provide collective or group experiences in order to provide the support necessary to overcome the effects of prolonged collective reinforcement that supports entrenched negative attitudes and stereotypes. Thus, it is proposed that negative attitudes and stereotypes toward various populations are primarily formulated through collective experiences (family, peers, society, etc.). If this is accurate, then it is logical to assume that having collective experiences that refute these negative attitudes and beliefs and that support more positive views can lead to changes in attitudes and beliefs about diverse groups. This is the primary rationale behind using group research experiences to study diversity competent practice.

It is interesting to note that experiences in teaching diversity competence in other classes seem different when the teaching comes primarily from the professor. For example, the author's African American colleagues are often seen by students as pushing a personal agenda when they discuss discrimination toward African Americans. Gay and lesbian colleagues are often seen in a similar way when discussing sexual minorities. However, when research is conducted and presented by fellow students and discussed in class, little if any of these perceptions have been evident.

A model for using group research projects to increase diversity competence

For the past decade or so research groups have been used to increase diversity competence in BSW students at Saginaw Valley State University (SVSU) located in the Great Lakes Bay Region of Michigan. Diversity awareness and diversity competence is infused throughout the curriculum. In addition, there is a concentrated study of diversity and privilege in the Human Behavior and the Social Environment II course. In a Social Work Practice I course during junior year, there is a study of an ecosystems strengths based change process with a focus on individuals and on developing diversity competent practice. Students are asked to identify various populations who have experienced prejudice, discrimination, and oppression. Inevitably this process includes women, African Americans, Hispanic/Latinos, sexual minorities, and people who are mentally or physically disabled. These are the major groups with whom social workers are likely to practice in the Great Lakes Bay Region of Michigan. Other groups typically identified are people who are older, children, Native Americans, Asians, and similar populations. If there are sufficient numbers of students, additional groups will typically study people who are older and possibly children. It is pointed out that these groups comprise probably 75-80% of the population of the U.S. In addition, members of these groups have no choice regarding their race, gender, ethnicity, sexual orientation or the like. This makes their treatment even more insidious and blatantly unfair.

Students are given a choice about how to form groups of three or four. One option is to select populations they would like to study and then form groups around these. The other option is to do the opposite, form groups and then choose populations. Most choose to form groups which is actually preferred because they tend to form groups around acquaintanceship. It is hoped that this might make the experience more intense. Groups of strangers might allow participants to dismiss findings or attitudes that are different from their own. This is more difficult when they are in groups consisting of friends and acquaintances. Of course there is a risk that a group might reinforce negative attitudes and stereotypes, but the structure of the assignment makes this difficult.

Groups are asked to choose their top three populations they would like to study. They are encouraged to include groups that are unfamiliar or might present challenges. Preference is given to their first choice followed by second and third. During the semester, time is set aside in class for groups to meet and discuss their work and they also do so outside class. The professor visits groups to assist in focusing on important issues or approaches to be considered. During the last four weeks of the semester, groups give Power Point presentations on their population followed by a discussion of diversity competent practice with that population. The assignment as it appears in the syllabus is as follows:

Research/Focus Group on Diversity Competence

Research/Focus Groups will research diversity competent practice with a diverse and disadvantaged and/or oppressed population. Diversity competent practice involves developing knowledge, values and skills that will allow the social worker to serve that population in a manner that is comfortable for the client. The main areas that will be covered by each group will include: 1) Describe the history of the population, especially in the U.S., its strengths, and the primary characteristics by which members are identified. Describe formal and informal mechanisms in American society that cause or reinforce discrimination and/or oppression (past and present). Describe attitudes and stereotypes (current and historical) of the dominant culture toward the population and the impact of these attitudes on the population (psychological, physical, political, economic, social, etc.); 2) Describe privileges and advantages that dominant groups have over the population (male privilege, white privilege, heterosexual privilege, wealth or class privilege, etc.). Identify personal and professional values and beliefs held by most social workers, values and beliefs held by the population and values and beliefs of the dominant culture that are relevant in becoming diversity competent. Describe how these values and beliefs are similar, different, and/or in conflict with each other. Describe how privilege and these differences or conflicts in values or beliefs might influence the helping process; 3) Identify knowledge and skills regarding relationship building, assessment, planning, actions, evaluation and termination that are necessary to become diversity competent; and 4)

Identify at least two direct and two indirect intervention methods that should be used with your population and describe how these would be used to serve them in a diversity competent manner. These areas should be divided by each group in an equitable manner according to the number of students. Each student is responsible for writing a research paper on their portion of the study and will participate in a group presentation. At least 5 professional sources must be used for your report. At least 3 of those sources must be articles from professional journals or historic chronicles. In addition, you may include interviews with people who have expertise with the population being studied. Each group will facilitate a class discussion regarding their population. The purposes of this assignment are: 1) to learn about diversity competent practice with a diverse population; 2) to learn how to conduct research about diversity competent practice with a diverse population; 3) to learn how to write a college level research paper; 4) to begin developing a professional identity that includes sharing knowledge with others; and 5) to use this class project as a means of enhancing cultural and diversity competence. (Yanca & Johnson, 2010)

During their senior year, students develop a portfolio in which they analyze their experiences in each course. Many identify their diversity research groups as the most significant learning experience in Practice I. Some identify this experience as life changing or attitude changing. The two populations that seem to generate this change most often are women and sexual minorities. Many female students were not aware of the history or the pervasiveness of discrimination toward women. For those studying sexual minorities, some students who have strong religious backgrounds have actually changed their attitudes and beliefs entirely. Others have moderated their positions sufficiently to allow them to be much less judgmental and more open to serving members of these populations while setting aside their religious teachings or beliefs.

It is proposed that the success of this activity lies in part in the use of small groups to form what DeLois and Cohen (2000) called 'an educational support group.' In addition, the use of a structured research assignment creates a context that influences the groups to study aspects of diversity that may not be well known and are almost certainly not the basis for the negative attitudes and stereotypes to which group members have been subjected. In addition, group presentations to the class can create a larger educational support group to support the development of diversity competent practice skills.

The combination of a structured group research project along with a group experience of studying and presenting information on diverse populations can enhance the development of diversity competence. This model is an example of how this can be accomplished. It may be that small group learning activities are a more powerful approach than instruction from teachers regarding topics that relate to attitudes and beliefs. Further study is needed to support this.

Examples of diversity research group projects

Nowhere is the transition to greater diversity awareness and competence more apparent than in some of the writings that are produced by students who have participated in the group research project in Social Work Practice I. The following are some excerpts from a sample of those papers. The first is by Autumn Ward (2009), a 20-something year-old female student who wrote the following to describe the connection between *The Bible*, European history, and the attitudes and treatment of women in early America:

> The notion that women were meant by God to serve mankind began the treatment of women as inferior beings without a voice. This led to the denial of a woman's right to vote, own property, work outside the home in many professions, go to college, bring suit to court, or even choose what to do with her own body (Rowland, 2004). As far back as the Middle Ages, women were valued solely for their procreative abilities, in other words, the ability to produce heirs so that their husbands could gain status in society (Rowbotham, 1997). This idea that women were only valued for their ability to bear children did not stop in the Middle Ages, this notion was passed down through generations. Early American society deemed women as dependents of their men folk, who would speak for them in economic, political, and legal affairs. When America was first founded, the leaders ... adopted the same rules regarding women that had worked so well in Europe ... to keep women submissive to their husbands, fathers, and masters. When a woman married a man, all of her moveable property she had owned previous to marriage became her husband's to sell, keep, or give away as he pleased, leaving women nothing to call their own (Rowland, 2004).

Ward (2009) pointed out the strong connection between reproduction and the oppression of women as she cited sources that described how attitudes toward bearing children were used to justify this.

A woman's destiny ... was to bear children. In early American society, a single female – one devoid of maternal instincts, or one who refused to have children – was a so called threat to society, as dangerous as terrorism, viral and contagious, and downright unpatriotic (Rowbotham, 1997). ... Women were not allowed to take contraceptives, or even look at information regarding any type of birth control. Birth control information was not to be distributed, and doctors could not even prescribe it. Anthony Comstock('s) ... efforts against contraceptives gave way to a law forbidding the use of the postal system to distribute any type of contraceptive paraphernalia. Women were not allowed to choose whether or not they would like to bear children, they were basically told they had to (Rowland, 2004). This idea that women should not have the right to choose to be a mother paved the way for thousands of botched abortions, deaths from childbirth, and suicides (Cook & Howard, 2007). So women did have a choice, they could choose not have children and die, or choose to have children and die anyway.

Ward (2009) concluded her paper as follows:

In conclusion, women have endured everything from being deemed a genetic flaw, to having leeches 'cure' her so called female diseases. Women have battled with discrimination for centuries, and finally put up a fight for their freedom from the role of submissive housewife. Women are strong, capable, intelligent, and contrary to what they have been told in the past, they are very useful in so many more ways than just to bear children. Although women have fought a few battles of inequality, and came out victorious, the war is yet to be won.

A second paper by Kelsey Clark (2010), a Caucasian female in her 20s, discussed the use of a feminist approach in the change process consisting of engagement, assessment, planning, action, and evaluation and termination:

... To build a successful relationship with a client who is a woman, it is important to understand that culture uses woman-blaming themes quite often. It is this type of problem that leads to and encourages gender oppression. Also, in many stories women are considered responsible for men's behavior (Hare-Mustin, 1994, as cited in Wood & Roche, 2001).

Clark (2010) added the following:

Women are often taught by society to internalize problems. From the time they are little girls, society creates the idea that many of the issues women deal with are caused by themselves, not those around them. It is this internalizing that needs to be addressed when working with a female client. Teaching a female client to externalize is very important. Externalizing is a process that separates a problem from the client who is dealing with it and makes it a separate entity. Teaching this to a client can help them to stand with the client and against the separate problem (Wood & Roche, 2001).

Clark (2010) concludes with the following summary:

... During the time the worker spends with the client he should continue to engage in radical listening, which includes listening attentively, listening to bear witness, deconstructive listening, and also listening with planned emptiness. . . The social worker should also continue to undermine the oppressive beliefs that the client has. This means the worker should help the client externalize issues. The worker should use deconstructive questioning with the client and seek resistant and defiant ideas and responses from the client. This will help to remind the client of times when she has resisted the oppression placed on her. Finally, the social worker should apply the principle of co-creating a revisioned self-story. By doing this the worker will bring about the process of honoring heroism and courage ... (Wood & Roche, 2001).

A third research paper is by Jennifer Miller (2009), a Caucasian female in her 20s as well. She wrote about using the change process with people who are members of sexual minorities:

... While individuals differ in the diversity groups they are most uncomfortable with, it is not uncommon for social work students to be uncomfortable when talking about working with clients who are not heterosexual. ... it was found that students with limited knowledge of these groups tend to distance themselves from these clients, potentially affecting the services that are provided. ... social workers are often unaware of relevant issues affecting this population and not adequately prepared to serve clients who are not heterosexual. Forty-two per cent of interviewed social work students reported feeling as though they lacked essential knowledge about the issues and challenges faced by gay, lesbian, bisexual, and transgendered individuals. It was mentioned that tolerance or sensitivity do not equal competence ... (Logie, Bridge & Bridge, 2007). Attempting to avoid work with clients is not effective, because it is inevitable that at some point, homophobic attitudes of the worker, if present, will need to be addressed.

Miller (2009) made the following observations:

Living with societal hatred and dealing with homophobic reactions by those in the client's environment are two issues that must be addressed. ... The worker must be comfortable discussing such issues and knowledgeable of the ways that individuals who are gay, lesbian, bisexual, or transgendered are affected by prejudices. One factor ... is the individual's religious affiliation. Belonging to a religion that condemns homosexuality adds psychological stress to the client, because he or she is believed to be immoral by those in the religious community. One study ... found that the more religious people claim to be, the more likely they are to possess homophobic attitudes toward the GLBT population (Rowatt, *et al.*, 2006). Significant differences have been found among religious groups concerning the level of homophobia present, with Protestant individuals reporting more negative attitudes than Catholic respondents (Logie, Bridge & Bridge, 2007). While these religions teach the principle of loving one's neighbor and stress the importance of brotherhood, divisive attitudes directed at people who do not fit the dominant group cause GLBT individuals to become further stigmatized. Being aware of these beliefs and the exclusion of homosexuals from many religious institutions will allow the worker to understand that even if the client is interested in practicing a religion, it may not be as easy for him or her to feel accepted and part of a church family as it is for a heterosexual individual. Even if the individual is accepted, they may be viewed as sinner and the client may hear messages against homosexuality, and the need to seek forgiveness for being homosexual. The client may not feel understood by the other members because it is assumed that he or she can change their 'sinful behavior'. It is assumed that they have chosen homosexuality over heterosexuality. This plays a role in the previously mentioned lack of support system for individuals in the GLBT community. A lack of spiritual institutions that accept individuals in this population further limits the support system that is available.

These excerpts from student research papers are presented to illustrate the quality of work and the insight that has been generated from their group research project experiences and evidence of advanced understanding of the concept of diversity competent practice. These are from young junior level BSW students.

Conclusion

In conclusion, modern social workers are expected to develop competence in working with diverse populations. These populations are at risk of being disadvantaged along with experiencing prejudice, discrimination, and oppression. Students need to be aware of their own attitudes, beliefs, and stereotypes toward these groups as well as the source of these misconceptions.

This paper accompanied a workshop on increasing diversity competence in students by using a group research project. It examined how altitudes toward diversity on the part of settlement workers may have been influenced by the collective experiences of living and working with each other and with the immigrants whom they served. It proposed that collective activities probably gave considerable support for having and acting on attitudes and beliefs toward those immigrants that were different from the larger society. Support from groups can be quite powerful in changing and sustaining attitudes and beliefs. This proposition has been applied to increasing diversity competence in social work students through the use of group research projects by the Social Work Department at Saginaw Valley State University. The paper presents a group research assignment along with examples from student papers.

More research is needed regarding the use of research groups to increase diversity competence and the effects of group research experiences on changing and shaping attitudes and beliefs about diverse populations. It is proposed that the use of groups can be a powerful tool in increasing diversity competent practice.

References

Cook, R. & Howard, S. (2007). Accommodating women's differences under the women's anti-discrimination convention. *Emory Law Journal*, 56, 1039-1092.

Clark, K. (2010, unpublished paper). Women and diversity. Submitted Winter 2009, Saginaw Valley State University, University Center, MI (SVSU). Quoted with permission.

DeLois, K. & Cohen, M. (2001). A queer idea: Using group work principles to strengthen learning in a sexual minorities seminar. *Social Work with Groups*, 23(3), 53-67

Dewees, M. (2001). Building cultural competence for working with diverse families: Strategies from the privileged side. *Ethnic & Cultural Diversity in Social Work*, 9(3), 33–51.

Diller, J. (1999). *Cultural diversity: A primer for the human services* (p.14). Belmont, CA: Brooks/Cole & Wadsworth.

Hare-Mustin, R. (1994). Discourses in the mirrored room: A postmodern analysis of therapy. *Family Process*, 33, 19-35.

Johnson, L. & Yanca, S. (2010). *Social work practice: A generalist approach* (10th edn.). Boston, Massachusetts: Allyn & Bacon.

Leigh, J. (1998). *Communicating for cultural competence* (pp.31–33). Boston: Allyn & Bacon.

Logie, C., Bridge, T.J. & Bridge, P.D. (2007). Evaluating the phobias, attitudes, and cultural competence of Master of Social Work students toward the LGBT populations. *Journal of Homosexuality*, 53(4), 201-221.

Lu, Y., Lum, D. & Sheying Chen, S. (2001). Cultural competency and achieving styles in clinical social work: A conceptual and empirical exploration. *Ethnic & Cultural Diversity in Social Work*, 9(3/4), 6.

Lum, D. (1999). *Culturally competent practice: A framework for understanding diverse groups and justice issues*. Pacific Grove, CA: Brooks/Cole.

Miller, J. (2009, unpublished paper). Social work with the GLBT community: A walk through the change process. Submitted Winter 2009, SVSU. Quoted with permission.

Nagda, B., Kim, C. & Truelove, Y. (2004). Learning about difference, learning with others, learning to transgress. *Social Issues*, 60(1), 195-214

Nichols, W. (2001). 'Portfolio,' unpublished paper (University of Vermont, Burlington), as cited by Marty Dewees in: Building cultural competence for working with diverse families: Strategies from the privileged side. *Ethnic & Cultural Diversity in Social Work*, 9(3), 41.

Norton, D. (1978). *The dual perspective*. New York: Council on Social Work

Education.

Okum, B., Fried, J. & Okum, M. (1999). *Understanding diversity: A learning-as-practice primer* (chaps. 2 & 3). Pacific Grove, CA: Brooks/Cole.

Rowatt, W., Tsang, J., Kelly, J., LaMartina, B., McCullers, M. & McKinley, A. (2006). Associations between religious personality dimensions and implicit homosexual prejudice. *Journal for the Scientific Study of Religion, 45*(3), 397-406.

Rowbotham, S. (1997). *A century of women.* New York: Penguin Books.

Rowland, D. (2004). *The boundaries of her body: The troubling history of women's rights in America.* Naperville: Sphinx Publishing.

Toseland, R. & Rivas, R. (2005). *An introduction to group work practice* (5th edn.). Boston: Allyn & Bacon

Ward, A. (2009, unpublished paper). Living with discrimination: A history of women's fight for rights. Submitted Winter 2009, SVSU. Quoted with permission.

Wilson, G. (1976). From practice to theory: A personalized history. In R. Roberts & H. Northern (Eds.), *Theories of social work with groups.* New York: Columbia Press.

Wood, G. & Roche, S. (2001). An emancipatory principle for social work with survivors of male violence. *Affilia, 16*(1), 66-79.

Yanca, S. & Johnson, L. (2008). *Generalist social work practice with families.* Boston: Allyn & Bacon.

Yanca, S. & Johnson, L. (2009a). *Generalist social work practice with groups.* Boston: Allyn & Bacon.

Yanca, S. & Johnson, L. (2009b). Generalist social work practice with groups: Sharing the past, present, and future. Paper presented at 31st International Symposium on Social Work with Groups, Chicago, June, 2009.

Yanca, S. & Johnson, L. (2010). *Instructors manual and test bank for social work practice: A generalist approach* (10th edn.). Boston: Allyn & Bacon: Sample Syllabus.

8

Group work at the heart of hospital social work practice: Creating inclusion and solidarity in the acute care environment

Joanne Sulman, Lieve Verhaeghe, Catherine Coulthard, Kristy MacDonell, Amber Oke, Aviva Werek Sokolsky, Trish Woodhead, Sue Worrod

Abstract: For patients and families attempting to negotiate care, fast-paced acute hospitals can be stressful and anxiety-provoking. Social workers and allied health staff often feel unable to provide the support that their clients need. Social group work skills can transform this perception by creating opportunities for inclusion, connection, social support and solidarity. This paper will describe examples of innovative group work practice with patients, families and staff in the obstetrical and neonatal intensive care units, the sarcoma program, surgical oncology, out-patient mental health, the inflammatory bowel disease program and the out-patient breast cancer clinic. Themes related to group purpose and worker role will be explored. The group work programs described here are themselves supported by a strong social work collective based on social group work principles, where the social work group is the fundamental structural and functional entity.

Keywords: group work, hospital, single mothers, breast cancer, sarcoma, NICU, inflammatory bowel disease, psychiatry, staff support

Patients and families facing serious illness can experience acute care hospitals as anxiety-provoking and depersonalizing. When the mandate of social workers and healthcare staff is to discharge patients as soon as possible, they may feel unable to provide the support that patients and families require. Social group work skills can transform this perception by creating opportunities for inclusion, connection, social support and solidarity. Based on worker descriptions of practice, this paper portrays and contextualizes social groupwork practice on several patient care services in an acute care university teaching hospital in Toronto, Canada. The paper outlines the historical and translational background of social group work practice in hospitals, special features of social group work models and skills used in these settings, examples of innovative group work practice with patients, families and staff, a discussion of themes related to group purpose and worker role, and a description of the sustainable group work structure of the social work collective that supports the practice.

Historical underpinnings of social group work practice in hospitals

Our roots continue to define our practice. Group work is a movement that emerged out of the late 19th and early 20th century work in settlement houses (Hull House, Henry Street Settlement, Toynbee Hall), community centers, Ys, camps, scouts and guides, informal education and labour union organizing (Breton, 1990; 1995). Group work's value base of advocacy, social action and community is associated with social work practice in any setting. However, according to Andrews (2001), group work's decision to merge with social work in 1955 provided unanticipated consequences for group workers and, 'ultimately, resulted in the disappearance of group work as an integral part of social work education and practice' (p.45). This deficit in social group work education (Jacobson, 2009; Kurland *et al.*, 2004) leaves social workers who have not had group work practice courses at a distinct disadvantage when they try to start groups in the tough acute care milieu.

Casework, following Mary Richmond's influential text, *Social Diagnosis*, patterned itself after the medical model of 'study, diagnosis and treatment' of an individual's particular problem (Richmond, 1917).

Richmond's legacy in medical and psychiatric social work, although more recently strengths-based (Berg & Miller, 1992; Saleebey, 2002), has evolved into a role that, in acute care, is characterized by being the member of the team who helps make discharge plans, finds resources and intervenes to help upset patients and families cooperate with treatment. Health maintenance organizations (HMOs) and hospital hierarchies tend to define the scope of allied health practice, including social work roles, to meet corporate objectives (Sulman, Savage, & Way, 2001). This can challenge anti-oppressive practice and patient advocacy (Dominelli, 2002), and lead to pressure on social workers in healthcare to act primarily as agents for the organization's bed turnover and/or revenue-generation goals. To challenge this trend, social work's objective in secondary settings is to find novel ways to accomplish value-based practice. As hospital social workers, it is our experience that social group work can generate powerful value-based interventions, even in a fast-paced acute care setting.

Translational features of social group work practice in acute care: Recreating the spirit of settlement house

The work of group work pioneers such as Jane Addams of Hull House in Chicago distinguished group work and settlement work from both the charitable friendly visiting model and the medical model, since the purpose of settlement work was to focus on strengths, to engage in social and political action and to build community (Pottick, 1989; Lee, 1993). At its best, social group work continues to be an anti-oppressive, anti-oppression practice based on social justice, social action, advocacy, community, and diversity (McNicoll, 2003). This is particularly important in hospitals because of the vulnerability of patients and families contending with serious illness, and because many healthcare settings serve diverse, at-risk populations.

For group work in acute care, there are several additional core features of practice that workers rely on to create groups. Social group work has always been strengths-based. When so much of acute care treatment is focused on illness, groups are empowering. From a group treatment perspective, social group work is a practice that activates group process even when using manualized or specialized group treatment models (Muskat, Mishna, Farnia & Wiener, 2010; Galinsky, Terzian & Fraser, 2006). Social group work utilizes purposeful activity and mutual aid to address needs articulated by a range of constituencies: individuals on a service; groups of patients, families and staff; the hospital as a community; and its neighbourhoods and catchment areas.

Social workers in acute care have the potential not only to be the group worker for their patients and families, but also for their teams. In addition, they can use their group work skills to be community workers on their services. A patient care service is a small community within the larger hospital community that is comprised of patients, their support networks, and staff members. By identifying issues related to patient care, staff morale or other common concerns, the social worker can animate key elements within this community to build solidarity and develop strategies to address the issues. Several of the practice examples included in this paper describe groups that were initiated in response to the needs of their patient-service communities.

Special issues for groups in acute care groups and collectivities

Although we refer to groups throughout the paper, in hospital settings, especially acute care, much of the practice that utilizes social group work skills takes place in collectivities rather than in small groups. Collectivity is a small social form consisting of a number of people gathered for a specific purpose, and has some of the features of fully-formed groups such as mutual aid, interaction, shared goals, and some sense of entity (Lang, 1986). It is similar to any group in its initial phases of development.

There are many examples of groups and collectivities in acute care, including the traditional open-ended groups for in-patients, out-patients and families, time-limited outpatient closed groups which may be manualized, and single session and waiting room groups. There are also entities such as rounds and team meetings, family meetings, and groups for education and discharge planning that offer potential for the use of groupwork skills.

Worker's role in collectivity

The social group worker is often, though not always, more active in collectivity in order to foster connection and belonging (Sulman, 1987). Workers give permission for members to engage, and provide safety to express feelings: this encourages group members towards authentic interaction. Collectivity can evolve over the course of several meetings, with members coming sporadically. The presence of even one member with previous experience in the group seems to provide continuity, and a peer co-leader is doubly helpful in this regard. The worker uses the rich experience from a changing cluster of core members to help integrate new members.

Social group work models in hospitals

Model description in social groupwork continues to evolve. The following are examples of broad categories of group work models in current practice that can combine with other purposes such as tasks, education, and evidenced-based manualized groups to deliver a wide range of outcomes:

1. The remedial model that promotes therapeutic and behavioural change (Vinter, 1974).
2. The mutual aid model that facilitates therapeutic peer support (Schwartz, 1961; Steinberg, 2004).
3. The social goals model that works to promote change beyond the group through collective action (Cohen & Mullender, 2006; Shapiro, 1992).
4. The self-directed model where members identify the major problems in their lives, why they exist, and how to tackle them (Mullender & Ward, 1985).
5. The mainstream model, characterized by free interaction, common goals and mutual aid, which often has program other than 'talk' as a central feature (Lang, 1979; Middleman & Wood, 1990; Papell & Rothman, 1980).

In the section that follows, there are descriptions of group practice illustrating features of these models that combine to create robust practice forms. The remedial model is used in therapeutic groups with vulnerable populations, such as persons with persistent mental heath issues. The mutual aid model that promotes peer support in a safe context is an essential tool for change, and all of the groups described rely on mutual support to deliver important benefits to members. In the social goals and self-directed models, social workers in acute care, when allied with patients, families and staff, can be a powerful force for patient and family centred care (PFCC). The groups in perinatology and inflammatory bowel disease (IBD) are active in fostering improved patient care throughout the hospital and community, and the staff rounds in oncology tackle difficult patient care issues. Several of the groups rely on activity-based program content wherein the mainstream model unleashes the creativity that is a trademark of social groupwork.

The group work program: Innovative practice with patients, families and staff

'A group is like a new universe for the member – it opens doors and possibilities that weren't in place before you (the member) joined it'. (N.C. Lang, personal communication, March 29, 2008).

The group work program in this acute care, downtown teaching hospital consists of groups on a variety of in-patient and out-patient services. This section will describe the work of each group. The social workers who facilitate these groups were asked for written descriptions of their programs, including quotes from participants that exemplified recurring themes. The quotes came from a variety of sources: qualitative research, quality assurance data including anonymous feedback forms, and vignettes from group process. Following the group descriptions, we will explore some themes related to purpose and worker role that emerge from the practice, and give some suggestions for creating successful groups in acute care.

Sarcoma patient and family/caregiver support groups

> '[It helps] being around people who are "in your shoes", with the same understanding of the caregiver experience'... 'The group is a unique, safe and comfortable place for personal sharing'... 'A way of healing oneself'... 'As much as I feel like I'm giving, I'm taking'. (Patient and family members' comments)

Affiliated with the orthopedic oncology service, both the sarcoma patients' group and the sarcoma caregivers' group provide an opportunity for mutual support. Many of the patients being treated for sarcoma come from out of town and are isolated from their friends, families and communities. In an environment of facilitated mutual aid, these groups provide the opportunity for both patients and support persons who are caregivers to offer and receive help from one another, and to talk about their hopes, trials and worries. The group facilitates an understanding of coping strategies, provides support through sharing experiences, and normalizes reactions and responses to crises. In circumstances where patients and caregivers are often trying to protect the feelings of the other, each of these groups gives individuals permission to express emotions without censoring.

Nursing and allied health caregiving rounds

> 'The group relieves the weight of stress'... 'Makes us feel cared for'... 'We share expertise and gain validation from each other,'... 'As a new nurse, I learn a lot from more experienced staff' ... 'Brainstorm, reflect and reminisce about patients we have cared for'. (Staff members' comments)

Nursing and allied health caregiver rounds are an open ended, monthly drop-in group that gives inpatient oncology staff the opportunity to acknowledge, share and reflect on their own experiences of providing care to patients and families in crisis. The group allows staff to experience validation for their work and to give and receive mutual support. The social worker begins each group by stating the purpose of the group, the time available, and by helping the group to acknowledge the names of patients who have died or are having complex needs since the last meeting. Towards the middle of each session, the group looks at obstacles, strengths, coping and ongoing opportunities for mutual support. This reinforces solidarity within the team. At the end of the session, the worker summarizes the process and encourages discussion of topics for future meetings.

Young mothers' prenatal group

'From all the groups and classes I have taken, this has been the most useful' ... 'All my questions were answered' ... 'I felt very free to ask anything'... 'The facilitator] was very helpful and fun'...'I didn't realize my boyfriend was abusing me till I came to this group'. (Participants' comments)

The purpose of the young mothers' prenatal group is to provide an intensive, two-day experience of prenatal education and mutual support to high risk, disadvantaged young pregnant women aged 16 to 24 years. The program runs 6 times a year. The ten participants are young women and their support persons who work in a group with a social worker, a prenatal nurse and a dietitian on issues that, over the years, they and the staff have identified as important in their transition to parenthood. The social worker facilitates discussion and mutual aid on topics such as coping as a single young parent, relationship issues, negotiating housing, subsidized day care, welfare, returning to school, child protection and domestic violence. Each group establishes its own agenda centered in the women's lives, and forms a peer social support network within a culture of respect.

Day treatment program: Three day program and transitional program

'I could not come to terms with the sudden death of my mother until I heard another group member talk about losing his father, who was killed by a hit and run driver while crossing the street.' (Comment from group member)

Social work was involved in the creation and development of day treatment groups in out-patient psychiatry. People discharged from hospital following treatment for depression, post traumatic stress disorder or bipolar illness needed a transition to productive lives in the community. The day treatment program was designed in 1990 as a stepping stone. Together the three-day program and the transitional program run groups five days a week, providing intensive psychiatric rehabilitation. The worker creates a positive, collaborative relationship with interdisciplinary co-facilitators. Together they ensure that the group is a place where members feel safe and where they can trust one another. The worker models non-judgmental empathy, encourages self reflection and self reference, and promotes mutual aid through the sharing of concerns, difficulties and successes. Topics include relationship issues and life skills that foster autonomous coping with everyday life tasks. Through the identification of group strengths and members' strengths, the process instills hope in a population that struggles with serious, chronic psychiatric illness.

Taking charge: Healthy lifestyle choices for women after breast cancer

'I didn't want to join a group when I was going through treatment because I didn't think a group could help me, but what I've learned by meeting with all of these women is that I'm not alone, and I'm not crazy'... 'I feel better knowing that it's not just me with these issues'...'I thought there was something wrong with me because I felt sad, lonely and angry'. (Comments from group members)

Taking charge is a quarterly, 10 week closed, educational group program for women who have completed treatment for early stage breast cancer. The goal of the program is to help them make research-based healthy lifestyle choices. Initially set up with only nursing, a dietitian and personal trainers, the program features diet, exercise and 'ask the experts'. However, from the outset many participants identified distress and anxieties that were preventing them from being able to 'take charge' and move beyond a preoccupation with medical treatment and prognosis. When the group leaders realized that they were unprepared for the emotions that members were experiencing (e.g. fear, sadness, anger), the social worker was asked to participate. Now, as part of the very first group session, the social worker facilitates discussion about the emotional transition that women experience after treatment, including the identification, sharing and normalization of feelings. Mutual aid is an effective process that helps members cope with emotions that come with a cancer diagnosis and share strategies for a more balanced life.

Inflammatory bowel disease (IBD) support network and daytime drop-in group

IBD support network

'People always say, "How are you?", but you can't talk to your family and friends about colitis at the dinner table'. (Comment from member) ... 'Doctors can tell you everything about the medical condition, but they can't tell you about the emotional yo-yo that you will be on for the next series of months. This group can tell you that, and they can help you through the ups and downs'. (Comment from spousal member)

This collectivity is a large, open intake, peer support and education network for persons affected by inflammatory bowel diseases such as Crohn's disease and ulcerative colitis. It meets several times a year, with attendance ranging between 20-80 people at meetings. The network has been running since 1994, after inpatients and families told staff that they needed support, information and continuity of care after hospitalization. For the past 10 years, the social group work strategy has been to redesign what originated as a professionally-led education program delivered to an audience of patients and families, and transform it into a peer support network with indigenous leadership. By inviting interested participants to become members of a small-group steering committee, the social work and nursing staff empowered them to take ownership of the group process, to create the programs and to facilitate the sessions. The staff members then became workers to the small group, and consultants providing logistical support and troubleshooting to a peer-to-peer mutual aid network. The network starts its two-hour meetings with a presentation from invited speakers, and then offers an hour of networking, after brief introductions of everyone in the room. Participants are encouraged to mention any special issue that they want to talk about during networking, and may also identify a need for a 'buddy' who has been in their situation. The program is a major patient-family centred care initiative in the hospital.

IBD daytime drop-in group

> 'I've never really talked to anybody else who understood what I was going through' ... 'Everybody with IBD should come to a group like this'. (Comments from participants with IBD)

The IBD daytime group is an offspring of the IBD support network. Often at network meetings, steering committee members and staff noted that some participants needed much more support than the large group format could offer. This observation led to the creation of the daytime group, now in its 7th year. The collectivity is a monthly, single session drop-in group for inpatients, outpatients and their support persons whose lives are severely affected by IBD. Inpatient staff and students also attend, many of whom have a personal as well as a professional involvement with IBD. Co-facilitated by a social group worker, the IBD research nurse and a volunteer social worker, who has family members with Crohn's, the group usually has between 7 and 25 participants. Some members come once, some attend regularly for a while, and others come periodically, including members from out-of-town. The format for the sessions covers a welcome and statement of purpose, brief introductions explaining why people are attending the group, and an open discussion of participants concerns and questions about living with IBD. Workers encourage mutual aid, and at the end of each meeting, they summarize and check for unfinished business.

Parent programs, neonatal intensive care unit (NICU)

Parent education and support group

> 'The group gives us a lot of information, for example, the fact that you could have your "Primary Nurse", or how to keep in touch with your baby, or things you could request, such as "Kangaroo Care"'... 'From the time my child was born, we were educated as to how to take care of him, and the booklets issued to us have been very, very useful'. (Comments from parents of very preterm infants)

The parent group, which has been meeting weekly for 20 years, provides educational and emotional support for parents with infants in the NICU. The social worker co-facilitates each group along with rotating interdisciplinary team members who take the lead on discussion topics. Features of the group include ongoing mutual support and information to help members cope with the crisis of prematurity, to bond with their infant, and to foster a positive relationship with the interdisciplinary team.

Perinatal parent association, parent advisory committee (PAC)

'We could use a meeting room where mothers can set a time to talk, because usually we see each other at the washrooms, cafeteria, pumping room or different places. If we have a meeting room where we can talk or cry together, that will be good and is necessary.' (Mother's recommendation)

The parent advisory committee of the perinatal parents' association is an exciting social goals group for 12-15 veteran parents to discuss initiatives to improve the NICU/Level 2 Nursery. Chaired by a parent and supported by the social worker and perinatal nurse, the PAC is also a peer support group. The parent advisory committee is closely connected to the perinatal parents' association, and keeps in touch with many other parents via email so that they can share ideas and suggestions for improving care in the NICU. In addition, the workers and group members recruit parents who want to give back to the hospital by volunteering their time to patient and family centred care initiatives related to their experience (e.g. delivery of bad news committee, transfer committee, training to become a parent-buddy).

Parent-buddy training group

'She told me first to take care of myself so that I could have the energy to take good care of my baby.' (Mother's comment about parent-buddy)

This single session training group facilitated by the social worker and perinatal nurse is closely affiliated to the other parent groups in the NICU. Parents who have prior experience in the NICU volunteer to be matched with a parent who has an infant currently in the NICU with similar diagnoses. Over 70 parents, representing 20 different languages and cultures, have participated in these training groups. The training groups offer additional opportunity for mutual aid for the participants.

Themes related to purpose and worker role

From the workers' descriptions of their programs, we found common themes along with some unique practice features in each group. It is beyond the scope of this paper to do a complete qualitative analysis of the narratives, but we will explore two categories, group purpose and worker role.

Group purpose

'Create a sense of purpose, the aspiration of the whole that impacts each one of the members. Free interaction allows for the whole to create something together - not only mutual aid, but going somewhere together - that's the power of the group.' (N.C. Lang, personal communication, March 29, 2008).

Similarities emerged in group purpose, even though the populations differ. In most of the groups, a primary purpose is the creation of a healing environment of caring, empowerment and mutual support for members (Glassman, 1991). Another purpose of most groups is to bring together persons who are disadvantaged in relation to medical or psychiatric illness. In the young mothers' group, the purpose is to support young women who are disadvantaged by early pregnancy and socio-economic circumstances, to provide an experience that can enhance their self-esteem and help them frame goals to move themselves out of poverty. Other purposes in all groups are to reduce feelings of isolation and provide help coping with current circumstances. The groups purposefully normalize members' responses and allow them to experience their own strengths, particularly when they work towards common goals and become providers of mutual aid to other members (Riessman, 1965). As in most health-related group programs, information-sharing is a purpose in all groups. Interactive education is a purpose in the breast cancer transition group and in the large group IBD and NICU meetings. Most of the groups purposefully provide continuity of care as a lifeline for members in the transition from inpatient to outpatient and from active treatment to independent functioning in the community. Groups which have unique purposes are the psychiatric day treatment groups that are designed for remedial personal growth and well-being, and the NICU parent advisory committee and the IBD network steering committee, whose social goals include program improvement and design. Another group with a unique purpose is the parent-buddy training group whose purpose is to take mutual aid on the road by training veteran parents to provide peer support for new parents in the NICU.

Social group worker role

Before facilitating program content, the worker frames each session with welcome for new and returning members, and orients everyone to the format of the meeting. By providing a climate of non-judgmental respect and free interaction that allows people to know each other, the group worker allows members to raise difficult issues such as distressing physical and psychiatric symptoms, and relationship abuse. These worker actions can facilitate the therapeutic factors that emerge in the group; e.g. imparting information, group cohesiveness, and the instillation of hope (Lindsay, J., Roy, V., Montminy, L., Turcotte, D. & Genest-Dufault, S., 2008). Other crucial roles of the worker are to monitor group interaction to ensure that all members have an opportunity to participate, and to troubleshoot interventions when problematic process occurs.

Since support is more authentic when the source is a peer, the worker creates space for other members to provide mutual aid. In all groups, the group worker focuses attention on helping group members become a system of mutual aid (Middleman & Wood, 1990; Steinberg, 2010). This gives members the comfort to identify obstacles that they may be facing, to normalize their experiences, to validate strengths and coping strategies and to explore new perspectives. When in-patients and families are in the hospital round-the-clock, another role of the worker is to help members extend their mutual support system beyond the limits of the group meeting. In the NICU and on the IBD service, workers have mobilized peer support steering committees and created effective networks of mutual aid.

The worker centers the group in the members' lives by fostering a sense of belonging, of membership in the group (Lang, 1979). Being attuned to the specific needs of the group as a whole, the worker promotes the role of group process as a primary force responsible for individual and collective change (Middleman & Wood, 1990). The worker attends to purposeful endings by summarizing issues, checking for unfinished business and, when appropriate, making plans for the next meeting.

Creating groups in an acute hospital

Start-up

Many opportunities for groupwork in this setting are still untapped, owing to overburdened caseloads (Carlton, 1986) and lack of experience (Gilbert, 1990). However, if a social worker decides to explore the feasibility of convening a group in an acute care setting, the following are some guidelines for a successful outcome.

Generating buy-in on your service

Involve colleagues on the interdisciplinary team as co-facilitators and resource persons for the group. Clarify expectations for potential members and staff; e.g., 'It's peer support, not a gripe session'.

Selecting a workable meeting place

For inpatient/out-patient groups, find a consistent meeting space – on the unit if possible – with outlets to plug in medical equipment such as IV poles. With after-hours groups, ensure that the group room is easily accessible, with good signage.

Recruitment

Recruit with the help of staff, students, and patients and families who have attended previous groups. Publicize wherever you can; e.g. flyers on the units, in doctors' offices, hospital websites. Send out reminders (email and snail-mail for members not online). Make an announcement

15 minutes prior to the group on the unit's public address system. For inpatient groups, personally recruit on the day of the group and remind staff to do the same when they are providing care. In some groups, it may be important to screen members for minimal capacity to empathize and contribute.

Value-added groupwork

While emphasizing the benefits of groupwork for patients, families and staff, describing its cost-effectiveness and promoting the group as vehicles for quality assurance and patient-family centred care, the group becomes even more valuable to the organization if it is open to staff and students as a participant learning experience with potential for research.

Creating a framework for group process: Beginnings, middles and endings

Especially for social workers who are less experienced in group, the thought of convening more than a family-sized collection of people in one place can feel daunting. However, designing a simple group format as a template for process can provide confidence. Beginnings are introductions, including some mention of the purpose of the group, what to expect, and a brief statement by participants of why they came to the group. Middles work on issues related to the purpose of the group. The worker can open the meeting for discussion of issues and/or pull in a program piece such as menu planning with a dietitian, or role play a new mom's first day home with her infant after discharge from the NICU. The worker role fosters interaction, highlights opportunities for mutual aid, supports people to share differences and explore new skills. Endings sum up what happened in the group; talk about plans for the next meeting; invite people back if it is an open-ended/ drop-in/ single session; check on unresolved issues; and find out if everyone feels O.K. to leave the group or go home. Similar to phases of group development (Garland, Jones & Kolodny, 1965; Schiller, 2007), every session's beginning, middle and ending can allow group purpose to unfold.

Group work skills social workers use everyday in healthcare settings

The workers in this setting reflected on the social group work skills that they use on a daily basis. When they enter their service, they assess the strengths of key players, climate and morale, the needs of patients and families, and the gaps in continuity of care. They build alliances for systems interventions, employ active listening and mediate conflicting needs among the organization, patients, families and staff. They encourage unassertive patients, and differences of opinion, and by organizing rounds and family meetings, they create a team. Awareness of such group work skills can enable social workers to use them purposefully.

Supporting social group work practice in acute care

The hospital referred to in this paper is fortunate in that it continues to have a department of social work. The department itself is based on a social group work model of administration. Thus, the group work programs described here are themselves supported by a strong social work collective where the social work group is the fundamental structural and functional entity. Staff members attend weekly management groups to process issues related to all aspects of practice, and team leaders meet weekly with the director to act on issues within the department, the hospital, and the community. The groups, including the administrative group, feature professional accountability, support, autonomy, advocacy and collaborative decision-making within democratic peer group structures (Sulman, Savage, Vrooman, & McGillivray, 2004).

Regrettably, professional support similar to that found in a departmental structure is no longer the norm for many hospital social workers. With the move to program management, social workers can find themselves without adequate backing for innovative social work practice. In this situation, social workers need to become their own group workers and come together as voluntary collectives to foster professional practice. Many healthcare organizations will support groups for staff whose purpose is professional development. Participation in these groups can promote experiential learning and develop group work talent to bring to multidisciplinary teams, the hospital, and the wider community. In the event that other social workers are not available to support group practice, the social worker can take on the role of the community development worker and co-create groups with patients, families and team members.

In healthcare organizations, social work groups that promote patient and family centred well-being, quality improvement, teaching and research have high value. By taking advantage of the many opportunities to use social group work skills in acute care, social work's professional profile within the organization is raised. This can significantly improve the health of social work practice in hospitals.

References

Andrews, J. (2001). Group work's place in social work: a historical analysis. *Journal of Sociology and Social Welfare, 28*(4), 45-65.

Berg, I.K. & Miller, S.D. (1992). *Working with the problem drinker.* New York: Norton.

Breton, M. (1990). Learning from social group work tradition. *Social Work with Groups, 13*(3), 21-34.

Breton, M. (1995). The potential for social action in groups. *Social Work with Groups, 18*(2/3), 5-13.

Carlton, T.O. (1986). Group process and group work in health social work practice. *Social Work with Groups, 9*(2), 5-18.

Cohen, M.B. & Mullender, A. (2006). The personal in the political: Exploring the group work continuum from individual to social change goals. *Social Work with Groups, 28*(3), 187-204.

Dominelli, L. (2002). *Anti-oppressive social work theory and practice.* New York, NY: Palgrave MacMillan.

Garland, J., Jones, H. & Kolodny, R. (1965). A model for stages of development in social work groups. In S. Bernstein (Ed.), *Explorations in group work: Essays in theory and practice* (pp.12-53). Boston: Boston University School of Social Work.

Galinsky, M.J., Terzian, M.A. & Fraser, M.W. (2006). The art of group work practice with manualized curricula. *Social Work with Groups*, *29*(1), 11-26.

Gilbert, M. Carlean. (1990). Developing a group program in a health care setting. *Social Work with Groups*, *12*(4), 27-44.

Glassman, U. (1991). The social work group and its distinct healing qualities in the health care setting. *Health and Social Work*, *16*(3), 203-12.

Jacobson, M. (2009). The faculty meeting: Practicing social justice-oriented group work. *Social Work with Groups*, *32*(3), 177-192.

Kurland, R., Salmon, R., Bitel, M., Goodman, H., Ludwig, K., Newmann, E.W. & Sullivan, N. (2004). The survival of social group work: A call to action. *Social Work with Groups*, *27*(1), 3–16.

Lang, N.C. (1979). Some defining characteristics of the social work group: Unique social form. In S.L. Abels & P. Abels (Eds.), *Social work with groups: Proceedings of the 1979 symposium on social work with groups* (pp.18-50). Louisville, KY: Committee for the Advancement of Social Work with Groups.

Lang, N.C. (1986). Social work practice in small social forms: Identifying collectivity. *Social Work with Groups*, *9*(4), 7-32.

Lee, J.A.B. (1993). Jane Addams in Boston: Intersecting time and space. *Social Work with Groups*, *15*(2), 7-21.

Lindsay, J., Roy, V., Montminy, L., Turcotte, D. & Genest Dufault, S. (2008). The emergence and the effects of therapeutic factors in groups. *Social Work with Groups*, *31*(3), 255-271.

McNicoll, P. (2003). Current innovations in social work with groups to address issues of social justice. In Sullivan, N., Mesbur, E.S., Lang, N.C., Goodman, D. & Mitchell, L. (Eds.), *Social work with groups: Social justice through personal, community and societal change* (pp.35-50). Binghamton, N.Y.: The Haworth Press.

Middleman, R.R. & Goldberg Wood, G. (1990). From social group work to social work with groups. *Social Work with Groups*, *13*(3), 3-19.

Mullender, A. & Ward, D. (1985). Towards an alternative model of social groupwork. *British Journal of Social Work*, *15*(2), 155-172.

Muskat, B., Mishna, F., Farnia, F. & Wiener, J. (2010). 'We may not like it but we guess we have to do it:' Bringing agency-based staff on board with evidence-based group work. *Social Work with Groups*, *33*(2), 229-247.

Papell, C.P. & Rothman, B. (1980). Relating the mainstream model of social work with groups to group psychotherapy and the structured group approach. *Social Work with Groups*, *3*(2), 5-23.

Pottick, Kathleen J. (1989). Jane Addams revisited. *Social Work with Groups*, *11*(4), 11- 26.

Riessman, F. (1965). The helper therapy principle. *Social Work*, *10*(2), 27-32.

Richmond, M.E. (1917). *Social diagnosis.* New York: Russell Sage Foundation.

Saleebey, D. (2002). *The strengths perspective in social work practice* (3rd edn.). Boston: Allyn Bacon.

Schiller, L.Y. (2007). Not for women only: Applying the relational model of group development with vulnerable populations. *Social Work with Groups, 30*(2), 11-26.

Schwartz, W. (1961). The social worker in the group. In B. Saunders (Ed.), *New perspectives on services to groups: Theory, organization, practice* (pp.7-29). New York, NY: NASW.

Shapiro, B.Z. (1992). Social action, the group and society. *Social Work with Groups, 14*(3), 7–21.

Steinberg, D.M. (2004). *Mutual aid approach to working with groups* (2nd edn.). Binghamton, NY: Haworth Press.

Steinberg, D.M. (2010). Mutual aid: A contribution to best practice social work. *Social Work with Groups, 33*(1), 53-68.

Sulman, J. (1987). The worker's role in collectivity. In N. C. Lang & J. Sulman (Eds.), *Collectivity in social group work* (pp.59-67). New York, NY: Haworth Press.

Sulman, J., Savage, D., Vrooman, P. & McGillivray, M. (2004). Social group work: Building a professional collective of hospital social workers. *Social Work in Health Care, 39*(3/4), 287-307.

Sulman, J., Savage, D. & Way, S. (2001). Retooling social work practice for high volume, short stay. *Social Work in Health Care, 34*(3/4), 315-332.

Vinter, R. (1974). The essential components of social group work practice. In Glasser, Sarri &Vinter (Eds.), *Individual change through small groups* (pp.9-33). New York, NY: The Free Press.

9

Challenges, strategies and rewards of an adaptation of trauma systems therapy for newly arriving refugee youth: School-based group work with Somali adolescent boys

Amanda Nisewaner & Saida Abdi

Abstract: Somalis are one of the largest group of refugees resettled in Massachusetts and across the United States. Many Somali youth experience war and violence prior to their arrival and continue to face ongoing acculturative and resettlement stress. Due to these challenges, Project SHIFA was developed to provide culturally appropriate mental health services for Somali youth and their families. A group for refugee children was experimented in order to work with these students to improve their social and coping skills so that they can better function in the classroom environment. This paper focuses on the issues that arise when leading school-based groups and on the intersection of cultural, clinical and institutional issues in the presence of co-leaders from different cultural backgrounds.

Introduction

The *United Nations High Commissioner for Refugees* (UNHCR) reports that as of 2009, there are approximately 12 million refugees and asylum seekers worldwide (UNHCR, 2009). In the United States (US) there are close to a million refugees and asylum seekers (UNHCR, 2009) and it has been estimated that over half of these are under the age of 18. Researchers in the mental health field report on the impact that war trauma has on the refugee youth and many state that refugees may be more vulnerable to mental disorders not only because of the war trauma but also due to the experience of displacement, separation from family, poverty, violence and discrimination in their new country (Bhui, Abdi, Abdi, Pereira, Dueleh, Robertson, Sathyamoorthy & Ismail, 2003; Heptinstall, Sethna & Taylor, 2004).

Since a civil war erupted in Somalia in 1991, which still continues today, Somalis have been one of the largest groups of refugees resettled across the US and in Massachusetts (Massachusetts Department of Public Health (MDPH), 2009). The immigration experience for many refugees, not excluding Somalis, is often an arduous and long journey that may result in long extended stays in refugee camps and uncertainty about their futures. Many youth who resettle with their families have an extensive trauma history due to their experiences in refugee camps as well as the violence they fled due to the civil war in Somalia. Although studies have shown that the rate of mental health symptoms is high amongst Somali youth in the US, very few actually access and receive mental health services (Ellis, Lincoln, Charney, Ford-Paz, Benson & Strunin, 2010).In Somali culture, as in many cultures, there is social stigma attached to seeking mental health services in a medical setting. Traditionally Somalis seek help from family, community, religious leaders or traditional healers for mental health symptoms (Guerin, Guerin, Diiriye & Yates, 2004). The combination of linguistic and cultural barriers, in addition to social stigma, contribute to Somalis' reluctance to pursue Western mental health services despite the high rates of mental health symptoms. In the post 9/11 era in the US, Muslims increasingly receive negative attention in the media, which may lead to alienation and isolation. As such, the successful integration of Somali youth has become a growing concern in the US (Ellis *et al*, in press). Project SHIFA (Supporting the Health of Immigrant Families and Adolescents) was developed in response to this need and to provide culturally appropriate mental health services for Somali youth and their families. There is a mental health disparity for ethnic minorities which makes programs like Project SHIFA and research in the refugee mental health field all the more necessary.

Project SHIFA developed the program with Somali cultural values in mind. Somali's highly value the family unit and one's individual identity is built upon his or her place in the community. Additionally, the community places a great deal of importance on the education of children. Talk therapy is largely unfamiliar to Somalis, and the idea of sharing your concerns or worries with a stranger is foreign. Sitting down with a group of friends and discussing a topic, on the other hand, is a very familiar concept. Therefore, group work is an ideal way to address mental health issues because it incorporates culturally accessible ways of relating to others. Emphasizing the educational benefit of addressing mental health issues and providing services in a school environment is also ideal as they allow the team to address the needs (of whom?) in a safe and culturally sanctioned manner (Guerin *et al*, 2004).

Project SHIFA, funded by the Robert Wood Johnson Foundation's Caring Across Communities Initiative, is a trauma-focused, school-based mental health program. This project is a collaborate effort between Children's Hospital Boston, Boston Public Schools, Boston University School of Social Work, local refugee agencies and other community partners. Project SHIFA is compromised of several components: a) parent and community outreach, b) school-based groups for students, and c) direct intervention using Trauma Systems Therapy (TST). Parent and community outreach is an essential component and allows the treatment team the opportunity to educate the community about the impact of trauma but also provides the opportunity to assess the needs of Somali youth, families and their community. The community outreach has also enabled us to build trust within the Somali community which allows us to engage both families and youth in services. Project SHIFA places social work clinicians and cultural brokers in a local middle school to provide individual and group clinical services to Somali youth and to educate the school staff about the impact of trauma and acculturation issues their students may be encountering. The school-based groups were developed to assist students with social skills and acculturation. These groups have afforded the clinicians both the setting and time to further evaluate the needs of the students while building rapport. Students who are identified for more intensive service receive TST, a therapeutic framework which incorporates two key elements, a traumatized child who cannot regulate emotional states and a social environment that is unable to sufficiently help the child regulate the emotional states (Saxe, Ellis & Kaplow, 2007).

This paper highlights the development of the school-based groups for students and incorporates several TST principles that have been utilized for the group environment. It will also address the issues that arise when leading a school-based group for a group of Somali boys and on the intersection of cultural, clinical and institutional issues in the presence of co-leaders from different cultural backgrounds and explores the challenges, strategies and rewards when implementing school-based group work for immigrant and refugee populations. The format of this paper will begin with background information on group participants, group content and co-leaders, followed by a description of the group sessions and concluding with the challenges that we faced when planning and implementing this group.

Group participants and content

The group met weekly for 15 sessions which were scattered throughout the school year and each group took place during the elective period which lasted an hour. The group was comprised of 10 Somali males aged 13-15, in seventh and eighth grade. The group members were told that being in the group was voluntary, they had the option to participate in group or not, and that at any point during group if they wished to discontinue participation they always had the option of returning to class. Most group members had a history of war trauma and were new to the country. All members attended an urban public school and resided in the inner city, thus exposing them to violence, gangs and drugs. Students were referred to the group by the school social worker, primarily because they were male refugee students in the English Language Learners (ELL) class who were struggling for numerous reasons. Most common referral concerns included disruptive behavior and peer conflict. It is important to note that many of the students who were referred to group had never been exposed to a public education system or formal education prior to their arrival in the US. Group offered these students a place to learn about the school's expectations and assist with the acculturation process.

Researchers Ellis and colleagues (2006) and Van der Kolk (2005) associate a history of trauma with peer and social difficulties. With this in mind, group was intended to promote healthy relationships and help students further develop and improve their social and emotional skills to enhance classroom performance. Additionally this skill building aimed to enable students to function effectively and positively in their families and communities. Somali youth, like many other refugee and immigrant youth, must navigate living in two cultures. At home they are expected to practice Somali culture and speak Somali while outside of the home and in the school environment they are expected to adhere to the American way of life. They have the difficult task of incorporating these two very different cultures into who they are and how they are perceived. Frequently issues arise for these students within the school environment due to cultural differences: the way an argument is settled, the relationship with a teacher, the relationship with their Somali peers, and how they respond to discipline (Osterman & de Jong, 2007). The group was intended to offer a safe and structured environment to address and learn about differences between American and Somali culture and to provide a space in which the students could explore their own identity as well.

The SHIFA group work approach was informed by Andrew Malekoff (2004) and his principles on group work with adolescents. The group sessions were also structured utilizing two key principles of TST – 'align with reality' and 'don't go before you are ready' – both of which allowed us to proceed with flexibility. We structured our sessions to include emotion identification, emotion regulation, and coping skills (Saxe *et al*, 2007). Each session included a check in, a goal for the session, an activity that would engage the group members and we would end group with a snack.

Group leaders

The relationship between group leaders proved to be an integral aspect of running groups with Somali youth. The group was co-facilitated by a Somali cultural broker/social work intern, and a non-Somali licensed social worker, both of whom were new clinicians in the field of social work. The cultural differences between the group leaders served many purposes including modeling a sense of trust to group members throughout the sessions. It was extremely useful to have the two different cultures represented in the group leaders since it mirrored the experience of these youth – the intersection of their Somali background and their new American life. When planning for group, this trust and respect between group leaders was equally as important. Clinical implications as well as cultural implications were always discussed when creating games, worksheets and activities for the group. The richness of different backgrounds and true collaboration allowed for lengthy discussions and typically ended with modifications of a Western tool that were appropriate for Somali culture. The group leaders' unique qualities and skills were complementary and the differences were harnessed to strengthen the relationship.

Prior to implementing the Somali boys group, both group leaders had worked for Project SHIFA and had the privilege of running groups with each other. As such, the team had already had the opportunity to develop ideas together, learn from past experiences and had developed a healthy dynamic in a group setting. The team had also learned that group was an ideal way to work with Somali youth; aside from group activities being a culturally normative activity, the group also created a sense of community in the school environment. As two females co-facilitating an all boys group, the group leaders were cognizant of the potential issues that could arise due to gender differences. In Somali culture, interactions between males and females are traditionally very specific and strict. A woman (especially an older woman) is often viewed as a mother regardless of the direct relationship and this garners much respect. Thus, the Somali boys would address the Somali co-leader as *habaryar* which means maternal aunt (literally small mother). The relationship between a Somali boy and his mother is a significant relationship based on respect and nurturing. Having a Somali 'mother' present created a safe environment for the boys to talk about their feelings and experiences. On the other hand, traditionally, Somali boys are disciplined by fathers and at times when group got out of control, the group leaders wondered whether the lack of a male leader was a deficit.

When working with a group from a culture different to your own, it is paramount to educate yourself as much as possible about its history, language and culture. In our case, understanding the history of the civil war, the legacy of immigration and the Muslim religion in addition to the complex gender and relationship dynamics all informed how the co-leader developed relationships with the students and understood the clinical work. Encouraging the group members to educate the non-Somali on their religion, music, poetry and language throughout the group sessions allowed the boys to feel like experts which boosted their self esteem, allowed for ownership of the group and helped strengthen the bond of the non-Somali with the group.

Challenges

Creating a program like Project SHIFA in a school setting is incredibly beneficial because, as Maria Saino (2003) argues, holding a group in a school setting allows 'members who would not otherwise receive services to receive services in a normalized and appropriate context' (p.72). In this case, the members are refugee children whose parents were unlikely to take them to a group located in a mental health setting due to the stigma attached to mental illness in the community. However, school settings can also create complicated logistical and relational issues that challenge school-based clinical work despite the support of the administration and the ready access to the children. The benefits of having groups at the school obviously outweigh the challenges but the challenges require attention.

Typical groups run for 8-12 sessions, but the SHIFA team had the task of creating a group that would last for an entire school year with numerous breaks due to holidays and mandatory academic testing. The team also faced the challenge of addressing not only the needs of the boys in the group but also those of the teachers and the school. On many occasions issues arose during the school day that affected group dynamics and problems that arose in the classroom were frequently brought to the group. Additionally, when there were urgent issues with group members in their classrooms, the teachers would expect them to be addressed in the group milieu. This proved to be very frustrating for the group leaders especially considering the time spent developing a curriculum and planning sessions. The group was not intended to be a place to manage daily school crises and doing so derailed plans to explore topics that could potentially prevent such crises in the future.

These issues are not unique to this group and point to the challenges of running a group in school settings. It is difficult for students and adults alike to separate the group from the classroom experience. In the SHIFA group, disruptive behaviors that were causing problems in students' classrooms were also happening in the group environment and the group leader-group member relationships began to mirror the teacher-student relationships making building therapeutic alliances challenging.

Another challenge was that the group was composed of a group of refugee children who had experienced or were exposed to enormous trauma in their native country, Somalia, which has been at war for the last 19 years. This history of trauma is particularly relevant because symptoms of trauma can manifest themselves as disruptive behaviors. Symptoms of trauma like distractibility, hypervigilence, rage, angry outbursts, and irritability can hinder group work as well as cause tension in the group environment (Carbonnell & Parteleno-Barehmi, 1999). In addition all of the group members lived in Boston neighborhoods with high-crime rates which continued exposure to violence. Carbonnell and Parteleno-Barehmi (1999) note that 'children cannot regain a feeling that the world is predictable and worthy of trust when that world continues to assault them' (p.287). Hence, the SHIFA team understood that in order to do effective group work, they would need to develop group methods that provided a safe space for children with trauma histories to function to the best of their abilities. Group success required that members had a space to build social skills, manage anxiety, and develop a sense of competence – skills necessary not only for overcoming trauma but also for mastering the developmental tasks of adolescence. The first four sessions gave us a lot of information about the group dynamics and some of the individual needs of the group members which eventually forced us to re-evaluate how we were running the group and examine our own objectives for the group.

Sessions 1-4

The goal of the first session was to get to know one another, generate a list of rules for the group environment, and have the group members leave with an understanding of why we were meeting as a group, as well as what we would be learning and the group structure. We explained to the group that we were meeting to learn some new skills that would help at school, at home and with different relationships. During the first group, it became apparent that our members were hesitant to participate and apprehensive about what it meant to be in group. The members had many questions such as why they were in group, what's the point and, most importantly, if they were going to have fun. We were asked if being in the group meant that they were 'bad' kids. It was explained that the group was created to help them and provide support and in no way meant that they were bad students and being punished. We used this opportunity to ask them what they would like to get out of the group and they had many different ideas such as improving their academics, creating art work and making music. We reminded them that as this would be their group; their ideas were very important to us and would help us prepare and plan for group. The activity that we had planned was well received and coincided with their suggestion for creating artwork. Each member traced his hand onto construction paper, cut it out and then wrote his name and two facts about himself on his hand. We then glued each hand onto a large poster board and created a circle with everyone's hand, including those of the leaders, to represent our group (activity adapted from Khalsa, 1996, p.5).

Overall we felt our first session was a success and we were able to observe quite a bit about the group dynamics and our role as leaders. We did not accomplish our task of generating a list of rules but it was clear that the group wasn't quite ready for that. As group leaders, we learned quickly the importance of flexibility when running groups for Somali boys. It was clear to us that there was apprehension about what the group meant and why they were chosen to be part of it. We later realized that explaining to the members that group was meant to help them only added to their apprehension about participating in group. They understood the word 'help' to mean that there was something wrong with them and our job was to fix them.

We now had the task of generating a list of rules and consequences for the group which became our main objective for the second session. Many of the members had prior experience with rule making and the group needed very little assistance from the group leaders. While the discussion on rules was taking place, each member had their own piece of paper and a marker to write down the rules for themselves. We noticed that for many members this helped keep them focused and engaged. There was a lot of thought and ideas contributed by the group members in the discussion but we frequently had to redirect and break up conflict between group members.

We used Session 3 to talk about the consequences of breaking the rules and used a similar format for generating a list. This was a lengthy discussion and there was a lot of debating and decision making taking place. We could already see that some of our group members were becoming frustrated and could have accomplished these tasks at a much quicker rate. There were also group members who became agitated and found it difficult to sit still for the entire hour. We ended session 3 with a very basic breathing exercise and explained how these exercises could assist when they needed to calm down or re-focus. This was quite successful! The group members responded well and it was decided that we would begin and end every session with a breathing exercise.

In session 4 our objective was to generate a list of goals for the group as well as for each individual. It was a long and painful session in which we had to constantly remind members of group rules and enforce the consequences. There was a lot of name calling, verbal insults, shuffling around, and the entire group appeared to be distracted and bored. Due to the challenges and the constant re-direction we did some breathing exercises in the middle of group and managed to generate three solid goals for the group.

Unexpected detour

Within the first four sessions the variability in academic abilities was clear; several of the boys struggled with writing the rules as sentences. There were group members who struggled to wait their turn and others who always raised their hand. The disruptive behavior and the peer conflicts were consuming all of our group time and the boys were leaving group more frustrated and confused. One of the main problems with our group was becoming quite clear; we had 10 boys with different needs who were developmentally and emotionally at different stages. Due to the group composition we knew we had to make some fundamental changes but we were struggling with how to restructure the group. Although we felt we were being flexible and had read the literature on group theory and stages, we believed that there were certain topics we had to review and necessary tasks to complete such as group purpose, rules, consequences, and goals. These are not fun tasks to accomplish and having rules and consequences just encouraged their belief that they were bad kids who needed help. The discussions we had, regardless of how short or simple they were, created an environment that mimicked their classroom environment which in turn fueled disruptive behavior.

We planned the group to be fairly structured with weekly tasks but it soon became obvious that some members could not adhere to this structure. It took us several sessions to realize that we had a huge problem with the group structure and content and we began trying to salvage the group in multiple ways by enforcing the rules and trying to adhere to the group structure. We also tried to limit conflict by interjecting ourselves and attempting to minimize group conflicts instead of letting the kids work through it. After much thought and discussion we came to the conclusion that the problems experienced stemmed from a variety of sources. First, the group composition was not ideal and we had the challenge of running a group with students who differed significantly in developmental and academic abilities. The needs and mental health status of our group members were also vastly different and, ideally, we would have run separate groups but due to time and space this was not an option. Second, the kids spent all day together and they had developed a culture of horse playing and verbal insults which they then brought to the group; and finally, our group rules which rewarded good behavior and punished breaking of group rules were so parallel to what the kids were experiencing in the classroom that they could not differentiate between the two.

We noticed that some members of the group were not able to follow the rules or accomplish the tasks. At first, we thought that this indicated resistance to doing the work and we tried to strictly adhere to group rules. There were group members who were quite capable of doing the work and focusing on the tasks while others, who struggled with the tasks, were immature and dealing with serious mental health issues. It got to the point where not only were we unable to move the group work forward but the safety of group members was threatened by the horse play and arguing and several of the more advanced members expressed a desire to quit as they found this to be a waste of their time.

In *Group Work with Adolescents*, Malekoff (2004) talks about the uncertainty and untidiness of group work with adolescents. 'Being able to label or categorize adolescents may give group workers an elevated sense of expertise in their own eyes, as well as those of others. However, the group worker must be much more than a fixer of broken objects,' (p.21) he advises. He reminds us that group work with adolescents is never easy or clean. Adolescents demand to be taken as a whole person and they resent being categorized, diagnosed, and placed in special groups (Malekoff, 2004). He also writes that: 'It is critical for group workers to hear the music behind seemingly unstructured activities such as spontaneous singing, rapping, dancing, and aimless horsing around' (p.24). Reading Malekoff's (2004) accounts of groups he had run, how he brought this idea of fun into the group space, how he gave up control and how he was able to see his own issues and fears being the problem, made us realize that there was a way out! First, we needed to accept that while the group problems started with the composition issues and the school culture that we as group leaders failed to face these problems head on and were so afraid of the possible chaos and disorder brought on by conflict that we did not allow the group to work through problems. We were so afraid of losing control of this group of boys, we tried to mask conflict by trying to impose order with group rules and by interjecting ourselves into moments of conflict. What we realized, after much discussion and examination, was that taking the group's success or failure as *our* responsibility rather than the *group's* was our first mistake. Defining presence of conflict, arguments and horsing around as a problem was our second mistake. Our final and fatal mistake was that we had somehow adopted the institutional way of looking at certain behaviors exhibited by the children as 'bad' and we had been, in our group milieu, reenacting punishment and failures that the children faced in the classroom. If the base of effective group work is building competence, safety and cohesion we were utter failures. More importantly, our model was not conducive to building these positive traits. What we were doing was putting an 'emphasis on controlling kids, shoving education down their throats, and stamping out spontaneity and creativity' (Malekoff, 2001, p.247). The problem was these methods had already failed with these kids. After much thought and consultation we decided that we would allow group members much more freedom in speaking, moving and being spontaneous. Our group required structure but with enough flexibility so that the group members felt they were contributing to the process and had ownership of it. .

At this point, we also realized that as new clinicians we were not prepared for the specific challenges that arise when running a group for traumatized boys. As group leaders we feel we should have been better prepared and more understanding of peer conflict and disruptive behavior. We also could have spent more time establishing relationships within the group and creating a safe group environment. Saxe *et al* (2006) contend that the therapeutic relationship is integral in effective treatment and traumatized children are constantly evaluating whether or not the relationship is safe enough. Somalis place a lot of importance on trust and establishing a trusting relationship takes time to build (Guerin *et al*, 2004). In retrospect we should have begun group with activities that focused on building confidence and team work and held off on some of the major group tasks until we had created a safe and trustworthy environment.

A new group: Sessions 5-15

Embrace the chaos

This was the beginning of a new group and after consulting with our Project SHIFA clinical team and reviewing the literature on group work with adolescents, we had some activities to try and, most importantly, a different attitude. We intended each session to build off the previous sessions. The ideas of team work, respect, integration of the children's own values and ownership of the group were essential. We shared with the group that we wanted to try some new things and we then proceeded to take the rules and consequence posters off the wall. We shared with the group that we trusted that they knew the rules and we were not going to worry so much about following them and breaking them. We did inform the group members that if conflicts came up in group, we would have to deal with them but as a group. We provided the group members with stress balls and explained that sometimes having an outlet or distraction and something to do with our hands can help us focus on talking about serious things.

Our initial plan was to have a session on communication skills and we began group with a game of telephone. The group members had a lot of fun and after a couple rounds of telephone everyone was able to engage in a conversation about how important it is to listen and how easy it is to not understand someone. We then played 'Simon Says' which was a great way to get the members moving around, laughing, and jumping up and down but in a very structured way. It also allowed group members to feel like leaders for a moment which contributed to confidence building. Over a snack we discussed different forms of communication and how Somalis often communicate through poetry and music. We discussed listening to music in group and they shared their favorite artists. We finished group with a breathing exercise and for the first time a group member asked to lead everyone in the breathing exercise.

Self esteem & teamwork

We learned from our previous session that several of the members enjoyed taking leadership roles and that it was a great way to build self esteem. We played a game called 'King for the Day' (adapted from Jones, 1998, p.96; Lowenstein, 1999, p.81) in which each student had a note card with another group member's name. They were instructed to write one nice thing about the person on the card and then read it to them when it was their turn. Crowns were passed out and co-leaders were very careful about who got who. On several occasions other group members chimed in something nice about the 'king' and we were able to talk about how it felt good to hear your peers compliment you. The conflicts were still present in group but they were not as time consuming or disruptive and in the next session we wanted to show the team members that they were very capable of working together, listening and, as a group, accomplishing a task. We adapted an activity known as 'Talk to Me' (Jones, 1998, p.148) to address the group needs and split the group into two teams. Each team performed various physical, mental and, most importantly, fun tasks that required them to listen carefully and make decisions as a team. These were quite simple but active instructions that they had to follow and it always involved working as a team. After the activity we talked about the challenges they encountered and what made this fun for them. They spent the rest of group making up raps for their teams and listening to K'naan, a Somali musician. We were apprehensive about using the teams again but we knew this would be a very organic way to have team work weaved throughout the next couple of sessions.

Conflict and personal space

Our goal for session 8 was to discuss with the group members how to safely deal with conflicts and we challenged each team to come up with a skit that showed what they would do if they were confronted with a peer conflict (adapted from Lowenstein, 1999, p.73). We had a set of criteria for the teams and we split up and each of us worked with one team on putting together a scenario, a script, and a final presentation. The group members on both teams got very creative, worked hard, and had fun putting together their skits. Over the snack they shared with us what fun they had and how it reminded them of a Somali variety show. It was suggested that in group we continue making skits like the variety show. We also had a very interesting discussion about how in their skits both teams said they would tell a teacher if someone was bothering them but they shared that, in reality, this is not what they did. We then discussed what some of the other options were and that conflict is inevitable and learning how to respond is the most important factor.

Building off our session on conflict we wanted to talk about personal space and the difference in cultural norms. We began group by having a couple of different activities that demonstrated what it was like when someone invaded your bubble or personal space. We were able to talk about some of the difficulties that group members were having in class regarding personal space and how it was challenging to keep your hands to yourself and often the group members found themselves horse playing and getting into trouble because of it. The two teams had a task of putting together another skit about what personal space meant to them. The two teams took very different approaches but the results were impressive with everyone engaged and working together. One team created a rap called 'Don't Touch Me' and the other put on a skit about going to court. Horse play for Somali boys is part of the ritual of boys becoming men but in the school environment it became a source of huge conflict and caused a lot of issues for the Somali boys. Addressing some basic cultural differences allowed the group members to open up about many of the differences they were experiencing and how challenging it was to adjust to all the differences.

Emotion identification and regulation

The goal of the next two sessions was to identify and discuss the different emotions that impacted their daily lives. We reflected on what it was like to feel good when they were kings for the day and discussed the many different feelings involved in conflict. We wanted to focus session 10 specifically on the differences between sad and mad; in Somali there is only one word for what we recognized as being sad and mad in English. The two teams had the task of creating a skit on what makes them sad and what makes them mad. Each group had a different emotion to work with. As excited as they were about creating skits and putting on their own variety show, it was obvious that this wasn't as fun as it used to be. Regardless the two teams still did an excellent job and identified the differences between the two emotions. During our snack we had an open ended discussion about emotions, body language and when it is important to tell others how you feel.

In session 11 we played emotion charades and each group member had to silently act out the emotion they picked out of a hat. Each group member had to guess what was being acted out and this facilitated a conversation pertaining to differences and how not everyone feels the same way about the same things. Over the snack we were able to engage the group in a discussion about what to do when they felt angry or sad and who to talk to when they felt this way.

Soccer: Using what we have learned

The next four sessions were spread out over the course of 10 weeks due to school vacation and the Massachusetts Comprehensive Assessment System (MCAS) testing schedule. As co-leaders we were concerned with how the breaks in our sessions would impact the group progression and we also wanted to address the request of having outdoor activities during group time. The group members from the very beginning were adamant about wanting group outside and over the course of the year we had heard a lot about how it was hard for them to always be inside not just because of the weather but mainly because of the neighborhood violence and they frequently talked about how life in Africa was often spent outside. The group members also talked a lot about soccer and asked if we could play as a group. We thought about all the work they had done over the year as a group and thought we could finish group by having a soccer tournament where they could show us what they had learned in terms of working together and resolving conflict. We also believed there was a lot to be said for the power of play, many of our group members didn't have the opportunity to play with their peers and to engage in healthy physical activity. The group members were ecstatic about the idea of playing soccer and understood that all of the lessons we discussed over the past year could be applied on the soccer field. Respect, team work, conflict resolution, and emotional regulation were all showcased during the soccer sessions. Conflict did arise and as a team they worked through these issues. Ultimately they agreed that conflict was inevitable and what was most important was how they dealt with the conflict. As co-leaders, watching these kids orchestrate captains, teams, rules, and ultimately work together to have a great time, was an ideal way to end the year.

Conclusion

When we began the planning for this group we were two newcomers to the field of social work. We had a lot of enthusiasm and energy but no idea of the journey we were actually about to embark upon. Ultimately in the process of running groups we learned as much as the group members did. Reevaluating our group work forced us to look at ourselves and our role in the group process. We learned a fundamental lesson that the group dictates the actual group work and that the leaders' job is to adapt to the needs of the group. The success of the group is determined by the ability of the leaders to learn from the group and make the necessary changes. In our case we had several challenges to address in order to make the group a success. When providing clinical services to refugee populations one must not only work from a trauma framework but it is essential to incorporate the specific culture into the intervention. In our case, the group was composed of refugee children whose cultural values and communication skills were completely different from those of American children. As group leaders, we needed to look at our group and ensure that these cultural values were integrated into the way the group was both constructed and conducted. The literature on working with refugee youth emphasizes the need to integrate familiar cultural practices and suggests that group activities should take place within a cultural context (Marsiglia, Cross & Mitchell-Enos, 1998). By integrating the culture, language and values of the group members, we were able to achieve group cohesion and we were able to build a sense of competence and commonality among group members.

References

Bhui, K., Abdi, A., Abdi, M., Pereira, S., Dueleh, M., Robertson, D., Sathyamoorthy, G. & Ismail, H. (2003). Traumatic events, migration characteristics, and psychiatric symptoms among Somali refugees. *Soc Psychiatry Epidemiology, 38.*

Carbonnell, D. & Parteleno-Barehmi, C. (1999). Psychodrama group for girls coping with trauma. *International Journal of Group Psychotherapy, 49*(3), 285-305.

Ellis, H., Lhewa, D., Charney, M. & Cabral, H. (2006). Screening for PTSD among Somali adolescent refugees. *Journal of Traumatic Stress, 19*(4).

Ellis, B.H., Lincoln, A.K., Charney, M.E., Ford-Paz, R., Benson, M. & Strunin, L. (2010). Mental health service utilization of Somali adolescents: Religion, community, and school as gateways to healing. *Transcultural Psychiatry, 47*(5), 789-811.

Ellis, H., Miller, A., Baldwin, H. & Abdi, S. (accepted). New directions in refugee youth mental health services: Overcoming barriers to engagement. *Journal of Child and Adolescent Trauma.*

Guerin, B., Guerin, P., Diiriye, R. & Yates, S. (2004). Somali conceptions and expectations concerning mental health. *New Zealand Journal of Psychology, 33*(2).

Heptinstall, E., Sethna, V. & Taylor, E. (2004). PTSD and depression in refugee children. *European Child Adolescent Psychiatry, 13*

Jones, A. (1998). *104 activities that build: self esteem, teamwork, communication, anger management, self discovery, and coping skills.* Richland, WA: Rec Room Publishing.

Lowenstein, L. (1999). *Creative interventions for troubled children & youth.* Toronto, Canada: Champion Press.

Khasla, S. (1996). *Group exercises for enhancing social skills & self esteem.* Sarasota, Florida: Professional Resource Press.

Malekoff, A. (2004). *Group work with adolescents: Principles and practice.*

New York, NY: Guilford Press.

Malekoff, A. (2001). The power of group work with kids: A practitioner's reflections on strength-based practice. *Families in Society: The Journal of Contemporary Human Services*, 243-249

Malekoff, A. & Laser, M. (1999). Addressing difference in group work with children and young adolescents. *Social Work with Groups, 21*(4) 23-33.

Marsiglia, F., Cross, S. & Mitchell-Enos, V. (1998). Culturally grounded work with adolescent American Indian students. *Social Work with Groups, 21*(1/2), 89-102.

Osterman, J.E. & de Jong, J.T.V.M. (2007). Cultural issues in trauma. In M.J. Friedman, T.M. Keane & P.A. Resick (Eds.), *Handbook of PTSD: Science and practice* (pp.425-446). New York: Guilford.

Saino, M. (2003). A new language for groups: Multilingual and multiethnic. *Social Work with Groups, 26*(1), 69-81.

Saxe, G.N., Ellis, B.H. & Kaplow, J.B. (2007). *Collaborative treatment of traumatized children and teens: The trauma systems therapy approach.* New York: Guilford.

Van der Kolk, B. (2005). Developmental trauma disorder. *Psychiatric Annals, 35*(5).

United Nations High Commission for Refugees (UNHCR) (2009). *2008 Global refugee trends: Refugees, asylum-seekers, returnees, internally displaced and stateless persons.* Geneva: UNHCR Geneva.

10

Men in India: Eliminating gender-based violence

Sanjay & Madhu Kushwaha

Abstract: Gender-based hierarchies and inequalities are deeply rooted in Indian social-cultural structure. Though all men are not perpetrators, most of the perpetrators are male. Males in Indian society are culturally tutored to be the 'protectors' of the family, women and children. Their socialization prepares them for this future social role which is based on the prevalent and hegemonic notion of aggressive masculinity. In the Indian social context, the violation of a woman's rights occurs in the name of her protection. This realization led to the idea of working with men and boys.

This paper is about the experiences of working with undergraduate men for three to four years (2005-09) in a state university located in northern India. The group work was focused the initiation of attitudinal changes among students by engaging them in critical enquiry regarding the notions of traditional masculinity and its consequences. Later the group worked as a support structure to facilitate little changes which were taking place in the university and in their personal lives.

The whole paper is divided into three main sections. The first section is about understanding gender-based violence in the Indian context. In the second section, the background of the MASVAW campaign is discussed. The third section deals with the formation of groups and group work at university level. A final part provides an analysis and evaluation of the group work.

Understanding the issue:
Gender-based violence in India

Gender-based violence means violence inflicted or suffered on the basis of gender differences. Gender-based violence is commonly used as a means of violence against girls and women. Nevertheless, the concept also applies to boys and other men too (Malik, Karlsson & Karkara, 2005). Factors such as age, caste, social class, ability, religion, and ethnicity also affect the likelihood of facing various forms of gender-based violence. Gender-based violence is related to power relations grounded in ideas of masculinity and femininity. It has many manifestations in Indian society such as son preference (Nabar, 1995; Jain, 2001), sex selective abortions, high incidence of maternal deaths, more malnourished girls than boys, unequal access to school education (NCERT, 2007).

The United Nations Declaration on the Elimination of Violence Against Women (1993) defined violence against women as any act of gender-based violence that results in, or is likely to result in, physical, sexual, or psychological harm or suffering to women, including threats of such acts, coercion, or arbitrary deprivation of liberty, whether occurring in public or in private life.

In India, the most extreme forms of violence against women take place within families including dowry related crimes (Nabar, 1995). Over 40% of Indian women have experienced domestic violence at some point in their married lives, and nearly 55% think that spousal abuse is warranted in several circumstances, slapping being the most common act of physical violence by husbands. Meanwhile, a substantial 35% of women thought they deserved a brutal beating at the hands of their spouses if they neglected to do the household chores or look after their children (NFHS-III, 2007). Several cultural specific reasons, such as deep rooted son preferences in Indian society leading to sex selective abortions, almost no decision making of women in reproductive matters and less access to schooling and health care facilities for women, make the situation worst.

A 2006 UNICEF report says 69 million children witness violence within homes in India. It is unlikely that a women will admit abuse unless the problem is serious or chronic (Ingoldsby, 2006; Leeder, 2004). Furthermore, living outside of marriage is not an option for many Indian women. The financial repercussions and the shame brought to a woman's family often preclude alternatives to remaining in the abusive husband's home (Ingoldsby, 2006; Leeder, 2004).

According to feminist theory, domestic violence is embedded in patriarchal systems that perpetuate men's dominance and control over women (Anderson, 1997; Leeder, 1994; Liddle, 1989; Nabar, 1995). Gender hierarchies and gender inequalities both reflect and perpetuate gender-based violence. Gender-based violence manifests itself primarily as male violence against women and girls and it takes a variety of forms. At the same time, research indicates that gender-based violence is also the most accurate descriptor for violence against men and boys. It is rooted in the pressure and the effect of dominant forms of masculinity around the world and in specific cultural manifestations. (Lena Karlsson & Ravi Karkara, 2005).Gender-based violence is rooted in these systems which provide men with a sense of entitlement that cuts across culture, class, caste, religion, and location (Sanjay, 2005).

From a feminist perspective, gender is socially constructed which means that society and culture perpetuate differential experiences for men and women, rather than biology (Leeder, 2004). While feminist theory brings together diverse schools of thought from liberal to radical perspectives, there is an element of universality in patriarchy and the oppressive social structures which justify men's dominance over women. According to Nabar (1995), patriarchal domination in India operates in a different value context than that of western countries. In India, women (and men) are taught to value the community over their own individualism.

While it is true that most perpetrators of violence against women (VAW) are male and the victims are female, it is not correct to say that all men are opposed to gender-based equality (GBE) and applaud VAW. Nor is it correct to say that only women are victims. Reality is complex and years of excluding men from the gender discourse has not helped matters. There is a growing international consensus on involving men and boys in gender equality. This has emerged strongly in many international forums such as the Beijing Conference on Women, 1995, the UNAIDS – World Aids Campaign on Men and AIDS, 2000-2001, the WHO initiatives on Boy's Health, 2001-2002, the USAID Conference on Men and Sexual Reproductive Health, 2003, the UN Commission on the Status of Women, 2003, the International Fatherhood Summit in the UK, 2003, and the Men Engage for Gender Equality, Rio de Janeiro, 2009, to name a few.

There are several ways to involve men in the discourse on gender equality. Involving men in childcare is one that has been advocated by Ruddick (1989). She said that men can be maternal thinkers by participating in childcare and maternal thinking does not necessarily entail physical childbirth. She argues that anyone who does what mothers do – cares for young children and prepares them for social acceptability – has an epistemological resource for developing maternal thinking. Thus everyone is a potential maternal thinker. She takes her argument to a political level to include men and in maternal thinking she sees a route to world peace. To reach that point, she urges men to share childcare with women, thereby becoming maternal thinkers. Hence including men is a political necessity.

There is not much research which addresses male socialization, masculinity and gender-based violence in a north Indian context. With this in mind, a campaign of men (MASVAW) was started in 2002 in North India.

Background of MASVAW campaign

In 2001, several women's groups in Uttar Pradesh State (northern Indian province) launched a state wide campaign 'Stop Tolerating Violence' followed by a public hearing attended by some twenty five thousand women and men. Several male activists were actively involved with this campaign. It was realized that violence against women (VAW) was not only a women's issue but a social issue, hence combating it was the responsibility of the entirety of society, not just of women. This led to the formation of a campaign 'Men's Action for Stopping Violence Against Women' (MASVAW) in October 2002, with the core objective of making men partners in the struggle for gender justice. The target groups of the MASVAW campaign were peer groups (male youths; students and adolescents) and different male stakeholders in society, such as teachers, media persons, community leaders, social activists, and lawyers. The underlaying assumptions of this campaign were that men are not violent by birth but learn gender norms through gender-based socialization; masculinity and femininity are socially constructed and can be deconstructed; men are privileged in a patriarchal system and hold the position of authority; all men are not perpetrators though most perpetrators of violence are men, they can also be the survivor of gender-based violence; and men have a decisive role in preventing and eradicating this pervasive form of social injustice.

At present MASVAW is actively working in the northern Indian states of Uttar Pradesh, Madhya Pradesh and Uttarakhand. These states have long been vilified as those with strongholds of patriarchal domination, in which men deny women their basic rights to health, education, mobility, dignity, and a life free from violence. All these states are known for their poor performance with regard to human development indicators.

Eminent researchers and activist working on gender issues at national level in India are on the advisory board of MASVAW. Members of the advisory board meet annually, and facilitate the process of goal setting and policy formulation. The governing board (Core Group), comprising the founders of this campaign, is a cohesive group whose basic tasks are policy level planning, budget allocation for activities, monitoring and evaluation of the programs conducted at district and institutional level.

Formation of group at university level

Educational institutions cannot remain insulated from social contexts and contours and the atmosphere at M.G. Kashi Vidyapith University was no exception and reflected patriarchal notions of society. The university environment was not gender inclusive, spaces in the university were gendered and male students would be seen flouting their 'male attitudes' everywhere without being aware of its negative impact. It was thought that the MASVAW campaign had relevance for this university. The first author of this paper, being a founder member of MASVAW campaign and in a teaching faculty in the university, was given the responsibility organising the groups by the governing body of MASVAW. An awareness program was started to make students familiar with the concept of the MASVAW campaign. For this a variety of activities, such as public lectures and meetings with students, were organized in various departments of the university. Subsequently this generated curiosity and debate among students regarding the relevance and usefulness of the program. Initially there was a lukewarm response but about two hundred students showed interest and participated in activities. After three months eighty students remained associated with the campaign and showed interest in gender issues, while others left. These students were recruited as group members for in-depth intervention.

Group members' profile

All the students were from the Social Work, Education, Fine Arts, and Law departments of the university. All the members were males aged 18-25 years and belonged to the middle and lower middle class. Regarding ethnicity, the group was heterogeneous and all the major castes and religious groups of Eastern Uttar Pradesh were represented. Two third of the members (62/80) lived with parents; the others lived in the university hostel. Only two members of the group were married. All the eighty members remained with the group for three to four years depending on the duration of their courses. The group members were called MASVAW men and they were expected to be role models for other youths. No new member was allowed to join the groups because group work and activities were predesigned and staged in nature. Four groups of 20 male students each were formed with the following objectives: first to educate members on gender issues; second to make the university environment gender inclusive; and third to develop zero tolerance for gender-based discrimination in the university. The objectives of the campaign had consonance with the MASVAW's broader objectives and were decided by the members and mentors of the groups during meetings. An orientation program was organized to share the vision, the objectives of the program, and the expectations of the members.

Group process

It was difficult to determine group typology in a rigid manner as several overlaps were observed in the actual practice situation (Toseland & Rivas, 1998). On the basis of the characteristics of the groups, such as purpose, leadership, focus, bond, composition and communication, each had the characteristics of a social action group as the intention was to devise and implement social change tactics and strategies, during the course of action. When group members faced conflict and got into dilemmas then the mentor and other members of each group helped them cope with the stressful situation and enlarge their coping abilities by motivating and reinforcing, then a group functioned as a support group. Since the groups focused on developing members' awareness, insight, and potential then groups were education and growth groups. To achieve our objectives we followed group activities designed and designated for the whole year by the governing body. After the formation of the groups, a verbal contract was developed among group members with regard to obligations, duties and expectations. For example, the members would not be involved in any kind of violence and discrimination against women in private and public spheres, if they observed any such incident they would register their protest or break the silence, they would convince others (non group members to make a behavioral change), they would maintain the confidentiality of each other but at the same time watch each other's behavior, and if any member's behavior was found to be against the objectives and contract, they would report it to the mentors.

Group activities began with trust building exercises, self disclosure exercises, contextually relevant simulation exercises. Workshops followed by group discussions and debates were organized as were brain storming sessions on issues like gender and sex, gender-based discrimination, the socialization process, masculinity, femininity, patriarchy, the location of power and authority in society, and sexuality. Fine Arts students were involved in group activities like poster making and exhibitions. Screening films, lectures by experts, rallies and street plays were other activities. During workshops and simulation exercises, innovative educational materials and improvised games developed by experts, were used. Simulation exercises were especially useful in focusing on relative privileges and powers available to men in Indian society, how these undue privileges affected women and constituted violence, and how social expectations from men and boys turned them into perpetrators of violence. Female students were also involved occasionally in the discussions to share their experiences regarding the gender-based discrimination they faced in university and in their day to day life. Students discussed openly their dilemmas, confusions, and personal tensions during these sessions.

Mentors and their role

A total of five mentors was involved. Two of them were university teachers and the authors of this paper. The first author from social work discipline had 17 years experience of teaching and research and was associated with the university where this campaign started. The second mentor was from the discipline of teacher education, having 12 years experience of teaching and research and having worked in a central university located in same city. The other three mentors were Ph.D. students who had been involved with MASVAW since its inception in 2002. All the mentors except one were male.

All the groups remained with their mentors for three to four years. The mentors' role was diverse in nature;each mentor worked as advisor, teacher, resource person, role model and facilitator of group discussions. They listened to members' personal problems and helped them to overcome the pain involved in the change process. Group members worked at two levels; first they developed their knowledge, capabilities and perspectives regarding gender issues. Second, group members were great support for each other by providing a platform for sharing experiences of individual accomplishments and challenges they faced during the change process. During the above period group members were engaged in some sort of collective action in the university, for example, they protested against the inactive nature of the 'Anti Sexual Harassment Committee' of the university and took initiatives to reactivate and revive it. Some cases of domestic violence in Varanasi and reported in the local media instigated the group members to participate in a rally and register their protest. It seemed that now group members were feeling a sense of accomplishment in their work.

Evaluation of the program

At the end of the group work when group members (students) were about to leave the university as their course had come to end, an external evaluation was carried out to ascertain the level of accomplished task in terms of its objectives. A three member team was formed for the evaluation, which comprised Ms. Liz Mogford Ph.D. student of Sociology, University of Washington, Seattle as principal researcher, Ms. Seema Parveen and Mr. Ravi Jeena, research associates, SAHYOG, a non government organization. In order to observe attitudinal changes in depth qualitative interviews of group members were conducted. All the interviews were recorded with the permission of the interviewees. Nearly half of the group members (38/80) were interviewed. Also, close friends (non MASVAW men), fellow female students, parents and spouses of the group members were also interviewed separately to seek their opinion about the changes they had perceived in the behavior of members of the groups. The interview focused on the changes members perceived in themselves after joining the group. Some of the questions asked were: 'what kind of changes do you perceive in yourself as a result of having joined the group?', 'what are the challenges and threats of this process', 'how do you cope with the challenges?' Friends, parents and spouses were asked, 'do you perceive any change(s) in the behavior of x?'

The data obtained were in the forms of narratives. Data were transcribed, coded, and content analysis was carried out. To check any kind of social desirability, data were triangulated to find out contradictions.

A Social Work student (MASVAW member) said,

We have to fight against the traditional definition of masculinity which implies that if you are a man, you can dominate and subjugate people. We must redefine masculinity in the university campus in such way that a real man is he who respects women'. In the university campus, a slogan of MASVAW which became popular says, 'Men of quality are not afraid of equality.

A Fine Arts student (MASVAW member) said,

after being a member, now I have come to know that there is nothing wrong with being emotional'. Another member student said that he had become polite.

A Law student (MASVAW member) expressed his conflict in following words:

> *now I know, what is being man but how can I change my parents and family members who forced me to confirm the traditional masculinity... it is causing pain.*

In response to the question did he perceive any change in his friend's behavior, the MASVAW member's friend said: 'he is a changed fellow now.... he does not pass and enjoy dirty remarks about girls'.

A parent said that now her son is helping her in domestic chores and it is strange new behavior. A female student said, 'it is good to talk to these groups of men ... they are more sensible'.

A close friend of a MASVAW member said: 'there is something happened to him as he is not aggressive as he was before'.

So it can be said that group members gained greater understanding about the structure of violence against women and their own complicity and responsibility in the whole process. They learned to use positive tools for managing conflict and anger incorporating a broader range of emotional expression.

Accomplishments

The MASVAW Campaign has been successful in bringing change to male students of the university at two levels:

Inter-personal level

At the inter-personal level, interaction among male and female students has increased and more female students have started sharing their problems with MASVAW members. Other non MASVAW member male students also started sharing their problems (mainly regarding sexuality) with MASVAW members and peer group learning was started in the university.

Intra-personal level

All members perceive themselves to be more sensitive towards gender issues and they said that their attitude towards sexuality, masculinity, gender division of labor, women's work, and particularly towards their female classmates has changed.

These changes can be linked to the campaign because, in the evaluation process, members attributed and acknowledged the role of MASVAW in their lives and the kind of experiences they had had during last three or four years were potent enough to change their perspectives.

Challenges faced during the program

Lack of cultural sanction and recognition is the biggest challenge. The MASVAW network finds negligible support from society in general and the university in particular. Besides this certain women's organizations working at local level are suspicious about the intentions of MASVAW as they believe that only women's organizations can do justice to the cause of eradicating violence against women. One of the major challenges is to monitor and follow up the changes among students after they have left the university campus.

But in spite of these challenges MASVAW model shows that it is possible to work with men and boys. Men can bring about changes at institutional and individual level. This example shows that young men (however few in number) are not opposed to change and their agency can be employed successfully in achieving the mammoth goal of gender equality.

References

Anderson, K.L. (1997). Gender, status and domestic violence: An integration of feminist and family violence approaches. *Journal of Marriage and the Family, 59*(3), 655-669.

Bond, B. (2006). *Voices against violence.* Sweden: Save the Children.

Ingoldsby, B.B. & Smith, S.D. (2006). *Families in global and multicultural perspective.*

Jain, A. (2001). *Right to inheritance vs son's right to inheritance.* New Delhi: Rajkamal.

Leeder, E. (2004). *The family in global perspective: A gendered journey.* Thousands Oaks, CA: Sage.

Liddle, A.M. (1989). Feminist contributions to an understanding of violence against women – three steps forward, two steps back. *Canadian Reviev of Sociology and Anthropology, 26*(5), 759-775.

Malik, B., Karlsson, L. & Karkara, R. (2005). *Working with men and boys: Methods, strategies, tools and practices.* Sweden: Save the Children.

Nabar, V. (1995). *Caste as women.* India: Penguin Books.

National Family Health Survey (2007). National Sample Survey Organization, Gov. of India. Retrieved from www.nfhsindia.org on 25.11.2010 at 7.10pm

Ruddik, S. (1989). *Maternal thinking.* London: Verso.

Sanjay (2005). Ending gender-based violence: Highlighting the role of men. In D.P. Singh & M. Singh (Eds.),*Women and empowerment: Experiences from some Asian countries.* Chandigargh, India: Unistar.

NCERT (2007). *Seventh all India school education survey, 2007.* New Delhi: NCERT. Retrieved on September 1, 2011 from http://www.ncert.nic.in/programmes/education survey/index education.html

Toseland, R.W. & Rivas, R.F.(1998). *An introduction to group work practice.* USA: Allyn and Bacon.

United Nations Declaration on the Elimination of Violence Against Women (1993).*The Human rights of women: A reference guide to official UN documents.* Retrieved from www.un.org on 01.01.2009

11

Group intervention work with Aboriginal youth preparing for adult living

Stéphane Grenier, Martin Goyette, Andrée-Anne Lemay & Alexis Pearson

Abstract: The transition towards adult life is a complex process for most young people, but it is even more complex for young people experiencing or having experienced family problems requiring placement or intensive follow-up. Group intervention is a useful approach to help these young people face this step in their lives. Indeed, it offers youth workers the advantage of using mutual support existing among peers to reinforce learning that will help the young people be independent once they become adults. This article will focus primarily on group intervention, as applied to Aboriginal youth. There is very little information existing on specific considerations that need to be taken into account when using group intervention, which should be adapted culturally. Indeed, group intervention with Aboriginal youth needs to be adapted culturally in order to allow for specific modes of group functioning within Native communities. In this article we present the preliminary results of a research project on the transition to adult life among Aboriginal youth and we take a look at the lessons drawn from research in order to apply them directly to group intervention programs with Aboriginal youth preparing for independent adult living.

Introduction[1]

The social integration of young adults can be understood, on the one hand, as a series of changes indicating transition towards adulthood: from their parents' home to their own home; from school to work; from being single to having a relationship and forming a new family (Coles, 1996). On the other hand, it can be understood as a process of conscious connection to oneself and to others. To achieve social integration means to build significant relationships and make a place for oneself within various social environments.

In many ways the social integration of youth in general has become more and more complex, but it has become a major issue for youth facing specific challenges, for example those entering into adult life after more or less prolonged placement in care (Goyette *et al.*, 2007a). Indeed, the pressures to find a job and an apartment arrive much sooner for young people facing an abrupt break with services offered by the youth protection system than for the general population of young Quebecois. Upon discharge from reception centres, these vulnerable youth, more often than not, lack both emotional and financial support from their family of origin (Collins, 2001; Courtney *et al.*, 2001; Gauthier *et al.*, 1999; Goyette *et al.*, 2007b).

Without knowing for sure if the process of social integration of Aboriginal youth produces more negative results than for of all young adults exiting care, it is reasonable to assume that Aboriginal youth are faced with additional challenges (Brassard, 2001; Bousquet, 2005; Conseil du bien-être social, 2007; Fox *et al.*, 2005; Long *et al.*, 2006). It is also reasonable to assume that specific cultural, social and structural factors come into play when considering how young people themselves understand their process of becoming an adult.

Data from Canadian studies do indeed paint a bleak picture for Aboriginal youth in terms of socio-economic status and opportunities for social inclusion. They are significantly more likely than non Aboriginal youth to develop addictions to alcohol or drugs, adopt violent behaviour, act self-destructively and experience unwanted pregnancy (Thatcher, 2001). Exposure to risk factors related to economic and social poverty is likely to drive many Aboriginal youth to criminal behaviour (LaPrairie & Stenning, 2003). Moreover, it is reasonable to believe that Aboriginal youth are especially poor in terms of concrete social support, despite the value traditionally attributed to large, community-based support networks (Long *et al.*, 2006). The capacity of Aboriginal communities to set themselves in motion in order to assist their young people is limited, primarily because of the social problems afflicting many adults and the gradual erosion of traditional values (Dion Stout & Kipling, 2000).

Likewise, certain culturally-enforced attitudes inhibit the use of professional services. Access to these services in the community is lacking (Fox *et al.*, 2005; Long *et al.*, 2006). Provision of health and social services in communities can be hindered by high turn-over rates among employees and miscommunication between sectors (Minore, 2004). Furthermore, non Native government authorities are viewed negatively as a result of the history of colonization and attempts at assimilating members of Native communities (Munsell, 2004). All of these factors, added up, are likely to harm the future of youth who are exposed to them. Aboriginal youth struggle with many widely documented issues: poverty, problems related to alcohol and drugs, low education levels, unemployment and single parenthood (Conseil du bien-être social, 2007).

The existence of these 'disintegrative pressures' should not, however, overshadow the fact that many Aboriginal communities have 'forces of cohesion' (Boone *et al.*, 1997), that allow for positive development to take place when the necessary ingredients are assembled. On a structural level, some authors have pointed out the power of collective and collaborative approaches to effect change within Native communities (Haig-Brown, 2000; Kral, 2009; Boone *et al.*, 1997; Minore *et al.*, 2003). These approaches require specific attitudes, particularly on the part of non Native intervention workers and researchers. They include flexibility (Boone *et al.*, 1997), reciprocity and trust (Haig-Brown, 2003; Minore *et al.*, 2002); acknowledgement and inclusion of indigenous knowledge and customs (Haig-Brown, 2000; Boone *et al.*, 1997), and mindfulness about one's own social position and history and its potential impact on the intervention and/or research relationship (Haig-Brown, 2000; Kral, 2009).

These authors argue that it is more productive to work with the 'natural' forces existing in the community rather than to base intervention solely on professional or academic knowledge and skills. Group intervention uses the forces of the group to help youth gain support for their process of transition. Group intervention strategies leave more room for 'horizontal' interactions occurring between young people. Among youth, peer relations bear a lot of weight; for example, youth are more open to receiving advice from peers than from adults (i.e. youth workers). Thus, group intervention work may have the potential to make up for weak support networks of youth having been placed in the care of the youth protection services, one of the factors most often pointed out when considering their transition to adult life. Group intervention may be a particularly powerful tool while working with Aboriginal youth because of the value given to reciprocal relationships both within Aboriginal culture and in intervention.

In addition, Turcotte and Lindsay (2006) indicate that group intervention strategies may offer specific opportunities for young adults lacking assistance when facing discharge from care. On a cognitive level, group intervention allows young people to perceive their reality as normal, to consider who they are through the image reflected by others, to discover a variety of ways of thinking and behaving, to identify with peers and to grow in interdependence. On an emotional level, group intervention decreases feelings of loneliness and isolation by putting youth in contact with people experiencing similar issues, and offers them a chance to develop a certain status which in turn improves their self-esteem. Finally, on a behavioural level, group intervention teaches social skills, regulates conduct through the criticisms and positive feedback of the other group members, and encourages youth to take action as they draw strength and encouragement from within the group. In short, group intervention produces benefits on many levels for youth transitioning to independence.

Research method

In 2008 we conducted a research project[2] consisting of a qualitative exploratory study with interviewees specialized in the social integration of young adults from the Algonquin communities in Abitibi-Témiscamingue (Goyette & Grenier, 2009). Data from the interviews led us to reinforce the idea that group intervention would be a useful form of social work action to be carried out with youth transitioning towards independent living.

From October 2007 to May 2008, 23 respondents were met on an individual basis. Three of these were specialists in group intervention. Furthermore, two group discussions were conducted with 11 youth workers from the external services of the Centre jeunesse (youth protection services in Quebec) based directly in the Algonquin communities. The local communities were involved throughout the research process and were consulted for the recruitment of experienced interviewees. Though most of the workers interviewed are non Native, many of them (7) are Native. To help carry out the interviews, guides for semi-directive interviews and discussion groups were developed and used, our goal being to let the interviewees' various representations of the realities facing youth emerge, since the process of social integration among Aboriginal youth has yet to be studied empirically. The three-hour interviews touched upon the youth's general circumstances in regards to work, schooling, parenthood and residential history; the specific reality of Aboriginal youth leaving care upon reaching the age of adulthood; the particularities of becoming an adult within Aboriginal communities; and intervention work among Algonquin youth. Finally, thanks to information gathered through interviews with specialists on group intervention, many elements were brought up that relate specifically to group intervention with Native peoples. These three specialists are particularly close to the communities in which they work; many times throughout the process, they corrected and improved our analysis. The elements from these interviews and group discussions will be discussed in the following section. In our opinion, they represent the main points of convergence between the information provided by Native and non Native sources.

Results

Since non Native perspectives do not match realities experienced by Native communities, we need to adjust how we understand social integration among Aboriginal youth. Common challenges relating specifically to young people transitioning towards adulthood in an Aboriginal setting must absolutely be taken into account when considering intervention with Native youth to help them prepare for their future. Three common issues emerge as the result of our research project.

Adulthood: Distinct meanings for Natives and non Natives

The first issue relates to the distinction between Native and non Native notions of adulthood. According to our informants, it is clear that the word 'adult' has a very different meaning for Native communities. Non Native young people tend to prolong their studies before entering the job market; they reach financial independence well after their 18th birthday. Algonquin youth are encouraged to become self-supporting very early on and their parents expect them to help out financially as soon as they begin receiving social assistance or salary.

The non Native notion of transition towards adulthood is associated with the period extending from the end of adolescence to a person's early twenties, where studies, employment and material possessions represent favoured paths towards self-fulfilment. This notion does not apply in a Native setting.

In Native communities, the beginning of adult life is marked by specific events: acquiring eligibility for social assistance and becoming a parent are important benchmarks indicating that one has attained the status of adulthood. Nevertheless, this status is not related to specific life events only. It also refers to the notion of self-fulfilment, described as a process of healing that gives rise to the desire to do more for the coming generations.

The path towards fulfilment, especially among older adults, often involves drawing closer to traditional culture. For young people, who have had less contact with traditional culture, interviewees speak instead of integration strategies responding to the need both to reinforce their unique identity and to set themselves into motion in order to make a positive contribution to their community. These strategies inevitably involve a process of redefining their identity. The words of an Algonquin worker reflect this difference well:

> [...] perhaps for some Aboriginal families, having children and being able to honour your responsibilities as a parent; maybe that's a successful adult life. You don't need to have gone to university; you don't need to have a trade, to go to College to learn a technical trade. [...] I think that for Aboriginals what is important when you are an adult is to be balanced and to be an example for others[3].

Search for self among Aboriginal youth

The second common issue illustrates the challenges facing Algonquin youth in their search for self. Proud of their roots but confronted with an 'idealized' culture they are unable to live out, Algonquin youth struggle to define who they are and make a place for themselves as both 'young' and 'Native'. A split between past and present generations contributes to the identity crisis facing young people. This split would be due to painful historical episodes and more recently to the age of boarding schools, where Aboriginal children were separated from their parents and uprooted from their culture[4].

This situation made it difficult for parents to pass on their traditions to their children; these children thus lacked solid grounding in their native culture. The respondents also point out that many aspects of traditional Aboriginal culture can no longer be lived out in the context of contemporary lifestyles. Faced with the loss of cultural bearings, young people struggle to define themselves. They experience pressure to perpetuate their culture but have not been given the tools to accomplish this goal; this, according to the respondents, generates feelings of anger and bewilderment. As a result, young people find themselves faced with difficult choices in terms of their identity, and unsure where to position themselves in the intersection between Native and non Native cultural paradigms.

Moreover, openness towards non Native mores and customs may bring young people to adopt external values that clash with the values of their elders. As young people ask themselves how to succeed in life while remaining 'Native', adults, afraid of seeing their children become 'White', fail to send them clear messages. The youth experience pressure to succeed in both worlds, though no one has given them the means to do so. Receiving no clear message as to what they must do in order to remain 'true Algonquins', young people have trouble envisioning their future. One intervention worker speaks in these terms about this reality:

> [...] young people lack role-models who show them that it's possible to have a trade and follow a path that allows them to stay 'Indian' while having a career.

Though traditional culture remains the foundation of Aboriginal identity, our informants agree that this culture has now been emptied of its meaning for those to whom it has not been passed on. Young people are thus forced to reclaim and redefine their own identity, by combining elements of traditional and contemporary culture, as one Algonquin worker puts it:

> [...] truly redefining and reclaiming Aboriginal culture: for them, healing depends on it. [...] We are living in the age of Internet, television and video games; they exist in the communities [but] don't go and take that away from them. On the other hand, we are also living in the age of 'I'm proud to be Anishinabe, [...] I have pride and I feel connected; I don't know why but it's there, and my pride is real'.

Specific social and political circumstances in Aboriginal communities

The last issue relates to the specific social and political circumstances in Native communities. The motivation for social inclusion and the opportunities offered to Aboriginal youth for social integration are closely linked to the sociopolitical conditions in which they live. The internal dynamics of Native communities may in some ways represent stumbling blocks. For example, the problem of – what may seem, from a non Native point of view, to be – collective inaction limits young people's ambitions and inevitably affects their future. The interviewees observe that, since they have few role models to follow in terms of success, the young people often reproduce what they've seen and have trouble aspiring to more. Some caution, however, should be used in interpreting these findings and one must not assume that communities have only a negative influence on young people. Kral (2009), in his study on youth suicide, demonstrated how powerful social change was achieved in a Native community through 'collective action'.

In order to respond to the challenges facing young people, youth workers involved with Algonquin communities try to set up various intervention strategies. This can require some effort, however, particularly in contexts where actions coming from outsiders are seen as unwelcome. These observations echo remarks made by Boone *et al.* (1997: p.20).

Many respondents also mentioned the issue of reliance on outside help, especially social services. Some even believe that the continuity and maintenance of existing strategies are threatened in the absence of non Native intervention. From these considerations, our interviewees question the potential of social initiatives introduced within communities who are unable to make them their own.

> When we consider if someone can be autonomous, it's because many adults here are not. They are dependent. Tomorrow morning they [could] break the cycle of services that are offered... [...] That's where we see the breadth of poverty. I think we don't fully grasp it.

What to do?

All of the above considerations suggest that a group intervention program based on mutual support is likely to promote a spirit of self-determination among Aboriginal communities. Self-determination is, as Kral (2009) points out, an important factor ensuring the well-being of individuals and groups. As was mentioned by the informants, some social initiatives fail to reach the Aboriginal communities and it is difficult to motivate the young people. Group intervention positions us far away from traditional intervention styles where the only potential for change stems from the relationship between the 'helper' and the 'helped'. In group intervention strategies based on a model of mutual support, the participants yield as much if not more therapeutic power as the professional. In intervention strategies founded on group dynamics, exchanges should be respectful of the potential of each member to influence the others. Indeed, our respondents observe that comments from other members of the group are greeted more readily than those from professionals, because young people may believe that workers from outside their community think of themselves as superior to them.

Considerations for group intervention work with Aboriginal youth

Before introducing group intervention strategies for Aboriginal youth transitioning towards independent living, workers must be aware of where they stand in regards to the culture in which they are called to operate (Haig-Brown, 2003; Kral, 2009). To this effect, Pinderhugues (1995: quoted in Turcotte and Lindsay, 2008) suggests that they need to be able to challenge their own beliefs, adapt themselves to the population's value system and consider the context in which they will be working. These concerns also came up during the interviews with the three specialists in group intervention. They stated that facilitators need to adapt themselves as best as possible to the experiences of Aboriginal youth. In order to do this, youth workers need to acquire relational know-how (*savoir-être*), technical know-how (*savoir-faire*) and theoretical know-how (*savoir*) specifically related to the transition to adulthood as it is experienced within Native communities.

Relational know-how

First of all, facilitators must think of themselves as full-fledged members of the group. They should participate as equals in group activities, instead of positioning themselves as leaders and/or observers (Haig-Brown, 2000). To foster a climate of mutual support, facilitators should be capable of creating space for the strengths of the group to emerge, therefore avoiding the risk of hindering the process of gaining individual and collective power. They should keep their expert role to a minimum and adopt a bottom-up, supportive, approach as the group continues to progress. We can parallel this attitude with what Haig-Brown calls 'listening mindfully', in which the professional '[starts] from a place of not knowing anything at all' (2003: p.429).

Secondly, the specialists underline the importance of using 'basic-level' language with Native people in order to ensure comprehension; not because Native people lack intellectual capacity, but rather because the same words can refer to different things for Natives and non Natives. Moreover, references to Aboriginal lifestyles help the young people better assimilate the workers' meaning because it is easier for them to picture what they are trying to explain.

It is also important for facilitators to be able to decode non-verbal communication because few Aboriginal youth will acknowledge their incomprehension of what the workers are trying to get across. Non verbal reactions from Aboriginal youth can be very different than reactions from non Native youth; the former could easily – and wrongly – be interpreted as signals that young people lack interest in building a relationship, while it is nothing of the sort. Different modes of expression may be partly explained by the fact that, as Haig-Brown reminds us: Native culture is based on oral history, while non Native culture relies heavily on the written word (2003: p.417).

Lastly, in order for successful intervention to take place, the young people must feel that facilitators are there for them when they need them; however they don't like to feel 'educated'. Native people react negatively to 'interventionist', 'professional' and 'individual' approaches that bring back recent memories of boarding schools and/or contradict their traditional culture. A holistic approach is more fitting. Since the notion of sharing on a personal level is well ingrained in Aboriginal culture, self-disclosure, which demonstrates workers' investment in a relationship, is regarded positively. To sum up, empathy, genuineness, knowledge of self, creativity, open-mindedness, adaptability and interest in knowing the other, are elements of success for group intervention within Native communities. The skills related to technical know-how described below are just as important.

Technical know-how

First of all, group strategies must be adaptable and flexible. For example, the rates of participation will probably increase for groups taking place within the communities themselves, because youth don't have to go into town on specific days at specific times. For many Native people, punctuality is of little importance. They don't feel the need to be on time since their whole community functions according to principles in which this notion has no value. Facilitators therefore need to make sure that young people understand the meaning of punctuality as it relates to the transition towards adulthood. Otherwise, young people may view intervention strategies as a way for non Natives to impose their own values, which could generate strong resistance. This ties in to historical imbalance in power relations as indicated by Haig-Brown (2000) and Kral (2009).

The specialists on group intervention also point out that in order to arouse interest for the group, facilitators may call on other members of the community, use different venues and give a festive air to the meetings (banquet, special activity, pot-luck, etc.) Facilitators should continually foster interest among the young people by giving them some freedom and letting them suggest activities they might enjoy. It is best therefore not to lay down a tight schedule for each meeting, but rather think of a few activities that could be suggested to the group depending on where the discussion leads.

The setup of the meeting place is very important to achieve a sense of belonging among the young participants. To help them feel at ease and relate to their environment, the respondents suggest that they be allowed to decorate the space themselves, perhaps with meaningful objects.

One of the group specialists, who has worked with Aboriginal communities for many years, relates how the harm reduction approach fits well within this context; the young people will be more willing to work on their problems if they feel they won't be punished or constantly reprimanded for their actions.

Learning through positive modelling and learning through play are two appropriate strategies. The first one involves speaking positively about the community and gives the young people a chance to connect with their origins. The second strategy uses writing, drawing, music and art, which are very effective means of expression among young people.

Theoretical know-how

When forming the groups, certain considerations must be taken into account. One specialist pointed out that due to rivalries existing between Native bands in Abitibi-Témiscamingue, group intervention workers should target young people according to their community of origin rather than to their profile in the youth protection services (in Quebec, *Direction de la protection de la jeunesse*, or DPJ). These rivalries have the potential to greatly harm the group intervention process. To this effect, Boone and her colleagues (1997) remark that non Native workers often wrongly view Aboriginal communities as homogenous; in other words, they fail to take into account important sociocultural differences occurring between communities.

Care should also be given to the different wishes of young people as they exit care, as some of them choose to return to their communities, while others choose life in the city. At present, the strategies involving transmission of functional skills to Algonquin youth prior to their discharge and transition towards independent living do not take into consideration their specific circumstances and the fact that a majority of youth return to their community upon exiting care.

Some instrumental skills related to everyday tasks in an Aboriginal setting need to be taught to young people wishing to live in their community (eg: woodcutting, preservation and preparation of certain traditional foods, the functioning of non electrical heating devices, etc.). These skills could be taught by the communities' elders: as was mentioned before, learning through positive modelling is an approach that has been proven effective. Moreover, encouraging other generations to participate in the group process could promote the passing on of traditional values, in addition to motivating more members of the community to take up collective action. The work of Haig-Brown (2000) supports both this holistic view of learning and the importance given to traditional skills as a means of reinforcing cultural identities.

Secondly, since rites and ceremonies are such an important part of Aboriginal culture, especially within the traditions of many First Nations, it would be interesting to adapt the group rituals to beliefs stemming from these traditions. According to the respondents, establishing a routine within the group could also create stability and a sense of security among the young people, and in turn help them develop sufficient confidence to open up to the group. The spiritual element so cherished in Native beliefs could be translated into rituals within the group. For example, the rite of purification with sage branches, or the rite of smoking the peace pipe are two traditional customs calling up protection, positive influences, peace and harmony.

As for young people wishing to live in the city, the notion of punctuality should be stressed, especially with a view towards integration on a social and professional level. As was mentioned above, punctuality is not a dominant value in the community, so young people find themselves caught between the lifestyle they have been taught all their lives, and a new way of life we try to impose on them so they may function within the system (work, school, social institutions, etc.).

Conclusion

In short, according to our data, we observe that the transition towards independent living within an Aboriginal setting differs from the same transition within a non Aboriginal setting and that in some programs targeting Aboriginal youth, specific cultural elements are not taken into account. Since existing programs are conceived according to individual approaches and within a non Native mind frame, these programs may be ineffective. For this reason, and after having completed our research with specialists working closely with Native communities, we have come to believe that group intervention strategies could present good alternatives. Based on existing literature and our interviews, it is reasonable to assume that by adapting this approach to an Aboriginal context, it would be beneficial not only for the young people, but also for workers and community members. As we have mentioned above, group intervention offers many advantages that individual intervention does not. It does, however, require a significant level of commitment on the part of workers, young people, and the community.

Bearing in mind all the above considerations, our research team has partnered up with many service providers in Abitibi-Temiscamingue, youth protection teams, as well as field workers offering frontline services in two local Aboriginal communities. In the fall, building from a broad perspective on the issues surrounding the transition to adulthood for Aboriginal youth, our working group introduced – in these communities – two group interventions based on mutual support following two training sessions. The training sessions were completed by a training manual and activity guide offered to youth workers (Grenier *et al.*, 2010).

The experience of performing group interventions is at the heart of our reflective process on how to best assist Aboriginal youth in their transition to adult living. In order to identify the advantages of this type of intervention compared to what is presently carried out (Goyette *et al.*, 2010), the team has also undertaken a larger assessment of the group interventions in which the points of view of both the youth workers and the young people are considered. Here, we are not fixed in a top down perspective like many expert programs; our approach in favour of participation is supported by the need to adapt the programs to different cultural and organisational settings. Consequently, the intervention process, as well as the materials that come with it (i.e. manual and activity guide) will be improved upon in light of results from our assessment.

The ethical positioning and pro-participative stance presented in this article, as demonstrated by our cooperation with field workers and, in this case, Native communities, is coherent with a vision of program development and innovation taking into account contextual factors. As we wait for results from the field experiments carried out in the Native communities, we find that many youth workers are expressing their support for broader implementation of this participative approach, which they see as an additional tool for intervention with vulnerable youth, once our current project is carried through.

Notes

1. Many thanks to Alexis Pearson who helped us in the correction and translation of the text.
2. This research project was funded by the National Crime Prevention Centre (NCPC) and originates from a partnership between the Association des centres jeunesse du Québec and the researchers involved.
3. All quotes from interviewees are translated from French.
4. For a detailed account of how history has (re)shaped social relations within Inuit communities of Nunavut, see Kral, 2009.

References

Boone, M., Minore, B., Katt, M. & Kinch, P. (1997). Strength through sharing: Interdisciplinary teamwork in providing health and social services to Northern Native communities. *Canadian Journal of Community Mental Health*, 16(2), 15-28.

Bousquet, M.-P. (2005). Les jeunes Algonquins sont-ils biculturels? Modèles de transmission et innovations dans quelques réserves. *Recherches amérindiennes au Québec, XXXV*(3), 7-17.

Brassard, D. (2001). *L'insertion socioprofessionnelle des jeunes autochtones.* Québec: Université Laval.

Coles, B. (1996). Youth transitions in the United Kingdom: A review of recent research. In B. Galaway & J. Hudson (Eds.), *Youth in transition: Perspectives on research and policy* (pp.23-31). Toronto: Thompson Educational Publishing.

Collins, M.E. (2001). Transition to adulthood for vulnerable youths: A review of research and implications for policy. *Social Service Review,* 271-291.

Conseil national du bien-être social (2007). *Agissons maintenant pour les enfants et les jeunes métis, inuits et des premières nations.* Ottawa.

Courtney, M.E., Pliliavin, I., Grogan-Kaylor, A. & Nesmith, A. (2001). Foster youth transitions to adulthood: A longitudinal view of youth leaving care. *Child Welfare, 80*(6), 685-717.

Daining, C. & DePanfilis, D. (2007). Resilience of youth in the transition from out-of-home care to adulthood. *Children and Youth Services Review, 29,* 1158-1178.

Dion Stout, M., Kipling, G. & Stout, R. (2001). *Aboriginal women's health research synthesis project, final report* Winnipeg: Centres of Excellence for Women's Health.

Dumaret, A.-C., Coppel-Batsch, M. & Couraud, S. (1997). Adult outcome of children reared for long-term periods in foster families. *Child Abuse & Neglect, 21*(10), 911-927.

Fox, K., Becker-Green, J., Gault, J. & Simmons, D. (2005). *Native American youth in transition: The path from adolescence to adulthood in two native American communities.* Portland, OR: National Indian Child Welfare Association.

Frechon, I. (2005). Les stratégies féminines d'entrée dans la vie adulte. In E. Callu, J.-P. Jurmand & A. Vulbeau (Eds.), *La place des jeunes dans la cité. Tome 2, Espaces de rue, espaces de parole* (pp.215-232). Paris: L'Harmattan.

Gauthier, M. (1999). La jeunesse: un mot, mais combien de définition. In M. Gauthier & J.-F. Guillaume (Eds.), *Définir la jeunesse? D'un bout à l'autre du monde* (pp.9-27). Sainte-Foy: Les Éditions de l'IQRC.

Goyette, M., Chénier, G., Royer, M.-N. & Noël, V. (2007a). Le soutien au passage à la vie adulte des jeunes recevant des services des centres jeunesse. *Éducation et francophonie. Revue scientifique virtuelle, 35*(1), 95-119.

Goyette, M., Royer, M.-N., Noël, V. & Chénier, G. (2007b). *Projet d'intervention intensive en vue de préparer le passage à la vie autonome et d'assurer la qualification des jeunes des centres jeunesse du Québec. Rapport final d'évaluation.* Montréal: Soumis au Centre national de prévention du crime (NCPC) et à l'Association des centres jeunesse du Québec.

Goyette, M., Grenier, S., Pontbriand, A., Turcotte, M.-È., Royer, M.-N. & Corneau, M. (2009). *Enjeux relatifs au passage à la vie adulte de jeunes autochtones : vers une meilleure compréhension de la particularité du contexte des communautés algonquines de l'Abitibi-Témiscamingue.* [Research report]. Montreal: National Crime Prevention Centre (NCPC). 82 pages.

Goyette, M., Turcotte, D., Mann-Feder, V., Grenier, S., Turcotte, M.-E. & Pontbriand, A. (2010). *Évaluation de la satisfaction, de l'implantation et des effets à la suite de la mise en œuvre des programmes d'intervention de groupe Droit Devant et Moi et Cie auprès d'adolescents des centres jeunesse : Rapport d'évaluation des groupes 1 à 4.* [Research report prepared for the National Crime Prevention Centre (NCPC 350-A19) and presented to the Association des centres jeunesse du Québec]. 102 pages.

Grenier, S., Pontbriand, A., Lemay, A.-A. & Goyette, M. (2010). *D'hier à demain: Programme d'intervention de groupe visant à faciliter le passage à la vie autonome des jeunes autochtones.* [Training manual and activity booklet prepared thanks to funding from the National Crime Prevention Centre (NCPC) and Ministère de la Sécurity publique du Québec]. 68 pages.

Haig-Brown, C. (2000). *Some thoughts on protocol in university/community partnerships. NALL working paper.* Toronto : Ontario Institute for Studies in Education. [Online], http://www.oise.utoronto.ca/depts/sese/csew/nall/res/16somethoughts.htm, Retrieved on December 9, 2010.

Haig-Brown, C. (2003). Creating spaces: Testimonio, impossible knowledge and academe. *International Journal of Qualitative Studies in Education, 16*(3), 415-433.

Jahnukaiken, M. (2007). Hi-risk youth transitions to adulthood: A longitudinal view of youth leaving the residential education in Finland. *Children and Youth Services Review, 29,* 637-654.

Kral, M. (2009). *Transforming communities: Suicide, relatedness and reclamation among Inuit of Nunavut.* [Doctoral Thesis]. Montreal: McGill University, department of Philosophy.

Kufedlt, K. (2003). Graduates of guardianship care: Outcomes in early adulthood. In *Child Welfare: Connecting Research, Policy and Practice* (pp.203-216). Wilfred Laurier University Press.

La Prairie, C. & Stenning, P. (2003). Exilés, rue principale : réflexions sur la sur-représentation autochtone dans le système de justice pénale. In *Des gens d'ici: Les autochtones en milieu urbain* (pp.195-210). Ottawa: Projet de recherche sur les politiques. Gouvernement du Canada.

Lanctôt, N. (2006). Les adolescentes prises en charge par le centre jeunesse: Que deviennent-elles au tournant de la vingtaine? *Défi jeunesse, 12*(2), 3-7.

Long, C., Downs, A., Gillette, B. (2006). Assessing cultural life skills of American Indian Youth. In L. Sight & E. Konen, *Child & Youth Care Forum, 35*(4), 289-304.

Maunders, D., Liddel, M., Liddel, M. & Green, S. (1999). *Young people leaving care and protection.* Hobart, Tasmania: Australian Clearinghouse for Youth Studies.

Minore, B. & Boone, M. (2002). Realizing potential: Improving interdisciplinary professional/paraprofessional health care teams in Canada's Northen Aboriginal communities through education. *Journal of Interprofessional Care, 16*(2), 139-147.

Minore, B., Boone, M., Katt, M., Kinch, P. & Birch, S. (2004). Addressing the realities of health care in Northern Aboriginal communities through participatory action research. *Journal of Interprofessional Care, 18*(4), 360-368.

Munsell, G. (2004). *Tribal approaches to transition.* Tulsa, OK: The University of Oklahoma.

Pauzé, R., Toupin, J., Déry, M., Mercier, H., Joly, J., Cyr, M. *et al.* (2004). *Portrait des jeunes âgés de 0 à 17 ans référés à la prise en charge des Centres jeunesse du Québec, leur parcours dans les services et leur évolution dans le temps (Section 5: Portrait des adolescents âgés de 12 à 17 ans dans le cadre de la Loi de la protection de la jeunesse ou de la Loi sur les services de santé et des services sociaux)*: Groupe de recherche sur les inadaptations sociales de l'enfance (GRISE).

Pecora, P.J., Kessler, R.C., O'Brien, K., White, C.R., Williams, J., Hiripi, E. *et al.* (2006). Educational and employment outcomes of adults formerly placed in foster care: Results from the Northwest Foster Care alumni study. *Children and Youth Services Review, 28*(12), 1459-1481.

Rutman, D., Hubberstey, C., Feduniw, A. & Brown, E. (2006). *When youth age out of care - Bulletin of time 2 findings.* Victoria: Research Initiatives for Social Change unit, School of Social Work, University of Victoria.

Thatcher, R. (Ed.) (2001). *Vision seekers part 1: A structured personal & social development program for first nations's youth at high social risk.* Craven, Sask. : Socio-Tech Consulting Services.

Turcotte, D. & Lindsay, J. (2008). *L'intervention sociale auprès des groupes.* Montréal : Gaétan Morin Éditeur,.

Tweddle, A. (2007). Youth leaving care: How do they fare? In V. R. Mann-Feder (Ed.), *Transition or eviction : Youth exiting care for independent living* (pp.15-31). San Francisco: Wiley Subscription Services.

12

French-Canadian version of the Wellness Recovery Action Plan (WRAP):

Preliminary report of its validity for mental health patients in a community teaching and research hospital

Jean-Philippe É. Daoust, Valérie Lemieux, Gilles Fleury, Danielle Perron-Roach, & Diane Lavallée

Abstract: In recent years there has been an interesting shift in the realm of social work intervention from individual (professional – patient) towards co-facilitation (2 or more co-leaders, including both professional and peer-helpers) social group work. Much like the name indicates, the Wellness Recovery Action Plan (WRAP) (Copeland, 2000) offers workshops where participants are able to personalize a recovery action plan in a social group setting. Since this type of service is now available in French in Canada, this study was to assess preliminarily feasibility, efficacy, and efficiency of the WRAP with 10 participants in a mental health community teaching and research hospital (Ottawa, Ontario, Canada). The results indicate that the services seem to have contributed to a decrease in psychological distress, an increase of subjective well-being and a positive path to recovery. The implications of this study are briefly discussed as well as ideas for further scientific investigation. This study was possible due to funds provided by the Mental Health Program of the Montfort Hospital.

Keywords: Wellness recovery action plan (WRAP), peer support intervention, recovery, validity, co-facilitation, social group work, mental health, hospital setting, French-Canadian version.

Introduction

With the new Mental Health Commission of Canada (2009) and other initiatives worldwide, it is now imperative that people living with mental health difficulties be actively engaged and supported in their recovery process and achievement of well-being. Providing opportunities that enable patients to develop a sense of self-advocacy, empowerment, security and personal growth while shifting the focus from problems towards recovery should be the cornerstones of any mental health and social work interventions. However, in order to achieve these ideals, it is necessary that social workers and other mental health care professionals acknowledge each patient's experience as a key component.

In the past decade, there has been an interesting shift in the realm of social work intervention from individual towards social group work. This shift in our health care system has prompted many researchers to manifest a renewed interest in studying social group work in various settings (Aronoff, & Bailey, 2005; Drumm, 2006; Sulman, Savage, Vrooman & McGillivray, 2004; Wright, 2002; Kostyk, Fuchs, Tabisz & Jacyk, 1993; Rose & Chang, 2010; Letendre, Gaillard & Spath, 2008; Andrews, 2001; Cohen, & DeLois, 2001) to illustrate its benefits and limitations for a precise population.

Due to socioeconomic pressures, cost saving rationales and the lack of resource availability, the dramatic surge of social group work has been propelled by a common misconception that this approach enables mental health care providers to maximise the number of patients treated, while minimizing changes to existing service infrastructures and methodology of practice (Wright, 2002). In reality, there are clear distinctions between individual and group interventions and Tropp (1968), amongst others, suggests that group work is fundamentally a different type of practice than individual work.

Papell and Rothman (1980) explain that social group work emerges from the interplay of a) the group, b) the members in the group, c) the activity and d) the worker with the group. Groups are also characterized by common goals, mutual aid and non synthetic experiences (Wright, 2002). Furthermore, Drumm (2006) suggests that social group interventions are complex systems with multi-dimensional tasks. The objective of social group work is not simply to widen the scope of patients treated but rather it serves each member in a very different way from an individual approach (Wright, 2002). Social group work engages every member in active participation through group building and facilitates the development of new relationships while striving to meet the needs of every individual rather than simply broadening the scope of patients treated (Wright, 2002).

In parallel, co-facilitation of groups is increasing in popularity in terms of both practice and research. The term facilitator is being revolutionized with the forthcoming of trained peer-helpers as social group work co-leaders along with mental health professionals (Cohen *et al*, 2001; Kostyk *et al*, 1993). According to Yoak & Chesler (1985) having peer-helpers co-facilitate groups supplies valuable cost-effective resources where gaps in the health care system currently exist and they seemingly offer more social support, formal group structure and more active learning styles. In fact, peer-helpers do not only serve as a role model to other members by offering guidance, hope and optimism but they also help bridge the gap between the group members and the professional co-leader. In addition, the peer-helper and professional co-facilitator dyad features a wealth of complementary abilities and skill sets characteristic of each co-leader's expertise and background (Kostyk *et al*, 1993).

The idea of including peer support in the delivery of clinical services is increasingly discussed and a number of group work theorists have explored the pros and cons (Kostyk *et al*, 1993). However, it is important to asses its impact before consistently implementing this practice in social group work in a hospital setting. It is in this context that this study was conducted to allow an assessment of the Wellness Recovery Action Plan (WRAP) (Copeland, 2000), a form of social group work intervention, with co-facilitation including both a peer-leader and a mental health professional.

Moreover, in an innovative and exploratory perspective, the WRAP workshops have been recently offered for the first time to a Franco-Ontarian adult population in the Ottawa region of Canada within a mental health community teaching and research hospital. In addition, the format of the WRAP workshops, from the model developed by Mary Ellen Copeland, is now available in French (*Plan d'action individualisé de rétablissement* – PAIR – initial translation by *l'Association québécoise pour la réadaptation psychosociale* and final translation by Perron-Roach & Lévesque; approval in process by the Copeland Center).

Wellness Recovery Action Plan

The concept of a Wellness Recovery Action Plan (WRAP) was developed in 1997 by Mary Ellen Copeland and a group of individuals having all lived with mental health problems. In fact, the idea of the WRAP workshops originates from Mary Ellen Copeland's mother and her reported experience of living in a psychiatric institution for eight years. According to her daughter, despite the pessimistic forecasts that professionals projected at that time, this woman opted to take charge of her own recovery process and managed to live an entirely fulfilling life.

Having witnessed her mother's success, Mary Ellen Copeland acknowledged that she too could achieve success throughout her life when she was confronted with a mental health diagnostic. She believed that the professional help that was being offered to her was insufficient if she was to attain her full potential. Thus, she began to question other people with similar difficulties to identify what strategies and tools they were employing in order to achieve and maintain a sense of well-being. This process led to the identification of the values and ethics that seems to guide people's recovery process: hope, self-advocacy, personal responsibility, education and support. In fact, these keystones of the WRAP process aid individuals to regain confidence and ownership of their lives, thus helping them reacquire the hope necessary for progressing in their recovery journey. However, the term *recovery* is not a fixed and easily attainable goal, but rather a gradual and complex life long process that encompasses both internal (attitudes and experiences) and external conditions (circumstances and events) in which an individual is immersed (Jacobson & Greenley, 2001). For this reason, she then defined a workable framework in which these values and ethics could be applied – an intervention *by* and *for* peers.

WRAP is a structured help tool that is offered in a group setting traditionally co-facilitated by one mental health practitioner and one peer-helper (who has experienced mental health issues), both having received official WRAP training by Copeland Center Certified Advanced WRAP Facilitators. The WRAP framework embodies many of the innate values of social work by enabling members to start their own wellness recovery action plan based on their individual experiences and where they are in their recovery process. The action plan also allows them to explore their options and meet new people so that they may be better equipped and empowered to take an active part in decisions which affect them (Wright, 2002; Kostyk *et al*, 1993; Copeland, 2000).

First and foremost, the WRAP is a structured system that assists individuals to identify and monitor uncomfortable and distressing signs of mental health issues and to develop personalized action plans to reduce or eliminate them. The polestars of the WRAP workshops are the individual and their recovery rather than the problem, the flexibility of conception and its inclusiveness to participants.

In 2010, the WRAP workshops were offered for a first time to a Franco-Ontarian population at Montfort Hospital, a community teaching and research hospital (Ottawa, Ontario, Canada). In total ten WRAP workshops were offered (plus two unstructured group sessions of individual action plan development and one debriefing and celebration session). Initially, all of the group members selected together the participatory conditions that would facilitate their ability to be involved comfortably and securely during the workshop which aided in the creation of meaningful interactions and set the stage for the social group work.

The format of each session starts with introducing the topic, then sharing the members' expertise, knowledge and lived experiences in each relevant domain which can then assist each individual in defining their own wellness recovery action plan. Furthermore, the intervention aims to enable participants to identify for themselves the tools that will help them feel as well as possible, despite the intricacies associated with their mental health difficulties. More specifically, the WRAP workshops enable participants to build a personalized wellness toolbox so that they may identify, take ownership, and make better use of the means that they already possess to help them feel as well as possible. In summary, participants are invited to:

a. develop a plan for daily maintenance;
b. identify the triggers and provide an action plan to manage them;
c. identify the warning signs of discomfort and an action plan to manage them;
d. define an action plan for crisis situations; and finally
e. develop an action plan for the post-crisis situations.

The research results conducted by Mary Ellen Copeland have also demonstrated that hope, personal responsibility, education, self-advocacy, and support are often essential components for the recovery process.

More specifically and concerning the functioning of the group during WRAP workshops, the following sequence was implemented in a flexible manner:

a.   welcoming, experience sharing and support between participants;
b.   topic overview and open discussion amongst the group;
c.   real life consolidation and completion of the action plan both individually and as a group; and finally
d.   wrap up and departure.

Objectives

This study has three complementary objectives namely:

a.   an assessment of the feasibility and appropriateness of offering WRAP workshops in a mental health outpatient program in a community hospital;
b.   a preliminary estimate of the potential effectiveness of such an intervention; and finally
c.   a summary measure of its efficiency.

Methodology

The participants (N = 10) were recruited at the Mental Health Program of the Montfort Hospital (Ottawa, Canada). Of the twelve individuals that were initially invited to join the group, ten accepted and signed a consent form for both clinical and program evaluation purposes. Several individual psychometric measures were then gathered at the beginning and at the end of the ten session intervention. The WRAP workshops took place on Monday afternoons for an hour and a half each week, except for holidays (from 22-02-2010 to 03-05-2010). Congruent with the instructions from the Copeland Center, the content of the workshops was faithfully followed and presented in both paper and MS PowerPoint presentation formats (see Table 1. for WRAP Workshops Titles and Brief Topic Overview).

Table 1 – WRAP workshops titles and brief topic overview

Workshop Titles	Brief Topic Overview
1. Introduction to the Concepts	Defining the *recovery process*
2. Values and Ethics of Recovery	*Hope, self-advocacy, personal responsibility, education* and *support*
3. Wellness Tool Box (1)	Definition of *tools* and *resources* used in the *past, present* and in the *future*
4. Wellness Tool Box (2)	Practical *application of tools* and resources
5. Daily Maintenance Plan	Elaboration of *thoughts* and *behaviours* that *facilitate* the *recovery process*
6. Triggers and Action Plan	Identification of *triggers* (events) and action plan
7. Early Warning Signs and Action Plan	Identification of *troublesome emotions* and *behaviours* and ways to *counter them*
8. When Things Are Breaking Down or Getting Worse and Action Plan	Identification of the *signs* that things have *gotten worse*, without being a crisis
9. Crisis plan	Definition of *needs, supporters* and *conditions* in which *help* may be requested
10. Post-crisis plan	Establishing the *resources* and *conditions* that will maximize the wellness *recovery process*

All the participants accepted to complete an auto-evaluation by using the following measures that have been selected in part by the Copeland Center's recommendations: the Recovery Assessment Scale (RAS-41; Corrigan, Giffort, Rashid, Leary & Okeke, 1999), the Mental Health Confidence Scale (MHCS-16; Carpinello, Knight, Markowitz & Pease, 2000), the Empowerment Scale (ES-28; Rogers, Chamberlin, Ellison & Crean, 1997), the State of Hope Scale (SHS-6; Snyder, Sympson, Ybasco, Borders, Babyak & Higgins, 1996), the Outcome measure (OQ-45.2; Lambert & Burlingame, 1992), the Satisfaction with Life Scale (SWLS-5; Diener, Emmons, Larsen & Griddin, 1985), the Emotions Scale (ES-16; Larsen & Diener, 1992) and the Social Support Scale (SSS-4; Health Canada, 1999) in the day to day life. The psychometric proprieties of these tests are reported to be generally adequate (Carpinello, Knight,

Markowitz & Pease, 2000; Corrigan *et al*, 1999; Diener *et al*, 1985; Lambert, 2005 ; Lambert, Smart, Campbell, Hawkins, Harmon, & Slade, 2006 ; Larsen, Attkisson, Hargreaves & Ngyuen, 1979; Rogers *et al*, 1997; Snyder, Sympson, Ybasco, Borders, Babyak & Higgins, 1996).

Four measures that were not available in French (RAS-41, MHCS-16, ES-20 et SHS-6) were translated by a comittee-type procedure (Lemieux, Daoust & Perron-Roach, 2010). Given some cultural differences between French-Canadians and Anglo-Americans and some comments of the participants at the pre-test, questions 4, 7, 10, 15 and 21 of the Empowerment Scale (ES-28) were translated but were not considered in the data analysis, which lead to a shortening of the scale (ES-23).

The participants also completed an evaluation of their level of satisfaction in regards to the services that they received by the French-Canadian version (Sabourin & Gendreau, 1988) of the Client Satisfaction Questionnaire (CSQ-8; Larsen, Attkisson, Hargreaves & Ngyuen, 1979). In parallel, the dynamic relation between the two facilitators (a peer-support individual and a social worker who both have been certified by the Copeland Center) was estimated by using a modified version (Daoust, 2010) of the Dyadic Adjustment Scale (DAS-16; Spanier, 1989). At the end of the intervention, a debriefing session was organized in order to get a better understanding of how each participant was able to benefit from a social group setting.

Finally, a small survey was conducted among staff of the mental health outpatient program to obtain their perceptions about the relevance of implementing such a service in a community hospital.

ANOVAs were conducted to examine differences between all participants at pre- and post-testing. Given the exploratory nature of the present study, the alpha level was set at .05. In addition, t-tests for dependent means were conducted. Given the relatively large number of analyses (9) performed, the alpha level of significance was then adjusted (.05 / 9 = .0056) in order to stay conservative.

Results

Sample description

Ten participants (N = 10) were included in the present study; 70.0% of which were women. The mean age was 39.7 years (SD of 3.4) with an age range from 34 to 43 years. The majority of them resided (70%)

in Ottawa (Ontario, Canada) while the other participants came from the outskirts of the city. They were mostly employed (40% active in the workforce at the time that the service was offered and 40% off work with financial compensation). All participants had at least a high school education and 60% of them had a college diploma. The annual income of the majority of the participants (70%) was located above $ 40,000 per year. Regarding marital status, 40% of the participants were separated/ divorced, 30% were single and 30% were married or common-law. Moreover, half of the participants had dependent children. Among the socio-demographic variables and in function of all the dependent variables available in this study, only the work situation seems to have a significant impact ($F = 9.01$, $df = 3/6$, $p < .012$) on the rate of social support reported at the end of the process. In fact, participants absent from work reported more gaps in their social support compared with those present at work or those studying part-time.

At the beginning of the intervention and in terms of class diagnostic axis I of the DSM-IV-TR (APA, 2000), 70% had a mood disorder, 60% an anxiety disorder, 20% a substance use disorder, 10% psychotic disorder and 10% an Attention Deficit Hyperactivity Disorder (ADHD). Among these diagnostic classes and according to all the dependent variables in this study, only the psychotic disorder might have had a significant impact ($F = 9.17$, $df = 1/8$, $p < .016$) on the reported feeling of confidence concerning an individual's mental health (poorer self-efficacy was reported).

In regard to the DSM-IV-TR (APA, 2000) axis II, 10% of participants presented a borderline personality disorder and 40% other types of personality disorders. Only the other personality disorders taken together seem to have had a significant impact ($F = 7.24$, $df = 1/8$, $p < .027$) on the satisfaction with life at the end of the process.

Furthermore, for 40% of participants, co-morbidity was present on the axis I and II of the DSM-IV-TR (APA, 2000). The main co-morbidities were related to anxiety disorders and mood disorders (40% of co-morbidity) with mood disorders and personality disorders other than borderline personality (30%) and with anxiety disorders and personality disorders other than borderline personality (30%).

Feasibility and relevance of the implementation of the WRAP workshops in hospitals

In retrospect, the WRAP workshops were easy to implement and the attendance at the various workshops was high (M = 83.3%, SD = 19.6%), which seems rather high for a service offered in a hospital. In addition, all participants were able to create their own action plan which was the primary goal of the WRAP workshops. Some participants even appropriated the creative process in a way where, for example, one participant made and decorated a wooden box in which she has carefully selected and incorporated objects in connection with her recovery and that put her in contact with important elements of her life experiences and her action plan.

Overall, the participants were satisfied with the services offered to 91.0% (SD = 4.5%), which is considered a high level of satisfaction (Perreault *et al*, 2001). In addition, all participants felt that WRAP should be offered again, a view that was also shared by the two facilitators.

In regards to the dyadic adjustment between the co-facilitators, they were generally very satisfied with their interaction (M = 100.0%, SD = 0.0%) and seemed to agree very much on the technical aspects related to the philosophy and content of the WRAP workshops (M = 94.0%, SD = 6.0%) and the level of interactions in their co-facilitation (M = 88.5%, SD = 1.0%). From a qualitative standpoint, it is interesting to note that with the evolution of workshop facilitation, co-facilitators seem to have gone from a more technical (covering the transmission of key elements of the program) to a more group supportive role further based on empathic listening and sharing a message of hope.

Moreover, contrary to their expectations, they were surprised to find that participants do not behave differently towards them according to their respective status. It seems as though there was a good pairing between the two co-facilitators, a factor which is postulated by the Copeland Center as being essential to the success of the WRAP workshops.

Although not scientifically sound, the debriefing seems to confirm that the social group work format was an effective element of the intervention especially in the establishment of mutual aid, common goals, guidance, hope, optimism and non synthetic experiences amongst participants.

Efficacy

Overall, the research data suggested that the services provided were helpful and, to some extent contributed, to the reduction of their psychological distress, an improvement of their subjective well-being and to the promotion of their recovery (see Table 2 for overall conclusions).

Table 2
Overall conclusions regarding pre and post WRAP intervention comparison

Concepts	Conclusions
Outcome measure (psychological distress)	Participants reported some *improved functioning* (positive impact of the intervention).
Hope	Participants reported significantly *more hope* at the end of the process.
Recovery	Participants seem to have made significant leeway in their *recovery*.
Negative emotions	Participants reported significantly *fewer negative emotions*.
Positive emotions	Participants reported significantly *more positive emotions*.
Life satisfaction	Participants seem to have reported *more life satisfaction*.
Self-efficacy in the management of mental health	Participants reported a significant tendency to feel more *confident in dealing and managing their mental health*.
Making decisions confidence	Participants reported a tendency of *improved ownership of their decision making*.
Social Support	*No* significant change.

First and foremost, it is important to review the typical psychopathology perspective by analyzing the decrease in the symptomatology level of participants (e.g. psychological distress). On average, they presented clinically significant difficulties prior to the WRAP ($M_{OQ\text{-}45total\text{-}pre}$ = 105.3 [58.5%]), which significantly decreased clinically and almost statistically (t = 3.44; dl 9; p < .011) at the end of the intervention ($M_{OQ\text{-}45total\text{-}post}$ = 84.8 [47.1%]). However, this relatively important change (large effect size; n^2 = .57) is to be nuanced from the fact that the difficulties presented by the participants at the end of the

WRAP workshops remained in the clinical range.

One of the most interesting outcome measures from this study indicates that participants had a significantly higher level of hope at the end of the WRAP intervention ($M_{SHS\text{-pre}}$ = 33.8%; $M_{SHS\text{-post}}$ = 57.1%; t = -5.54; dl 9; p < .000; large effect size; n^2 = .77). Also, participants reported significant progress in their recovery process ($M_{RAS\text{-pre}}$ = 52.6%; $M_{RAS\text{-post}}$ = 67.1%; t = -3.79; dl 9; p < .004; large effect size; n^2 = .61). Moreover, an overall significantly higher proportion of positive emotions ($M_{ES\text{-positive-pre}}$ = 38.8% ; $M_{ES\text{-positive-post}}$ = 53.0% ; t = -3.71 ; dl 9; p < .005 ; large effect size ; n^2 = .60) and a significantly lower proportion of negative emotions ($M_{ES\text{-negative-pre}}$ = 76.0% ; $M_{ES\text{-negative-post}}$ = 57.2% ; t = 3.77 ; dl 9; p < .004 ; large effect size ; n^2 = .61) were reported by participants. In addition, higher satisfaction with life ($M_{SWLS\text{-pre}}$ = 7.1 [20.3%]; $M_{SWLS\text{-post}}$ = 12.7 [36.3%%]; t = -3.20; dl 9; p < .011; large effect size; n^2 = .53) was reported and reflected a significant trend, although participants still remained somewhat dissatisfied at the end of the process from a normative point of view.

It must be noted that another significant trend ($M_{MHCS\text{-pre}}$ = 45.1%; $M_{MHCS\text{-post}}$ = 59.9%; t = -2.81; dl 9; p < .021; moderate effect size; n^2 = .47) was observed concerning the participants' self-efficacy in terms of the management of their mental health state. Also, there was seemingly a tendency ($M_{ES\text{-pre}}$ = 60.2%; $M_{ES\text{-post}}$ = 66.1%; t = -2.03; dl 9; p < .073; small effect size; n^2 = .31) for participants to feel more empowered in their decision making process. Finally, no statistically significant changes ($M_{SSS\text{-pre}}$ = 80.0%; $M_{SSS\text{-post}}$ = 92.8%; t = -1.02; dl 9; p < .335) were observed concerning the reported social support in their social network outside the group work.

Among all the dependent variables in this study, only the participants' attendance to workshops seem to have a significant impact (F = 8.60, df = 5/4, p < .029) on self-efficacy of ownership of decision making and a significant trend (F = 5.90, df = 5/4, p < .055) of a sense of confidence in one's ability to face his/her mental health.

Efficiency

In terms of efficiency of the WRAP workshops in a mental health community hospital, the intervention was relatively inexpensive to provide (approximately 35 hours of pay for the social worker co-facilitator, about 32 hours of pay for the peer support individual, approximately 15 hours for the supervising psychologist, reimbursement travel and parking costs for the peer support individual, a small charge for photocopies, utilization of a therapy room and a few hours management time from the administrative secretariat of the Mental Health Program). Based on previously reported evidence of efficiency, it is reasonable to say that the WRAP workshops could be efficient in hospital settings. Obviously, further investigations will be needed here to get a clearer and more detailed picture.

Survey description

The survey participation rate was relatively small, given 35.3% of the 17 people originally invited (4 psychiatrists, 4 psychologists, 3 support staff members, 2 social workers, 2 occupational therapists, 1 nurse and 1 manager) returned their completed survey sheet. The results of this survey show that 100% of respondents felt that WRAP has a certain legitimacy and should be offered again in hospitals. However, 66.7% of survey respondents believed that there may be negative elements associated with offering this service in hospitals for the following reasons:

a.   there might be some sort of competition among participants and the peer support individual because of his/her special status or between the co-facilitators if they were a mental healthcare professional and a peer support individual;
b.   there are costs associated with providing services by the peer support individual, and this might present a particular challenge in hospitals where a comparable support service may already be offered by volunteers;
c.   it is possible that some participants could raise issues beyond the level of clinical skills and knowledge of the peer support individual that could create a potential problem especially in a mental health facility; and finally
d.   it is possible that the peer support individual might be struggling with a relapse of his/her mental illness and is no longer available to co-facilitate the group, which could have an impact on group dynamics.

It is interesting to note here that the peer support individual who co-facilitated WRAP workshops as part of this study had just lived a difficult period, during her co-facilitation, when her personal difficulties had lead her to distance herself from regular work. That being said, she was adamant in wishing to continue her facilitation of WRAP workshops as it allowed her to practice her skills directly related to the recovery process while also finding some comfort in the peer group. According to comments reported by participants in this study, it was an inspiring model for them.

Finally, survey respondents shared some recommendations concerning the framework to provide for the facilitation of WRAP workshops in hospitals:

a.   set clear guidelines in regards to the type of interventions that peer support individuals can perform (e.g., suggestions vs. recommendations, support vs. psychotherapy);
b.   ensure the presence of a triple-level supervision of the clinical, medical and administrative aspects as for example, coverage of professional liability insurance should be extended to include the peer support individual; and finally
c.   ensure adequate training of the peer support individual for the management of relatively likely crises in a mental health outpatient clinic.

Conclusion and Discussion

Although this study has obvious limitations (pre-experimental design, very small sample, no comparison group, no re-evaluation after delay to assess learning retention and/or use of the action plan in a time of crisis, no direct assessment of the social group work dynamic amongst the participants which it was decided to be defer to a later phase of investigation, etc.), the services offered under the WRAP intervention seem to have been profitable for the group as a whole and reflect the best interest of each participant.

In fact, the main objective to engage and support a group of individuals living with mental health problems appears to have been reached by including a peer support individual in a care giving team in hospitals and support the restoration of eleven (peer helper and participants) of our fellow citizens in need. The latter are probably better equipped to deal with potential relapses of their mental illness thus, potentially, reducing their need to use hospital services. This assumption, which is currently inferred, is in itself interesting for the clients themselves and for all citizens, since they could represent savings for all. As a result of the debriefing, participants and the co-facilitators seem to have benefited from their mutual interactions, an intricate component of the social group work that was offered, and reported that this type of intervention was qualitatively different from their usual individual and group format experiences.

What is more, several currently existing intervention models are inspired from the Negative Psychology school of thought, where the focus is drawn to the reduction of harmful behaviours/thoughts/principles (for instance, decreasing an individual's symptoms and their level of psychological and/or functional distress). One should, nevertheless, consider the psychotherapy and help interventions from another angle. Perhaps if the construct of such interventions where to be based on newly emerging Positive Psychology theory, which aims to highlight individuals' subjective well-being and recovery process as the primary focus, more optimistic clinically and statistically significant data would become known. It is very clear that from these observations, the WRAP workshops showcase well–being and the recovery process as its main preoccupations and that further studies of these types of positive philosophy interventions need to be explored and studied to determine and compare their feasibility, efficacy and efficiency with those of the Negative Psychology realm. Generally, at the end of the WRAP workshops, participants reported better overall well-being and less psychological and functional distress which interestingly seems to have an effect on both positive and negative mental health.

The present study would also suggest that the WRAP workshops may have their place in hospitals and not just in the community where they are usually provided. Interestingly, a change in intervention practices in recent years could have allowed a sort of homecoming in the sense that the philosophy behind WRAP workshops have possibly influenced the professional mental health community exactly where Mary Ellen Copeland's mother thought there was a need.

Moreover, the results of this study confirm the findings of many other researchers in regards to the overall success of social group work and co-facilitation of groups. In addition to confirming the findings of various studies, our conclusions denote that the combination of a peer-helper and a mental health professional co-facilitated social group work intervention is not only conducive to the overall success of the group in allowing each member to meet their specific needs in their recovery process but also it remains a cost effective practice and allows the broadening of available resources within the existing service infrastructure.

In years to come, furthering the investigation to include assessment tools to better understand the dynamics of social group interactions would be very interesting and fundamental both in qualitative and quantitative research designs. The latter could be achieved through offering the WRAP workshops in varying randomized control trial formats (i.e. individual, group with no interactions between participants, and a social work group).

Based on this preliminary validation of the WRAP workshops in community teaching and research hospital, it seems appropriate to pursue the scientific investigation to be able to offer this type of clinical service with confidence and this, in a philosophy of development *by* and *for* peers. It is currently planned to continue the investigation with more substantial samples of participants and through longitudinal studies or implementation of WRAP workshops in various settings and in different formats. It would be interesting to confirm the appropriateness of using the WRAP workshops to facilitate the return to the community and support of community facilitators after a hospitalization for example.

References

American Psychiatric Association (2000). *Diagnostic and statistical manual of mental disorders* (4th edn; DSM-IV-TR). Washington, DC: Author.

Andrews, J. (2001). Group work's place in social work: a historical analysis. *Journal of Sociology and Social Welfare, 28*(4), 45-65.

Aronoff, N. L. & Bailey, D. (2006). Partnered practice: building on our small group tradition. *Social Group Work, 28*(1), 23-29.

Carpinello, S.E., Knight, E.L., Markowitz, F.E. & Pease, E. (2000). The development of the Mental Health Confidence Scale: A measure of self efficacy in individuals diagnoses with mental disorders. *Psychiatric Rehabilitation Journal, 23*, 236-243.

Cohen, M. B. & DeLois, K. (2002). Training in tandem: co-facilitation and role modeling in a group work course. *Social Work With Groups, 24*(1), 21-36.

Copeland, M.H. (2000). *Wellness recovery action plan.* United States of America: Peach Press.

Copeland, M.H. (2000). French-Canadian translation by Perron-Roach, D. & Lévesque, L. (in revision). *Plan d'action individualisé de rétablissement.* United States of America: Peach Press.

Corrigan, P.W., Giffort, D., Rashid, E., Leary, M. & Okeke, I. (1999). Recovery as a psychological construct. *Community Mental Health Journal, 35*(3), 231-239.

Daoust, J.P. (2010). Modified version of the Dyadic Adjustment Scale (DAS-Mod). Unpublished document.

Diener, E., Emmons, R.A., Larsen, R.J. & Griddin, S. (1985). The satisfaction with life scale. *Journal of Personality Assessment, 49,* 71-75.

Drumm, K. (2006). The essential power of group work. *Social Work With Groups, 29*(2), 17-31.

Health Canada (1999). *Social support scale.* Ottawa: Author. Unpublished documents.

Jacobson, N. & Greenley, D. (2001). What is recovery? A conceptual model and explication. *Psychiatric Services, 52*(4), 482-485.

Kostyk, D., Fuchs, D., Tabisz, E. & Jacyk, W. R. (1993). Combining professional and self-help group intervention: collaboration in co-leadership. *Social Work With Groups, 16*(3), 111-123.

Lambert, M. (2005). Emerging methods for providing clinicians with timely feedback on treatment effectiveness: An introduction. *Journal of Clinical Psychology, 61*(2), 141-144.

Lambert, M. & Burlingame, G. (1992). *OQ*(R) *45.2 – Adult outcome measure (age 18+).* Salt Lake City: OQ Measures.

Lambert, M., Smart, D.W., Campbell, M.P., Hawkins, E.J., Harmon, C. & Slade, K.L. (2006). Psychotherapy outcome, as measured by the OQ-45, in African American, Asian/Pacific Islander, Latino/a, and Native American clients compared with matched Caucasian clients. *Journal of College Student Psychotherapy, 20*(4), 17-29.

Larsen, D.L., Attkisson, C.C., Hargreaves, W.A. & Ngyuen, T.D. (1979). Assessment of client/patient satisfaction: development of a general scale. *Evaluation and Program Planning, 2,* 197-207.

Larsen, R.J. & Diener, E. (1992). Promises and problems with the circumplex model of emotion. In M. Clark (Ed.), *Review of personality and social psychology, 13,* 25-59.

Lemieux, V., Daoust, J.-P. & Perron-Roach, D. (2010). Translation of the RAS-41, MHCS-16, ES-28 and SHS06 according to a committee type process. Unpublished documents.

Letendre, J., Gaillard, B.V. & Spath, R. (2008). Getting the job done: use of a work group for agency. *Groupwork, 18*(3), 52-68.

Mental Health Commission of Canada (2009). *Toward recovery and well-being: A framework for a mental health strategy for Canada.* Ottawa: Author.

Rogers, E.S., Chamberlin, J., Ellison, M. & Crean, T. (1997). A consumer-constructed scale to measure empowerment. *Psychiatric Services, 48*(8), 1042-1047.

Sabourin, S. & Gendreau, P. (1988). Assessing client satisfaction with mental health treatment among French-Canadian. *Applied Psychology: An International Review, 37*(4), 327-335.

Snyder, C.R., Sympson, S.C., Ybasco, F.C., Borders, T.F., Babyak, M.A. & Higgins, R.L. (1996). Development and validation of the State Hope scale. *Journal of Personality and Social Psychology, 70*(2), 321-335.

Spanier, G.B. (1989). *Manual for the dyadic adjustment scale.* North Tonowanda, NY: Multi-Health systems.

Sulman, J., Savage, D., Vrooman, P. & McGillivray, M. (2004). Social group work. *Social Group Work, 39*(3), 287-307.

Wright, M.M. (2003). Co-facilitation: Fashion or function? *Social Work With Groups, 25*(3), 77-92.

13

Research with and about groups: Overcoming obstacles to creativity and solidarity

Alice Home

Abstract: Research with community groups can have benefits for all when carried out collaboratively. It can address relevant issues, provide practical results, foster mutual learning and promote solidarity among researchers, practitioners and community groups. This kind of research also faces significant challenges, including scant recognition from funders and employers, lack of time and organizational support for practitioners and volunteers. Similarly, research about groups can stimulate creative solutions to practice problems while providing understanding and empirical support for observations in the field. It can highlight the complexity of group work while raising critical issues for practitioners and scholars but the difficulty of carrying out such research can be daunting. This paper presents some principles and challenges of these two types of research, drawing on case studies involving groups for parents of children with hidden disabilities.

Keywords: research, community, parent, groups, benefits, challenges

Introduction

Many group workers are hesitant to get involved in research, even though practice-focused studies can foster reflection, creativity and innovation. Research that is relevant to practice concerns and carried out collaboratively can bring benefits to scholars, practitioners and community groups while building solidarity between them. However, such gains do not come automatically any more than bringing people together guarantees the emergence of mutual aid (Shulman, 2005). Practice-relevant research faces significant challenges, including scant recognition and funding, incompatible time frames and priorities as well as limited organizational support. This paper examines principles, benefits and challenges of research carried out either in collaboration with community groups or on group work practice. The author outlines why such research is needed yet difficult, illustrating with examples from her work on groups for parents of children with hidden disabilities.

There is considerable agreement that social work needs to find more effective ways to overcome the persistent gap between research and practice. Arguments stem both from ongoing critiques of existing research and from international agendas. There are longstanding concerns about the marginal role research plays in practice. Critics have pointed out that social work research rarely arises from practitioner concerns, informs or guides policy/practice decisions, strongly involves students or leads to cumulative knowledge building (Rosen, Proctor & Staudt, 1999; Macdonald, 1999). Traditional research is often focused more on discovery and analysis than on findings that can be integrated into practice (Allen-Meares, Hudgins, Engberg & Lessnau, 2005). While there is recognition that research can no longer be an 'optional extra' in social work practice (Crisp, 2000), there is little agreement on how to move forward.

On the one hand, there are increasing pressures for social work to strengthen evaluative research and outcome studies, despite incompatibility with professional values. Those pressing for evidence-based practice disagree on what constitutes valid evidence and how to collect it. While some argue particular approaches are superior or more compatible with social work values, others claim client/context diversity requires methodological pluralism (Ainsworth & Hansen, 2002; Tsang, 2000). Similarly, calls to demonstrate programme effectiveness are often silent about who should participate in or control the evaluation process. On the other hand, participatory-action and anti-oppressive approaches attempt to balance knowledge development against community benefit, bringing to the fore such issues as ownership, location and context (Allen-Meares *et al,* 2005). Their central focus on partnership with communities in defining, planning and carrying out research relevant to community problems (Brown & Reitsma-Street, 2003) is highly compatible with social work values. However, this type of research involves managing power, role and resource differences (Lee, 2008), while ensuring time commitments are realistic for non-academic partners. This type of research can also have limited credibility in academic circles.

Social workers attempting to develop approaches that promote collaboration across 'town-gown' boundaries face many obstacles. In academic settings, there is little recognition or support for community-based research, despite an official discourse promoting practical research and knowledge transfer to consumers. University tenure and promotion structures tend to reward projects that attract prestigious funding and result in highly visible, peer-reviewed publications (Rubin, 2000). However, community research can succeed only if scholars invest their time in the invaluable but invisible work of trust-building, negotiation and consultation. While group workers have the interest, experience and skills for these activities, the latter delay more observable outcomes such as scholarly publications. This can penalize social work academics, who already tend to have fewer publications because their scholarship is done 'around the edges' of intense teaching, field consultation and community service commitments (Fraser, 1994). Funders unimpressed with social work scholars' productivity are even less inclined to support research that focuses on issues emerging primarily from practice or community needs.

Even if research is practice-focused, finding ways to involve graduate students and practitioners is another daunting challenge. In contrast to graduate students in disciplines such as psychology or sociology, MSW students often lack confidence and competencies in research. Many choose to concentrate on practice and those choosing research prefer small, individual projects over working in a research team. While this attests to their passion and commitment, it makes cumulative knowledge-building difficult and impedes later involvement in practice-research. Practicing social workers face obstacles of their own if they attempt to maintain or develop some type of research in the agency. As their experience is mainly in the practice arena, they too can lack confidence in their research abilities or competencies that are relevant to practice-based enquiry. Furthermore, agencies rarely have a research-friendly climate. Given competing demands for scarce time and resources, most agencies see research as a low priority compared to the 'real work' of service provision (Moseley & Tierney, 2005; Allen-Meares *et al*, 2005). Workers seeking research involvement can face managerial ambivalence or resistance (Fouche & Home, 2009), which translates into unwillingness to grant the time or resources needed.

Community collaborative research: One way around the obstacles

Collaborative research can narrow the gap between research and practice while circumventing some of these obstacles. It represents a compromise between traditional approaches controlled entirely by the researcher and ideologically purer, sometimes impractical participatory-action (Lee, 2008). It is designed to encourage power-sharing and mutual learning, through respecting and mobilizing the different kinds of knowledge contributed by scholars, practitioners and consumers, without negating real power and role differences. Respective roles and time commitments are clarified from the outset, with the researcher retaining final decision-making power over focus, method and management. Community partners are consulted initially and throughout the project, to ensure the research remains relevant to community needs. This arrangement avoids unreasonable demands on consumers or professionals' scarce time, while the researcher's clear leadership enhances the likelihood that the work will be taken seriously by funding bodies and the scholarly community (Home, 2008).

This type of collaboration has potential benefits for social work researchers and practitioners alike. It offers an opportunity for scholars to strengthen their community visibility and their connection to practice, while hands-on community research can be more attractive to graduate students, increasing their motivation and lasting commitment to integrating research into practice. Community partners can have a rare opportunity for creating new programmes and service delivery models while monitoring their effectiveness. This type of research fosters recognition and mobilization of forgotten knowledge and skills, which may lead to further practitioner learning and involvement in research-related activity (Fouche & Home, 2009). However, collaborative research is not a panacea; indeed it is 'fraught with challenges' (Rubin, 2000). Practitioners and community groups may hesitate to engage because of past research experiences that provided few benefits. Initial lack of trust can reflect low familiarity with this type of research or confusion around differing agendas and types of expertise. In addition, both academics and agency partners can be concerned about the slow pace required for successful collaboration, given competing pressures for quick results coupled with time and resource constraints (Fouche & Home, 2009).

Collaborative research with a community group: A case study

An example is research undertaken in collaboration with a parent self-help group/organization which offers support, education and information to families of children with Attention Deficit Hyperactivity Disorder (ADHD) and to professionals working with them. This prevalent, primarily genetic disorder brings cross-situational learning and social impairments, usually accompanied by other disabilities (Barkley, Edwards, Haneil, Fletcher & Metevia, 2001). Families live with high stress yet are often blamed or excluded because their disruptive but normal-appearing children are unable to meet social expectations (Segal, 2001). Mothers of children with disabilities often assume leadership roles in self-help groups, where they learn advocacy, community education and social analysis (Moorish & Buchanan, 2001). However, their accomplishments and unpaid community service are often unrecognized and undervalued.

To raise awareness of these mothers' experience, the researcher sought to learn how they see their maternal and multiple roles and to identify factors influencing their perception, using a mixed methods approach that combined interviews with a national survey. To ensure this project would be relevant to parents and professionals, the researcher consulted a national self-help organization regarding proposed focus, goals, methods and adapting data collection to this population. While promoting research was part of the organization's mandate, previous involvement had been limited to recruiting participants and presenting findings. To ensure community group input would be ongoing rather than only for recruitment purposes

(Brown & Reitsma-Street, 2003), the board appointed an advisory committee that worked with the researcher throughout the project. This committee was consulted on all important decisions, helped develop an instrument from the interview data and co-presented a research poster at an international conference. In return, the researcher published updates and early results in community group newsletters, enabling research participants and users to quickly learn findings of immediate, practical use.

Two innovative features strengthened collaboration. Firstly, interviews revealed mothers need to share experiences and resources with peers in a small group, as 'no-one understands my challenges' (Home, Kanigsberg & Trepanier, 2003). This led the researcher to approach a family agency about offering a mutual aid/empowerment group especially for mothers of children with ADHD. A researcher-practitioner team planned, co-facilitated and evaluated a short-term group, which produced positive results that were disseminated in presentations and publications (Home & Biggs, 2005). Secondly, feedback sessions in four Canadian regions allowed research participants, community group representatives and professionals to hear and respond to early survey results. Over 100 people provided input on the relevance and implications of key findings and suggested action. A summary of main themes was distributed to those who attended, posted on the organization's website and published in newsletters of several community groups (Home, 2005).

Benefits and challenges of this collaborative research

In addition to reflecting on her own experience, the researcher carried out telephone interviews with the other partners regarding benefits and obstacles they noted. As an 'insider' who has lived this mothering situation (Lee, 2008), the researcher wanted to use her time and skills to help community groups that had supported her in the past. This experience brought new appreciation for the courage, strengths and commitment of self-help leaders who support and advocate for others despite their own difficult family situations. Planning and co-leading a group in response to mothers' needs afforded a rare opportunity to be involved in innovative practice, while sharpening her group work practice skills and providing new material for teaching. Finally, feedback from other hidden disability groups opened up possibilities of strategic alliances to promote social change and undertake further collaborative research.

This study succeeded in attracting two graduate students who completed their MSW research on this study, as well as acting as research assistants. One of them presented her work at a national conference, while the other conducted and analyzed the French interviews and co-authored a publication which made her work available to practitioners. She reported learning how to adapt textbook methods to the realities of community research and discovering how easily she could use her practice skills in qualitative data collection. Interviewing mothers made her appreciate their resilience and strategies in difficult family situations and prepared her for school social work. As she understood what these mothers were going through, she was careful to avoid blaming them, working instead to increase supports and to educate colleagues about the impact of this disorder.

Professional partners reported various types of learning. The social worker who co-facilitated the mothers' group increased her knowledge of ADHD and the family impact of hidden disabilities, which helped her respond to the increasing numbers of agency referrals around child behaviour problems. Working with a group work educator strengthened theory-practice connections, especially in the mutual aid approach (Moyse-Steinburg, 2004). Participating in data analysis, presentations and publications led her to rediscover solid but latent research skills, while publications increased her agency's visibility. Finally, advisory committee members also learned from their experience. The national board member, a school consultant and parent of adolescents with ADHD, enjoyed the stimulation of working across boundaries that can separate scholars from practitioners. Key findings validated his observations in the community, while deepening his understanding of difficulties facing groups like his. Co-presenting a research poster at an international conference brought recognition rarely afforded self-help group leaders, while publications strengthened his organization's credibility in professional and scholarly circles (Kurtz, 2004). The professional board member, a clinical psychologist specializing in ADHD found collaborating with a social work scholar 'provided a refreshing change from clinical work'. He learned qualitative research skills and gained appreciation for researchers, after witnessing the 'intricacies and stumbling blocks' that had to be dealt with.

However, these benefits did not come without obstacles. The researchers faced incompatibilities with their institution's expectations and time frames. The huge time investment and slow pace of collaborative research was not understood by the university, whose priorities, workload levels and ethics procedures were geared to more traditional research. Funders approached for later projects did not take into account that community dissemination had delayed scholarly publications. The graduate student had difficulty completing her degree within the prescribed time period, which did not allow for the slow progress of community research. The social worker had some initial concerns about being the only 'outsider' in the 'Just ADHD Mom's' group (Home & Biggs, 2005). She later found her expertise in family/child development helped members put their problems into perspective, while her 'typical' mothering experience balanced the researcher's powerful dual role. However, organizational priorities restricted the time she could devote to research-related activities. Once agency service terminated with the group's end, she had to use personal time for research activities related to evaluation and dissemination.

Advisory committee members faced their own set of challenges. The national board member noted that findings did not provide quick solutions to problems faced by his organization. He also had difficulty finding the 'bursts of time' required to collaborate, given his heavy commitments. Both he and the psychologist sometimes wondered 'do I know my stuff?', when grappling with new tasks such as developing a research instrument, even though their contribution turned out to be invaluable. Nevertheless, collaborating *with* a community group brought benefits to all that helped outweigh the many obstacles. In the next section, we look at whether this is the also the case for research *about* groups in the community.

Research about groups: Relevance, benefits, challenges and a case example

If the need to carry out research *on* group work is well documented so too are the challenges. Proponents point out that practice cannot be improved until outcomes are evaluated and that this must be accompanied by sufficient detail about intervention (Tsang, 2000). There is agreement on the potential of groups to bring about change, yet their complexity and the number of potential influences on outcome discourages researchers from undertaking studies. As a result, group work research literature is dominated by behavioural or educational interventions which are easier to measure (Tolman & Molidar, 1994). While the latter are effective in certain situations, they do not cover a full range of social work problems and contexts nor do they reflect group work's social action, strengths-based and preventive traditions (Breton, 1990). The following is a rare example of a study that reflects group work values, while moving beyond purely descriptive accounts to explore outcomes and factors that may influence them.

This project had its origins in the community feedback sessions of the previous research (Home, 2005). Facilitators of self-help groups for parents of children with Fetal Alcohol Spectrum Disorder (FASD) and Autism Spectrum Disorder (ASD) noted similarities between findings on ADHD mothering and their members' experiences. They suggested that working together *across* hidden disabilities might enhance public/professional awareness while increasing impact on policies and services. A literature review supported the need for research on parenting children whose disabilities are not readily apparent. As early diagnosis is rare and appropriate services elusive, these parents face exhaustion from constant vigilance, frequent crises and the perpetual need to advocate (Russell, 2003; Morrissette, 2001) and they are often blamed for their children's problems. However, there is little research on parents' common experiences across hidden disabilities or on group and other interventions to address their needs.

In response, two group work scholars undertook a small, exploratory study of groups for parents whose children had one of three hidden disabilities (ASD, ADHD or FASD), using qualitative methods to explore the perceptions of both peer and professional group facilitators. Goals were to learn how they view parents' needs, different groups' attempt to meet them and main benefits and challenges. As the researchers were unable to obtain funding, it took several years to locate, recruit and interview a contrast sample of 16 groups (8 peer-led) in Ontario and British Columbia. Interview themes included agency context, member and group characteristics, benefits, challenges, resource and access issues. Thematic content analysis allowed identification of similarities and differences by type of group, by child disability and along cultural/linguistic lines. The following discussion is illustrated by findings from the latter analysis and data on groups for parents dealing with FASD.

Benefits and challenges of this research on groups

This innovative, difficult project brought two main *benefits*: it provided understanding and empirical support for practice observations, while raising important questions for group workers. The first is illustrated by the findings from six groups set up specifically for parents from cultural or linguistic minorities (three for French speakers in an English milieu, two for care givers of First Nations children, one for Chinese parents). Like the groups designed for 'mainstream' parents, members arrived with a 'burning issue' and came away with information, skills and support. They valued sharing in this safe place, seeing meetings as a 'special time' when they could be fully themselves but struggled with some members' challenging behavior. Like the others, they faced precariousness due to lack of resources or 'new blood'. However, these issues were both more complex and more urgent in minority groups, due to the intersection of culture and disability. Having a 'safe place' was critical when the disability was not accepted in the culture, while sharing in one's language and getting accessible resources was crucial for French and Chinese-speaking parents. Finally, creative use of cultural traditions and values was an essential way to reach and engage First Nations care givers, particularly in the light of cultural taboos and history (McNicoll & Home, 2010).

The six groups for parents of children with FASD had some distinct features that illustrate the off-cited adaptability of group work in responding to populations with varying needs. As FASD is more misunderstood and stigmatized than ADHD or ASD, the goal of learning advocacy was added to those of providing support and information on the disability, resources and parenting strategies, these groups found innovative ways to accommodate the unusually difficult family situations faced by their members. As the lifelong impairments of FASD can interfere with adult role functioning, some self-help groups welcomed a wider range of members, including parents, grandparents, trustees, spouses and affected adults. To help parents unable to leave adolescents safely or find competent sitters, all these groups offered either on-site child care or allowed cell phones to stay on for emergencies.

Benefits and *challenges* were subtly different in these groups as well. Hope to keep going came from hearing about successful outcomes ('so he can work? I need to hear that!'), while the group became a critical 'anchor in my stormy family life'. These groups went beyond reducing isolation (Shulman, 2005) to camaraderie, which helped replace friendships lost during intense parenting. Empowerment was perceived as a more prominent outcome by facilitators of these groups. Members realized they had been 'doing the right thing all along' acting as their child's 'external brain', which validated their sense of parenting competence. Members of some groups found their voice as individuals ('now I can speak to teachers, police'), spoke publicly on behalf of their group, started new ones or educated professionals or the community. Just as some benefits seemed stronger, so were certain challenges. Widely differing ages of affected children enriched the experience in some groups but others had to split in two because parenting older adolescents and young adults presented such unique issues (Home & McNicoll, 2010). Attracting and retaining parents presented greater obstacles as well, because of the stigma of FASD, some parents' lack of readiness, chaotic family situations and child safety concerns.

This study also pointed to the complexity of groups, thereby raising important questions for which there are no easy answers. This research showed groups can use many ways to address similar needs and to adapt to subtly different ones. The finding that one size definitely does *not* fit all suggests that the predominant models, prescriptive parent training and entirely peer-led groups, may not be the best way to serve these parents. However, this small, exploratory study did not allow identification of what type of group is most useful for whom or in which situations. Professionally-led groups seem to help more at certain times and peer-led groups at others, while emphasizing education, support or both may be relevant to different populations depending on gender, culture or type of disability.

One innovation emerging from this study is the 'hybrid' group that combines some features of peer and professionally-led formats. One group was organized, managed and facilitated by a parent, while a specialist in the relevant disability attended meetings, playing an important role in group crises and offering on-the-spot help or referral for individual parents. Another adapted format was an on-line group developed to help parents of autistic children who had difficulty attending meetings. The parent facilitator vetted membership, posted messages and sent out information but 'would never try to moderate a chat room', fearing it could be too explosive with some parents themselves 'on the spectrum'.This format provides more connection than 'listserv', which some groups use to e-mail information (Kurtz,

2004). One peer-led group combined the latter with face-to-face meetings, as the two rarely attracted the same people. It will be important to learn more about such on-line innovations, as they increase accessibility for overloaded parents, especially those who are alone, geographically isolated or reluctant to engage. However, just as short-term and open group structures can reduce group development and mutual helping, so do formats that eliminate face to face interaction (Moyse-Steinberg, 2004).

This exploratory study directs our attention to the critical issue of *precariousness*. Like research, group work has low priority in agencies and is treated as a non-essential 'extra' to be done when resources and time can be freed up. What support professionals get for their work with parent groups is often very limited or short-term. For example, the psychologist who acted as co-facilitator and consultant in the 'hybrid' group was paid only for the time she spent in meetings. Similar issues plagued other groups led by facilitators with some professional training. As many were on short-term grants, they spent a great deal of time trying to secure stable funding so the group could continue. In peer-led groups, precariousness was a survival matter. As these groups function with little to no funding, they depend on a few resilient, deeply committed volunteers to carry the load for a long time. As these leaders share the same stressful situations as other members, they worry the group might collapse if a family crisis left them unable to continue. Another study of self-help groups for parents of special needs children also found lack of new committed leaders and access to resources to be key challenges (King, Stewart, King & Law, 2000). Despite their accessibility to diverse populations and their important supportive role, the continued existence of these groups held together by volunteers is taken for granted. Several parent facilitators noted that a little training ('we need group work education too!'), access to professional consultation and to small but stable grants would make a huge difference.

Some concluding remarks

These examples illustrate the creative but demanding nature of research with and about groups in the community. In the first case, collaborating with a community group led to mutual learning, increased respect for participants' expertise and alliances across 'town-gown' boundaries. The experience provided intrinsic satisfaction for all and promoted both creativity and solidarity. In the second case, group work scholars discovered that professionally and peer-led parent groups show the adaptability and creativity for which group work is known. Researching these groups provided the scholars with invaluable data from those on the front-line, who in turn had the opportunity to have their voices heard and their views respected. Participating in this practice-focused research helped facilitators identify their competencies and skills and recognize that their challenges were common to many group leaders. Participants identified their own need for support and consultation, which the scholars are making visible in their publications.

It is hoped other group workers will pursue some of the issues that require further study. Group work practice-researchers need to undertake a larger scale study incorporating the parental perspective, to understand more fully what types of groups work best with different populations. A study comparing traditional and on-line parent groups could clarify how to maximize the benefits of innovative formats while minimizing their disadvantages and risks. Collaboration between university and agency-based group workers could allow such research to go ahead, while managing some of the challenges discussed in this paper. For example, researchers and group facilitators could try to find solutions to the precariousness that comes from the low value placed on both community research and on group work, compared to what is seen as 'real work'.

At the same time, these shared challenges strengthen the researchers' credibility in the eyes of community groups, and researchers' solidarity with the struggles of group facilitators. As one self-help leader said 'We understand what it's like to just do what you can despite no time or resources. We salute your commitment and value your work!' Despite the obstacles scholars and group facilitators grapple with, group work traditions and values give them the basis to find creative, flexible ways to work together towards better serving people in need.

References

Ainsworth, F. & Hansen, P. (2002). Evidence-based social work practice: A reachable goal? *Social Work and Social Services Review, 10*(2), 35-48.

Allen-Meares, P., Hudgins, C., Engberg, M. & Lessnau, B. (2005). Using a collaboratory model to translate social work research into practice and policy. *Research on Social Work Practice, 15*(1), 29-40.

Barkley, R., Edwards, G., Haneil, M., Fletcher, K. & Metevia, L. (2001). The efficacy of problem-solving communication training alone, behavior management training alone, and their combination for parent-adolescent conflict in teenagers with ADHD and ODD. *Journal of Consulting and Clinical Psychology, 69*(6), 926-941

Breton, M. (1990), Learning from social group work traditions. *Social Work with Groups, 13*(3), 21-34.

Brown, L. & Reitsma-Street, M. (2003). The values of community action research. *Canadian Social Work Review, 20*(1), 61-78.

Crisp, B. (2000). A history of Australian social work practice research. *Research on Social Work Practice, 10*(2), 179-194

Fouche, C. & Home, A. (2009). Building practice-relevant research across university-community boundaries: Lessons from two innovative approaches, *CASWE/ACFTS Conference*, Ottawa, May 2009.

Fraser, M. (1994). Scholarship and research in social work: Emerging challenges. *Journal of Social Work Education, 30*(2), 252-266.

Home, A. (2005). Mothering children with ADHD: Brief feedback session summary. *The National, 20* (Fall).

Home, A. (2008). Recherche en collaboration: Joindre recherche, formation et pratique. *Pensée Plurielle, 1*(17), 37-44.

Home, A., Kanigsberg, J. & Trepanier, G. (2003). Always on duty: Employed mothers of children with ADHD. Research Poster presented at the 15th CHADD International Conference, Denver, Co., October 2003.

Home, A. & Biggs, T. (2005). Evidence-based practice in the real world: A group for mothers of children with invisible disabilities. *Groupwork, 15*(2), 39-60.

Home, A. & McNicoll, P. (2010). Evolving needs: Parenting adolescents and young adults with hidden disabilities. Poster presented at 4th National Conference on Adolescents and Adults with Fetal Alcohol Spectrum Disorder, Vancouver BC, April 14-17 2010.

Home, A. (2009). Groups for parents of children with FASD and other hidden disabilities: A study of facilitators' views. Research Poster presented at 3rd International FASD Conference: Integrating research, policy and promising practice. Victoria BC, March 2009.

King, G., Stewart, D., King, S. & Law, M. (2000). Organizational characteristics and issues affecting the longevity of self-help groups for parents of children with special needs. *Qualitative Health Research, 10*(2), 225-241.

Kurtz, L. (2004). Support and self-help groups. In C. Garvin, L. Gutiérrez & M. Galinsky (Eds.), *Handbook of social work with groups* (pp.139-159). New York: Guilford.

Lee, B. (2008). Will the real community research please stand up? Some critical issues. *Canadian Social Work Review. 25*(1), 5-21.

Macdonald, G. (1999). The practitioner as scientist. In F. Turner (Ed.), *Social work practice: A Canadian perspective* (pp.546-554). Scarborough, On: Prentice-Hall, Allyn and Bacon.

McNicoll, P. & Home, A. (2010). Groups for parents of children with invisible disabilities: similarities and differences across cultural/linguistic boundaries. Paper presented at the 32nd International Symposium on Social Work with Groups. Montreal. June 6, 2010.

Morrissette, P. (2001). Fetal alcohol syndrome: Parental experiences and the role of family counselors. *The Qualitative Report, 6*(2), 1-16

Morrish, M. & Buchanan, N. (2001). Women's empowerment and adult education. In D. Poonwassie & A. Poonwassie (Eds.), *Fundamentals of Adult Education* (pp.256-270). Toronto: Thompson.

Moseley, A. & Tierney, S. (2005). Evidence-based practice in the real world. *Evidence & Policy, 1*(1), 113-120.

Moyse Steinberg, D. (2004). *The mutual-aid approach to working with groups* (2nd edn.). Binghamton, N.Y.: Haworth.

Rosen, A., Proctor, E. & Staudt, M. (1999). Social work research and the quest for effective practice. *Social Work Research, 23*(1), 4-14.

Rubin A. (2000). Social work research at the turn of the millenium: Progress and challenges. *Research on Social Work Practice.* January, 9-14.

Russell, F. (2003). The expectations of parents of disabled children. *British Journal of Special Education, 30*(3), 144-149.

Segal, E. (2001). Learned mothering: Raising a child with ADHD. *Child and Adolescent Social Work Journal, 18*(4), 263-279.

Shulman, L. (2005). *The skills of helping individuals, families and groups* (5th edn.). Itasca, Ill.

Tolman, R. and Molidar, C. (1994). A decade of social group work research: Trends in methodology, theory and program development. *Research on Social Work Practice, 4*(2), 142-159.

Tsang, A. (2000). Bridging the gap between clinical practice and research: An integrated practice-oriented model. *Journal of Social Service Research, 26*(4), 69-90.

14
Research!
What we can do to advance it in social work with groups

Mark J. Macgowan

Abstract: *Despite a growing movement towards evidence based practice, many group workers do not systematically utilize the best available evidence. In addition, there are scant publications about the effectiveness of social group work processes or interventions. This paper describes actions group workers can do right now to advance group work research. Using the acronym R-E-S-E-A-R-C-H, these actions begin with 1) a Regard for the value of research in practice, followed by a response to 2) Evaluate (measure) at least one outcome; 3) Sway (or modify) one outcome with methods that have rigor, impact, and applicability; 4) Evaluate (measure) one group process; 5) Alter one group process; 6) Recharge one's knowledge bank - get connected to electronic group resources; 7) Collaborate with a university or community partner 8) Herald one's findings in a journal. Examples and resources are offered in each of these areas to advance Research!*

Keywords: *Group work, group work research, evidence-based group work*

Introduction

Despite a growing movement towards evidence based practice, many social workers do not systematically utilize the best available research. An agency-based survey of practitioners reported that most social workers were poorly informed about practice guidelines, rarely used findings in practice, and seldom read the literature but instead sought direction primarily from supervisors, experienced workers, or consultants (Mullen & Bacon, 2004). Although these sources might yield the best available evidence, the research suggests that workers do not follow a systematic, critical process to find the best available evidence. In addition, there are few research-based publications about social group work processes or interventions, or teaching methods. This paper describes actions group workers and group work educators can do right now to advance group work research. Using the acronym R-E-S-E-A-R-C-H, this paper identifies eight actions to advance research in practice and in teaching. This paper is intended for practitioners, learners, and for those who influence group work learners. Readers are encouraged to identify at least one area in which they can add to their research.

It is first important to define what is meant by "research," which is both a noun and a verb. As a noun, it is a systematic collection of information and knowledge. It is also a process of inquiry that is rigorous and systematic, whether the inquiry utilizes "precise, objective, and generalizable findings" (Rubin & Babbie, 2008, p. 643), as in quantitative research, or utilizes methods "that emphasize depth of understanding and the deeper meanings" (Rubin & Babbie, 2008, p. 643), as in qualitative research – and research can be both quantitative and qualitative. Either way, it is a systematic process of inquiry that follows commonly accepted scientific practices.

Regard for research

These actions begin with a **Regard** for the value of research in practice and in teaching.

The ethical mandate for research is clear in both NASW and in other ethical guidelines for the practice of group work. For example, increasing knowledge and skills by using the best evidence available is part of Social Work's values and Code of Ethics:

Social workers should critically examine and keep current with emerging knowledge relevant to social work. Social workers should routinely review the professional literature and participate in continuing education relevant to social work practice and social work ethics. Social workers should base practice on recognized knowledge, including empirically based knowledge, relevant to social work and social work ethics. (National Association of Social Workers, 1999, standard 4.01)

It is also part of the Association for the Advancement of Social Work with Groups' Standards for the Practice of Group Work. According to the Standards, group workers should include in their practice "monitoring and evaluation of success of group in accomplishing its objectives through personal observation, as well as collecting information in order to assess outcomes and processes" (AASWG, 2006, section 1F).

There is evidence that groups can be harmful (Dies & Teleska, 1985; Galinsky & Schopler, 1977, 1994; Schopler & Galinsky, 1981; Smokowski, Rose, & Bacallao, 2001) and it is our ethical mandate to avoid practices that are harmful and to adopt those that are beneficial. The regard for research is at the same time a regard for those *involved* in the practice of research – our group members. Thus, our actions have a simultaneous concern for utilizing research findings and/or methods, and to ensure they are relevant and appropriate for our groups and their members.

There is also the need for a regard for using research in evaluating our teaching of group work. There are very few empirical studies on teaching group work. There is no shortage of recommendations about teaching approaches or surveys about social work education related to group work, but there are scant empirical studies of teaching approaches that improve learning group work knowledge or skills. If we are going to advance education about social work with groups, we must develop an appreciation for and utilization of research methods to determine the effectiveness of teaching approaches about social work with groups. To have regard for using research in practice we should also have an equal regard for using research in teaching about group work.

Evaluate an outcome

With the solid foundation of a regard for the value of research in practice and the value of group- and member-appropriate methods, we Evaluate (measure) at least one agreed-upon *outcome*. These can be proximal, measured within group life, or distal, which are measured at the end of group or beyond. Accurate measurement is at the heart of demonstrable change. Many issues and challenges group members have are measurable, which can be problem- or strengths-based. An example of the former is monitoring depression over time, and an example of the latter is monitoring a group member's social support network. These can include those measured at the individual level and, to capture the essence of group work, can be aggregated at the group level to measure group-level change.

Where do we find outcome measures for clinical practice? We can utilize existing clinical instruments, such as those compiled in Fischer and Corcoran's Measures for Clinical Practice and Research (Fischer & Corcoran, 2007). Another source is the CORE Battery-Revised (Burlingame *et al.*, 2006), a compendium of vetted clinical assessment tools for group work. One measure of general functioning is the Outcome Questionnaire, available for adults and youth, both of which are included in the CORE Battery-Revised. If *existing* measures are inadequate or inappropriate, measures can be tailored for the individual, developed in collaboration with group members, such as self-anchored rating scales (Toseland & Rivas, 2009).

Where can we find outcome measures for teaching? The Educational Policy and Accreditation Standards (EPAS) states that "assessment is an integral component of competency-based education" (CSWE, 2008, p. 16) and establishes "thresholds for professional competence" (p. 1) in the Standards. Group work should be at the forefront of that process in defining foundation competencies. That has been done with respect to the AASWG Standards for the practice of social work with groups. In consultation with AASWG, the author has developed a preliminary 82-item inventory based exclusively on the standards, which assesses perceived knowledge and self-efficacy of group work skills (Macgowan, in preparation). On each item, respondents rate how important they think the item is for successful group work (very unimportant, unimportant, important, very important) and how confident they are they could successfully carry this out (very unconfident, unconfident,

confident, very confident)(following Wilson & Newmeyer, 2008). Examples of items from the Inventory include, "Reaches out to and recruits potential group members," "Seeks to cultivate mutual aid," "Accesses and uses supervision;" and, "Identifies and discusses direct and indirect signs of members' reactions to endings," which draw from the planning, beginning, middle, and ending phases of the Inventory, respectively. This instrument can be used as an outcome measure for teaching, which fits in with the new competency-based learning required in the new EPAS.

Sway (modify) one group outcome

Having created a marker for change, we work to Sway (or modify) one group outcome with methods (e.g., interventions, techniques) that are based on the best available evidence. As discussed in detail elsewhere (Macgowan, 2008), best available evidence is the product of a critical process that determines evidence's (a) rigor (likelihood that the action will lead to a desired outcome), (b) impact (direction and strength of the outcome), and (c) applicability (how the evidence relates to my group and group members). Each has equal weight in determining whether methods get utilized. Thus, determining the best evidence is an iterative process between weighing the merit and impact of external research findings, with practice considerations. Best available evidence is the result of a critical process that each group worker engages in and is not, necessarily, a randomized clinical trial or a manualized group therapy. The process is not "the mindless application of rules and guidelines" (Haynes, Sackett, Gray, Cook, & Guyatt, 1996, p. A-15), but is guided by the worker's thoughtful consideration of the research evidence, professional ethics, knowledge, skills, and experience, and client and group situation. There are many different terms for the current "evidence" movement, such as evidence-based, evidence-driven, and evidence-informed. There are important distinctions between these words and we should all inquire of their meaning. Practice should be evidence-based, which is also evidence-informed, if it is the critical process described above and in detail elsewhere (Macgowan, 2008).

We should also make an effort to sway outcomes related to group work education. Alarming findings indicate that faculty and students need to learn more about basic group work principles and skills. A survey of faculty who teach group work courses were asked about their knowledge in teaching practice (Birnbaum & Wayne, 2000). Although faculty assigned high self-ratings for their teaching, many had problems identifying key group work concepts. A second study reported the findings of a survey of foundation MSW students (Sweifach & LaPorte, 2009). Less than one third of the students :

> ... perceived that they had basic group work skills, such as understanding how to select group members, how to identify tasks and goals for the group to accomplish, and how to assist the group members in problem solving. Of note is that only 16% of respondents felt that they possess the ability to use mutual aid as a tool. (Sweifach & LaPorte, 2009, p. 307).

These findings suggest we need teaching approaches that demonstrably improve foundation group work knowledge and skills, which presumably will also help educators who teach them.

One approach to increasing group work skills over time is to use a measurement-based approach using an inventory of foundation group work skills, which is based on the AASWG Standards, noted above (Macgowan, in preparation). The teaching approach involves students first identifying specific knowledge and skills deficits using the Inventory, and then participating in assignments intended to increase perceived knowledge and competence in utilizing the skills in practice. A study reported significant changes in knowledge and perceived self-efficacy from the beginning to end of semester (Macgowan, manuscript submitted for publication).

Evaluate on group process

It is also important to Evaluate (measure) one group *process*. Process here simply means what occurs during the time the group is meeting. Traditionally most group work research virtually ignored group processes. A 1973 study titled "the use and misuse of groups" reviewed 61 publications in social work over a 15-year period, and found that 90% focused on work with individuals in the group to the neglect of group structures and processes (Levinson, 1973). Subsequent reviews have documented similar findings (Tolman & Molidor, 1994) and most researchers using groups today still tend to emphasize group outcomes over processes. Process variables become proximal markers of progress towards achieving ~positive outcomes, but they are also important to measure in their own right.

There are potentially many areas one can measure, and there are different sources for reviews about group-based measures (Beck & Lewis, 2000; DeLucia-Waack & Bridbord, 2004; Toseland, Jones, & Gellis, 2004) and compendia of group-based measures (Burlingame, *et al.*, 2006). So which ones should be measured? Burlingame and colleagues (2006) have identified several processes we should attend to related to outcomes. These three areas are the bond with the worker and group, a working relationship with the worker and the group, and negative factors that interfere with the bond or the work (Burlingame, *et al.*, 2006). To economize, the focus should be on the bond and working. There are several instruments that could be selected, all of which are included in the CORE Battery-Revised. One is the Working Alliance Inventory (for the bond between worker and member and a measure of the working relationship); another is the Group Climate Questionnaire (MacKenzie, 1981, to measure the bond with the group and the group working relationship); and a third is the cohesion subscale of the Therapeutic Factors Inventory (Lese & MacNair-Semands, 2000). Another instrument to consider is the Group Engagement Measure (Macgowan, 2006; Macgowan & Newman, 2005), which also measures both bond and working.

Alter group processes

In addition to working to change one agreed-upon outcome in groups or in teaching, we should strive to Alter one (or more) group process. Sheldon Rose (1984) outlined a systematic process of solving particular group problems involving a partnership between the group leader and group members. Macgowan (2003) outlined a process of using a measure of group process (Group Engagement Measure) and specific strategies derived from the literature for increasing engagement in groups. As noted earlier, another process tied to outcomes that could be measured and improved within groups is cohesion (Burlingame, *et al.*, 2006). Cohesion could be measured using the brief cohesion subscale of the Therapeutic Factors Inventory (Lese & MacNair-Semands, 2000) and there are many strategies and techniques for increasing cohesion have been outlined in the literature (Burlingame, Fuhriman, & Johnson, 2002, p. 75; Corey & Corey, 1997, pp. 153-154; Fehr, 1999, appendix titled Structured Exercises for Developing Group Cohesion; Robbins, 2003; Rose, 1998, pp. 372-377). There are examples of how to use the process measures in the CORE Battery-Revised (Strauss, Burlingame, & Bormann, 2008).

Recharge one's knowledge bank

An important component of advancing research in group work is getting and staying connected to group work knowledge and evidence, to Recharge one's knowledge bank. The inaugural issue of *Social Work with Groups* was intended to help connect practitioners with latest research. The first article within the first issue, by Margaret Hartford, pointed out the state of groups in the social services in which she wrote, "There is a growing body of knowledge about small group behavior [Hare, 1976], based not only on hunches and armchair theory development and upon findings of experimental collectivities of individuals convened for research, but also empirical research on groups constructed for treatment, help, growth, change, and self-management" (Hartford, 1978, p. 8). At the end of the same journal (pp. 115-118) there was a section of recent literature, with the intention of connecting practitioners to the latest research. Thus, from the first issue of *Social Work with Groups*, there has been a call to get connected to latest findings in group work.

With the internet, there is an explosion of easily-accessible, electronic resources. There is, indeed, too much information, and much of it is unfiltered. An essential component of evidence-based practice is finding *best* available evidence. Where and how does one find this and stay connected? Where does one find group-related evidence? One such source is www.EvidenceBasedGroupWork.com (also www.EBGW.org), created by the author. The site "is intended to be a link to research-based evidence about group work. The purpose is to make research evidence available to those who want to make group work demonstrably more effective and beneficial to participants" (from the website). The site includes a section on searching for evidence, including common search terms that can be copied and pasted, and locations for searching for evidence, such as links to ten scholarly group work journals, meta-analyses, and other sites. Also included is a link to a social bookmarking site of group work resources. As defined by Wikipedia, "Social bookmarking is an activity performed over a computer network that allows users to save and categorize personal collection of bookmarks and share them with others. Users may also take bookmarks saved by others and add them to their own collection, as well as subscribe to the lists of others - a personal knowledge management tool" (http://en.wikipedia.org/wiki/Social_bookmarking). The social bookmarking site http://delicious.com/EBGW includes many published materials, such as systematic reviews, links to major group work journals, and guides to publishing in group work.

Collaborate

Another important way in which research can advance in group work, is for academics and practitioners to Collaborate. These are not just piecemeal or opportunistic relationships to take advantage of funding opportunities, but strategic relationships to improve group work research and teaching. There are examples in the literature of strategic, reciprocal, university-community organization partnerships in general (Allen-Meares, Hudgins, Engberg, & Lessnau, 2005; Borkovec, 2004; Sherrod, 1999) and in group work in particular (Fouché & Lunt, 2009; Home & Biggs, 2005). A recent special issue of *Social Work with Groups* was dedicated to the use of evidence-based group work in community settings (Pollio & Macgowan, 2010). There are several purposes for such collaborations; namely, to develop and answer research questions relevant to local practice concerns; to increase the utilization of systematic methods and rigor of research done in the community; and to improve the dissemination of research findings in scholarly outlets (conferences, publications). One approach that is useful for developing and testing group work knowledge is the translational research (TR) model, developed in medicine but expanding into other disciplines, which is essentially the clinical application of scientific research knowledge ("bench to trench" or "bench to bedside")(Hait, 2005; Hudgins & Allen-Meares, 2000). Importantly, the academic-practitioner relationships is *bidirectional*; basic research is applied in the field, and clinical observations are used to provide the impetus for further scientific research ("bench to bedside and bedside to bench")(Marincola, 2003). Whether in the format of TR or in another, equally strategic form, the research enterprise is improved by a strong, bidirectional relationship between the university-based educator and community setting. Thus, if one is an academic, identify an agency or individual to form a strategic partnership with. If one is a practitioner or a student-practitioner, reach out to a former or current professor.

Herald research findings in a journal

An academic partner can help to Herald research findings in a scholarly, peer-reviewed journal. Such partnerships could create writing clubs. Too many conference presentations go no further than the live audience. If one has never published, submit to the next AASWG symposium. If one has presented at a symposium or symposia, take the next step and submit a paper to a scholarly, peer-reviewed journal. If one is not sure how to do it, ask an academic partner. To which journals should one submit? It depends on the purpose and target audience. The website www.EvidenceBasedGroupWork.com has links to all the journals and their submission requirements. The journals listed there include, *Group Analysis, Group Dynamics, Group Processes & Intergroup Relations, Groupwork, International Journal of Group Psychotherapy, Journal for Specialists in Group Work, Journal of Groups in Addiction and Recovery, Small Group Research*, and *Social Work with Groups*. Consider *Social Work with Groups* or the British journal *Groupwork*. If one's paper is highly technical in research methodology, consider *Small Group Research*. Other journals in social work that publish technically rigorous research-articles include *Research on Social Work Practice* and a new open-access, peer-reviewed Journal of the Society for Social Work and Research.

If one is not sure how to write a research article, there are guides. Andy Malekoff, the Editor-In-Chief of *Social work with Groups* has written one (Malekoff, 2006). There are guides to publishing qualitative and quantitative studies in the *Journal of Specialists in Group Work* (Asner-Self, 2009; Rubel & Villalba, 2009). A guide for publishing research articles has been written by Bruce Thyer, Editor of *Research on Social Work Practice* (Thyer, 2008). These resources for publishing in group work journals are cited in the social bookmarking site http://delicious.com/EBGW/group-work-journals.

An important issue in writing about group work is including sufficient information about the groups so that adequate interpretations and replications may be made. The lack of information creates two problems. First, "the large number of studies that fail to provide the basic details of the study and its components significantly attenuates the possibility of offering substantive conclusions" (Burlingame, Mackenzie, & Strauss, 2004, p. 680). It also makes it difficult if not impossible to make comparisons with one's group situation. Thus, group work studies need to provide even basic information about the structure of the group (e.g., group size, number of sessions, timing), group composition (e.g., gender, age, ethnicity/race), and leadership (e.g., gender, training and experience, adherence)(see Macgowan, 2008, p. 188 for more details). In sum, ensure that sufficient details about the groups are provided in one's paper.

Summary and conclusions

In summary, these eight components that make up R-E-S-E-A-R-C-H are intended to advance the research enterprise in social work with groups. Readers are encouraged to select one recommendation or letter that is new to them. These are certainly not all the ingredients, but they are important for improving the utilization and generation of group work research.

References

AASWG. (2006). *Standards for social work practice with groups* (2nd edn.). Retrieved July 19, 2010, from http://www.aaswg.org/files/AASWG_Standards_for_Social_Work_Practice_with_Groups.pdf

Allen-Meares, P., Hudgins, C.A., Engberg, M.E & Lessnau, B. (2005). Using a collaboratory model to translate social work research into practice and policy. *Research on Social Work Practice, 15*(1), 29-40.

Asner-Self, K.K. (2009). Research on groups: Writing your quantitative study so that JSGW will publish it; researchers, academics, and practitioners will use it; everyone will benefit; and good quality groups will proliferate. *The Journal for Specialists in Group Work, 34*(3), 195 - 201.

Beck, A.P. & Lewis, C.M. (Eds.). (2000). *The process of group psychotherapy: Systems for analyzing change.* Washington, DC: American Psychological Association.

Birnbaum, M. L., & Wayne, J. (2000). Group work in foundation generalist education: The necessity for curriculum change. *Journal of Social Work Education, 36*(2), 347-356.

Borkovec, T.D. (2004). Research in training clinics and practice research networks: A route to the integration of science and practice. *Clinical Psychologist, 11*(2), 211-215.

Burlingame, G.M., Fuhriman, A. & Johnson, J.E. (2002). Cohesion in group psychotherapy. In J.C. Norcross (Ed.), *Psychotherapy relationships that work: Therapist contributions and responsiveness to patients* (pp. 71-87). New York: Oxford.

Burlingame, G.M., Mackenzie, K.R. & Strauss, B. (2004). Small group treatment: Evidence for effectiveness and mechanisms of change. In M. J. Lambert (Ed.), *Bergin and Garfield's handbook of psychotherapy and behavior change* (5th edn., pp.647-696). Hoboken, NJ: Wiley.

Burlingame, G.M., Strauss, B., Joyce, A., MacNair-Semands, R., MacKenzie, K.R., Ogrodniczuk, J. *et al.* (2006). *CORE Battery - Revised: An assessment toolkit for promoting optimal group selection, process, and outcome.* New York, NY: American Group Psychotherapy Association.

Corey, M.S. & Corey, G. (1997). *Groups: Process and practice* (5th edn.). Pacific Grove, CA: Brooks/Cole.

CSWE (2008). *Educational policy and accreditation standards (EPAS).* Alexandria, VA: Council on Social Work Education.

DeLucia-Waack, J.L. & Bridbord, K.H. (2004). Measures of group process, dynamics, climate, leadership behaviors, and therapeutic factors. In J.L. DeLucia-Waack, D.A. Gerrity, C.R. Kalodner & M. Riva (Eds.), *Handbook of group counseling and psychotherapy* (pp.120-135). Thousand Oaks, CA: Sage Publications.

Dies, R.R. & Teleska, P.A. (1985). Negative outcomes in group psychotherapy. In D.T. Mays & C.M. Franks (Eds.), *Negative outcome in psychotherapy and what to do about it* (pp.118-141). New York: Springer.

Fehr, S.S. (1999). *Introduction to group therapy: A practical guide.* New York: Haworth Press.

Fischer, J. & Corcoran, K. (2007). *Measures for clinical practice and research: A sourcebook* (4th edn. Vol. 1, 2). New York: Oxford University Press.

Fouché, C. & Lunt, N. (2009). Using groups to advance social work practice-based research. *Social Work With Groups, 32*(1), 47-63.

Galinsky, M.J. & Schopler, J.H. (1977). Warning: Groups may be dangerous. *Social Work, 22*(2), 89-94.

Galinsky, M.J. & Schopler, J.H. (1994). Negative experiences in support groups. *Social Work in Health Care, 20*(1), 77-95.

Hait, W.N. (2005). Translating research into clinical practice: Deliberations from the American Association for Cancer Research. *Clinical Cancer Research, 11*(12), 4275-4277.

Hartford, M.E. (1978). Groups in the human services: Some facts and fancies. *Social Work with Groups, 28*(3/4), 7-13.

Haynes, R.B., Sackett, D.L., Gray, J.M., Cook, D.J. & Guyatt, G.H. (1996). Transferring evidence from research into practice: 1. The role of clinical care research evidence in clinical decisions. *ACP Journal Club, 125*(3), A14-16.

Home, A. & Biggs, T. (2005). Evidence-based practice in the real world: A group for mothers of children with invisible disabilities. *Groupwork, 15*(2), 39-60.

Hudgins, C.A. & Allen-Meares, P. (2000). Translational research: A new solution to an old problem? *Journal of Social Work Education, 36*(1), 2-4.

Lese, K.P., & MacNair-Semands, R.R. (2000). The therapeutic factors inventory: Development of a scale. *Group, 24*(4), 303-317.

Levinson, H.M. (1973). Use and misuse of groups. *Social Work, 18*(1), 66-73.

Macgowan, M.J. (2003). Increasing engagement in groups: A measurement based approach. *Social Work with Groups, 26*(1), 5-28.

Macgowan, M.J. (2006). The group engagement measure: A review of its conceptual and empirical properties. *Journal of Groups in Addiction and Recovery, 1*(2), 33-52.

Macgowan, M.J. (2008). *A guide to evidence-based group work.* New York: Oxford University Press.

Macgowan, M.J. (in preparation). Development and preliminary test of an instrument to measure group work knowledge and skills based on the

AASWG Standards for the Practice of Group Work.

Macgowan, M.J. (manuscript submitted for publication). *Teaching standards-based group work competencies to baccalaureate students: An empirical examination.*

Macgowan, M.J. & Newman, F.L. (2005). The factor structure of the group engagement measure. *Social Work Research, 29*(2), 107-118.

MacKenzie, K.R. (1981). Measurement of group climate. *International Journal of Group Psychotherapy, 31*(3), 287-295.

Malekoff, A. (2006). Putting ideas to paper: A guideline for practitioners (and others) who wish to write for publication. *Social Work With Groups, 29*(2), 57-72.

Marincola, F.M. (2003). Translational medicine: A two-way road. *J Transl Med, 1*(1), 1.

Mullen, E.J., & Bacon, W. (2004). Implementation of practice guidelines and evidence-based treatment: A survey of psychiatrists, psychologists, and social workers. In A.R. Roberts & K. Yeager (Eds.), *Evidence-based practice manual: Research and outcome measures in health and human services* (pp.210-218). New York: Oxford University Press.

National Association of Social Workers. (1999). *Code of ethics of the National Association of Social Workers*. Retrieved June 20, 2004, from http://naswdc.org/pubs/code/code.asp

Pollio, D.E. & Macgowan, M.J. (Eds.). (2010). *Evidence-based group work in community settings*. New York: Routledge.

Robbins, R.N. (2003). Developing cohesion in court-mandated group treatment of male spouse abusers. *International Journal of Group Psychotherapy, 53*(3), 261-284.

Rose, S.D. (1984). Use of data in identifying and resolving group problems in goal oriented treatment groups. *Social Work with Groups, 7*(2), 23-36.

Rose, S.D. (1998). *Group therapy with troubled youth: A cognitive behavioral interactive approach*. Thousand Oaks: Sage Publications.

Rubel, D. & Villalba, J.A. (2009). How to publish qualitative research in JSGW: A couple more voices in the conversation. *The Journal for Specialists in Group Work, 34*(4), 295-306.

Rubin, A. & Babbie, E.R. (2008). *Research methods for social work* (6th edn.). Belmont, CA: Thomson Brooks/Cole.

Schopler, J.H. & Galinsky, M.J. (1981). When groups go wrong. *Social Work, 26*, 424-429.

Sherrod, L.R. (1999). 'Giving child development knowledge away': Using university-community partnerships to disseminate research on children, youth, and families. *Applied Developmental Science, 3*(4), 228-234.

Smokowski, P.R., Rose, S.D. & Bacallao, M. (2001). Damaging experiences in therapeutic groups: How vulnerable consumers become group casualties. *Small Group Research, 28*(1), 9-22.

Strauss, B., Burlingame, G.M. & Bormann, B. (2008). Using the CORE-R battery in group psychotherapy. *J Clin Psychol, 64*(11), 1225-1237.

Sweifach, J. & LaPorte, H.H. (2009). Group work in foundation generalist classes: Perceptions of students about the nature and quality of their experience. *Social Work With Groups, 32*(4), 303 - 314.

Thyer, B.A. (2008). *Preparing research articles.* New York: Oxford University Press.

Tolman, R.M. & Molidor, C.E. (1994). A decade of social group work research: Trends in methodology, theory, and program development. *Research on Social Work Practice, 4*(2), 142-159.

Toseland, R.W., Jones, L.V. & Gellis, Z.D. (2004). Group dynamics. In C.D. Garvin, M.J. Galinsky & P.M. Gutierrez (Eds.), *Handbook of social work with groups* (pp.13-31). New York: Guilford.

Toseland, R.W. & Rivas, R.F. (2009). *An introduction to group work practice* (6th edn.). Boston: Pearson/Allyn and Bacon.

Wilson, F.R. & Newmeyer, M.D. (2008). A standards-based inventory for assessing perceived importance of and confidence in using ASGW's core group work skills. *The Journal for Specialists in Group Work, 33*(3), 270 - 289.

15
Some ethical and legal challenges in researching groupwork practice

Michael Preston-Shoot

Abstract: This chapter emphasises the importance of ethical and legal literacy, and of reflecting on organisational culture, when contemplating groupwork and research projects. It draws from research findings, legal judgements and inquiries to alert groupworkers to disconcerting practices in organisations where groupwork and research projects are unfolding. It identifies questions which groupworkers and researchers might ask in order to ensure ethical practice and to realise the potential of groupwork practice and research to improve outcomes for service users and staff.

Keywords: ethics, law, groupwork, research, organisational culture.

Introduction

This chapter draws from personal experience as a university researcher inquiring into local government organisations with social services responsibilities in the United Kingdom (UK), and into the effectiveness of social work education and groupwork practice. It also draws from experience of researching the interface between law, ethics and professional practice, and from reviewing the literature about the lived experience of work of social welfare professionals. Some parallels are also drawn with episodes in health care organisations.

The chapter begins with some observations about research ethics, prompted by experiences when conducting research within social services organisations. To broaden the focus on ethical and legal challenges surrounding practitioners and managers, it then connects these observations with research findings, legal judgements and conclusions from inquiries into serious case failures. Here the paper addresses some disconcerting and, arguably unasked questions about aspects of practice in social work agencies, including the under-utilisation of research findings. The focus then moves to questions that researchers might ask of themselves and of the organisations commissioning or hosting their explorations.

On approving research ethics

Groupworkers who have obtained ethical approval for research projects will have experienced the challenges of completing forms and defending submissions. With the increasing emphasis on accountability and on safeguarding service users, ethical approval processes have become more rigorous. However, the focus of ethical scrutiny will have been predominantly on the researchers and their proposals, on the time period before research projects commence, and on their processes for securing the active consent of participants and ensuring protection of their well-being. There appears to have been much less focus on the organisations commissioning or hosting the research. Indeed, a pervading assumption appears to be that the organisational context is benign and hospitable. In the foreground will have been the researcher's competence, motivations, capacity and behaviour. Kept in the background are the ethical issues that might arise once the research has begun and how these might be negotiated should they arise (Preston-Shoot *et al.*, 2008).

The argument here is not whether the process of ethical scrutiny and approval actually safeguards or guarantees research standards. That debate may be held elsewhere. The proposition advanced here is that the ethical questions, asked when approval for research studies is sought, should be broadened. Thus, when researchers seek contracts, grants and permissions, they might consider the environment into which they will be entering. For instance, what might be the challenges of entering an organisation that has been judged to have acted unlawfully or unethically, in respect of its workforce and/or people using its services? They might question also the commissioning or hosting organisation's competence, capacity and motivations. For instance, research may be commissioned and utilised to improve services, delay or seek justification for a particular policy or practice change, or influence quite selectively how contested issues might be framed (Weiss, 1979). This may partly explain the scepticism that researchers and practitioners sometimes articulate, namely whether political and management commitment exists to change policy and practice in line with research findings (Humphreys *et al*, 2003; Joint University Council Social Work Education Committee [JUCSWEC], 2006). How, then, does the research proposal fit into the organisation's context or tasks? Equally pertinent might be the knowledge and skills of agency managers to maintain an environment suitable for research, and the degree to which an organisational culture values and uses learning.

When seeking approval for research projects and when navigating through subsequent dilemmas and challenges, codes of research ethics (Economic and Social Research Council [ESRC], 2005; Association for the Advancement of Social Work with Groups [AASWG], 2006) highlight everyone's responsibility to maintain standards and safeguard ethics, for example when exploring whether people are consenting to participate. However, this responsibility for ensuring quality and accountability is usually placed on researchers rather than organisational managers. The organisational context is assumed to be unproblematic. Contextual impacts may be acknowledged but are not elaborated. For instance, groupwork standards (AASWG, 2006) include in core knowledge for practice the capacity of members to contribute to social change in the community beyond the group. Whether this includes the organisation hosting the group is uncertain. What the response should be if the organisation is not open to learning and change is also unclear. Groupworkers are held responsible for assessing the likely impact of the community and agency context, and for exploring the institutional barriers that may impact on the development of groupwork. Parallel responsibilities are not given to agency managers. Why should this matter?

Ethics in an organisational context

Groupwork standards (AASWG, 2006) focus squarely on the ethics of the groupworker's actions and on the rights of group members. Quite appropriately the emphasis is on obtaining the informed consent of potential group members, ensuring that they perceive a freedom to exit the programme, and maintaining appropriate levels of confidentiality. Attention is drawn to assessing and managing risks that may arise in groups, and to how power is exercised by groupworkers. The standards also require groupworkers to orientate their practice around current knowledge and research. Workers are responsible for systematically monitoring and evaluating group processes and outcomes. This requires knowledge concerning methods of evaluation and goal measurement. Left unexplored is whether there are organisational responsibilities regarding any of these components of groupwork and research practice.

In the UK, for instance, long-standing concerns remain about the availability of continuing professional development, and the degree to which some employers value research knowledge as opposed to procedural knowledge (Marsh and Triseliotis, 1996; Karban and Frost, 1998; Social Work Taskforce, 2009). Newly qualified social workers report frustration at being unable to use social work skills and whether they work for learning organisations (Bates *et al*, 2010). Equally, there is limited evidence of effectiveness for three models for promoting research-mindedness and use in organisations (Walter *et al*, 2004): the research-based practitioner model where responsibility resides with the individual professional; the embedded research model where responsibility rests with policy-makers and managers to construct and maintain systems for disseminating knowledge; and the organisational excellence model where partnerships and culture feature strongly. A whole system approach may be the best way forward, involving managers and practitioners, researchers and policy-makers. Currently, however, just how research-minded an organisation is could be questionable, with a lack of familiarity with current research among practice teachers, supervisors and managers potentially affecting the confidence that practitioners can place in taking forward their training into practice and in discussing the interface between research and practice.

Codes of research ethics will be mirrored by more general

codes (National Association of Social Workers [NASW], 1996; General Social Care Council [GSCC], 2002) and, to varying degrees in different countries, supported by national legislation and international conventions, which lay out standards for practice. Thus, the European Convention on Human Rights and Fundamental Freedoms, incorporated into UK law by the Human Rights Act 1998, provides for the right to private and family life, the right to liberty and the right to live free of inhuman and degrading treatment. So, when researching groupwork, and social services interventions more generally, researchers as well as practitioners and managers should emphasise human dignity and worth, enhance people's well-being and ensure their protection, and promote their rights. They should challenge and work to improve organisational procedures and service provision, highlighting particularly when resource shortages or other difficulties impact on safe working practices.

Employment law and codes of practice may also articulate organisational responsibility for the well-being of staff. In the UK (GSCC, 2002) employers must inform staff about relevant legislation for their work and provide effective supervision. They must provide an environment that is committed to social work values, principles and knowledge, and support practitioners to avoid putting their registration at risk. They should establish systems to facilitate the reporting of operational difficulties. Clearly, practitioners are employed because of their knowledge and skills. The practice (and research) environment should facilitate the deployment of such knowledge and skills. Additionally, codes and benchmarks also stress the place of research in practice. The NASW code (1996) emphasises research-based service. In the UK, practice should be based on evidence, or be research-informed, with practitioners knowledgeable about, and skilled in reviewing their effectiveness in meeting need and in evaluating intervention outcomes (GSCC, 2002; Quality Assurance Agency [QAA], 2008).

Several critical questions arise here. The first relates to the interface between law and ethics. When groupworkers and researchers encounter practice that is both lawful and ethical, or unlawful and unethical, their response may not feel problematic. However, two scenarios are more challenging. One concerns how to respond when actual or proposed practice is lawful but unethical, as possibly when requiring a parent with day-to-day responsibility for a child to comply with court orders mandating contact with a non-resident parent with a history of domestic oppression. The other focuses on practice that is unlawful but ethical. Assisting failed asylum seekers with financial and social support illustrates this position in England. It could be the ethical thing to do but is currently unlawful. Social workers are enjoined, including when practising as groupworkers and researchers, to act lawfully and ethically. The lived experience of work may be more complicated than the codes give guidance for. The interface between law and professional ethics is not as unproblematic as codes assume (Preston-Shoot, 2010).

The second critical reflection relates to the nature of some groupwork programmes. For various "client" groups, including involuntary service users, off-the-peg groupwork models are used. Some evidence indicates their effectiveness but ethical questions arise surrounding the imposition of preset plans and the focus on set tasks, which may not take account of how people learn and work, or of their needs and valued outcomes, or of processes and dynamics within the group (Preston-Shoot, 2007). More generally, for groupwork and other forms of practice, although practitioners have an ethical obligation to keep up-to-date with research into how individual and social problems might be understood and tackled, the evidence of research use is disappointingly variable (Sheldon and Chilvers, 2002; Macgowan, 2006; Walter *et al*, 2004). In the UK also, at least, the degree to which groupworkers are adding to, and synthesising research findings also appears weak (Preston-Shoot, 2004).

The third relates to whether the reach of ethical codes is sufficient and whether they provide adequate protection (Preston-Shoot, 2010; 2011). There is disconcerting evidence, in the UK, the United States, Australia and elsewhere, of social workers feeling unsupported within and pressurised by a management culture that proves hard to resist. There are disturbing parallels too with health services, with examples of poor practice, the absence of dignity and respect, failure to monitor performance adequately, and deep reluctance to investigate complaints (Kline & Preston-Shoot, 2012). Both research into law and ethics in an organisational context, and hearings before tribunals to consider whether or not to revoke a social worker's licence to practise, uncover evidence of inadequate supervision, chaotic departments, absence of support, workloads that exceed the competence and capacity of staff, lack of resources to cope with the volume of demands, and lack of an effective management response. Published standards for service providers appear unable to ensure moral probity or ethical and effective practice, and currently in the UK lack statutory force. Thus, the sanctions against individual registered social workers who transgress the code of practice (GSCC, 2002) are clear. They include removal from the register and, therefore, loss of the ability to practise as a social worker. The sanctions against employers, whose actions can affect profoundly the confidence and well-being of staff, are far from obvious.

Moreover, in the face of management pressures, practitioners may lack the confidence to assert the requirements of their practice codes in an effort to ensure ethical, lawful and evidence-based practice, especially since the codes may not be embedded in employment contracts. They may not feel the autonomous agents, able to act independently of their organisational context, that the codes seem to assume (Lonne *et al*, 2004). Equally, for those practitioners who whistle blow, the outcomes can be depressingly negative in terms of how they are treated subsequently (Preston-Shoot and Kline, 2009), with research (Hunt, 1998; Musil *et al*, 2004) also finding that organisations are willing to play down ethical breaches. Finally, in their failure to draw attention to problematic practice contexts, the codes may oversimplify the challenges that social workers, including groupworkers, encounter.

Judgements on practice

Most social workers, including groupworkers, are conscientious, performing valuable work and demonstrating care, skill and dedication in meeting people's needs. However, they are often overworked and lack the resources to practise as they would like and as they have been trained for. Thus, a mixed picture emerges from the evidence, both national and international, when researching judicial decisions and inquiries into cases where people's health and well-being have not been protected (Preston-Shoot, 2010). Whilst there are examples of excellent practice, often in difficult circumstances, there are also examples where practice has been unlawful and/or unethical, and where decisions have not been care-ful. The need to achieve targets or to manage within limited resources can dominate or distort decision-making. Attitudes may convey indifference to people's situations. Legal rules on assessment and care planning have been ignored. Research evidence also reveals bullying in health and welfare organisations (Balloch *et al*, 1999; Preston-Shoot, 2010), and negative responses from managers towards staff who whistle blow (Kline & Preston-Shoot, 2012).

Internationally research evidence (Lonne *et al*, 2004; Strom-Gottfried, 2000; Musil *et al*, 2004; Preston-Shoot, 2010) points to some organisations where there is an erosion of ethical practice, resistance to the requirements of the legal rules, and erratic supervision and continuing professional development. Practitioner and service user concerns and complaints are dismissed or inadequately investigated. Challenge is not welcomed. Research evidence also points to practitioners and managers colluding with unacceptable practice (Horwath, 2000) and foregrounding organisational procedures and policy rather than legal rules and ethical principles (Braye *et al*, 2007). The dominance of agency procedures presupposes that they are an accurate interpretation of legal rules and ethical principles when, as judicial judgements and inquiry reports have shown, reliance on such confidence might be seriously misplaced.

Once again, the disconcerting practice outcomes of the interface between law, ethics and professionalism are not restricted to social work alone. A systematic review of the international literature on law teaching to medical students also identified concerns about the reach into practice of law and ethics teaching in medical academic curricula, and drew attention to the existence of a hidden or silent curriculum where, effectively, health care staff feel too uncomfortable to challenge the instructions of their superiors and where organisational policies and decision-making hierarchies undermine a professional's knowledge base and formal education (Preston-Shoot and McKimm, 2010). In such contexts ethical codes and legal rules have insufficient reach to guarantee standards – their wording is too general, their relationship to employment contracts unclear, their guidance inadequate for tricky "what if?" situations, and the sanctions against employers unclear whilst those against registered practitioners are much starker. What is essentially taking place is the erosion or distortion of professional formation (Green, 2009).

Two research examples from adult protection reinforce the argument. Manthorpe and colleagues (2007) report on neglect and mistreatment of older people by residential care staff, the lack of attention to people's basic needs, and the negative attitude towards those who complain. Flynn (2006) points to system-wide failures and structural lethargy in one organisation that amounted to inhumanity and deprived the agency concerned of authority and legitimacy. She found out-of-date, inflexible and ineffective policies and procedures, and managers with no sense of how damaging or impoverished the organisation's services were. Complaints had been poorly investigated and, with parallels to how whistle blowers have been regarded and treated in social work and health care more generally (Stephenson *et al*, 2001; Kline & Preston-Shoot, 2012), no recognition of the bravery of practitioners and managers who do challenge organisational failings. Threats, subtle or otherwise, of disciplinary measures and exclusion, create pressures to comply with the directives of managers and senior colleagues, undermining human agency and moral responsibility (Green, 2009). In such environments, can groupwork and research achieve their transformational potential? In this context too, it is additionally disturbing that practitioners may perceive the law as difficult to understand and/or implement, particularly in respect of information-sharing and human rights (Perkins *et al*, 2007; Pinkney *et al*, 2008). They may also perceive values in the same light when encountering management expectations that erode the capacity to maintain an ethical orientation (Marsh and Triseliotis, 1996; Hunt, 1998; Banks and Williams, 2005; Preston-Shoot, 2010).

Finding the viruses

When overturning a decision by one local authority to restrict the services being offered to a disabled young woman and her mother, a judge compared it to a computer system that had been infected by a virus (R (CD and VD) v Isle of Anglesey County Council [2004] 7 CCLR 589). The judge did not articulate what the virus might be but the metaphor is powerful. How might the evidence be explained that organisations established to act care-fully can demonstrate actions that are care-less? Then, if legal rules on whistle blowing, coupled with the ethical codes, are designed to counter viruses, why do they seem to fail to act protectively?

Wardhaugh and Wilding (1993) seek to explain this corruption of care. They focus on how professionals react to the issues that service users bring, the dynamics that occur within organisations, and the incompleteness of a framework that can hold both individuals and agencies accountable. The components of their model coalesce around four themes, namely:

- "Client" characteristics lead to a neutralisation of moral concerns;
- Power and process in enclosed organisations;
- Complexity of work exacerbated by constraints;
- Absence of accountability.

Adams and Balfour (1998) focus much more on the dynamics within and between organisations, and on the organisational impact on individual staff. They shine a light on administrative evil, which comprises:

- Conformity to organisational procedures;
- Dulling of conscience and absence of independent critical thought;
- Erosion of personal judgement;
- Public policy-making encouraging moral inversion.

These two models, together with the research findings reported above on the sometimes collusive relationship between practitioners and managers, and the tolerant silence surrounding poor practice and the distortion of professionalism, require groupworkers and researchers to engage in personal as well as organisational appraisal. Social work is meant to be a moral activity, promoting social change, individual well-being and human rights (QAA, 2008). To what degree have practitioners and managers become prisoners of bureaucracy? Or, are they still able to hold conversations that cross hierarchies and positional status? Nor should these only be questions for social work. Health care has also been prone to ethical erosion (Branch, 2000; Kroll *et al*, 2008).

Perhaps what these questions and models also bring to mind is the notion of groupthink (Janis, 1972) and what can happen to organisations when people coalesce around one perspective and discount contradictory evidence. This raises the interesting thought of the degree to which communities of researchers and groupworkers have accessed the literature on power within groups and organisations, and have embedded within their knowledge and skill set such a groupwork literacy.

The models do not fully capture, arguably, another virus that has entered state social work. Ethical codes assume that practitioners are autonomous. However, the lack of autonomy, actual or perceived, in their terms of employment, may prove a barrier to research utilisation. Many practitioners do not draw on research findings (Sheldon and

Chilvers, 2002; Walter *et al*, 2004; Bellamy *et al*, 2006; Macgowan, 2006). Common explanations for this feature of practice include the lack of fit between research outcomes and the work environment, the poor translation of research methods and findings into viable practices, suspicion of research and a (misplaced) conviction that research and practice skills are different, and limited awareness of how to access and evaluate findings. Phrased more positively, research findings should be accessible, and synthesised where a body of knowledge exists (Walter *et al*, 2004; JUCSWEC, 2006; Macgowan, 2006), with social services organisations supporting actively their generation and use (Sheldon and Chilvers, 2002; Macgowan, 2006; Bellamy *et al*, 2006). Put another way, research has to capture the uniqueness and complexity of the problems that practitioners encounter (Humphreys *et al*, 2003; Macgowan, 2006).

What is then proposed is a partnership between researchers and practitioners, the creation of tools for dissemination of findings, and methods designed to improve the capacity and confidence of practitioners to undertake research, to read reported studies critically, and to discern the relevance of findings to their context of service delivery (Marsh and Fisher, 2005; Carpenter, 2005). This last point is crucial because a training deficit exists, with practitioners voicing a lack of knowledge, skills and confidence for conducting research about their practice (Preston-Shoot, 2004; Bellamy *et al*, 2006). However, whilst not disputing the value of these analyses, alone they will prove insufficient. High workloads, the target-driven pace of decision-making and time constraints on reflective space combine to deter the search for and application of evidence about what works, for whom, in what situations. Groupworker researchers disseminating their findings ever more actively, and therefore not just through journal papers, is only a partial solution. The lived experience of work for social workers and groupworkers, including their standing as professionals rather than as employees, also has to be addressed.

Questions before researching practice

To be asked to evaluate practice can be quite seductive, especially if accompanied with a sizeable grant. However, experience (Preston-

Shoot *et al*, 2008) has reinforced the importance of asking critical questions when contemplating whether to accept particular research commissions. The questions are just as applicable for groupworkers contemplating whether to run a group. The first explores what led to the proposed research commission and possibility to run a group project. Essentially, this is a systemic focus on the referring person and their context. It expresses curiosity about the timing, content and focus of the proposed brief. The second tackles how these ideas might be perceived by all those who might be involved – researchers, groupworkers, staff and service users. It continues the systemic inquiry and may include convening all those surrounding the proposal in order to keep communication channels open and facilitate scrutiny of key relationships. The third encourages outsider and insider researchers to appraise the organisational context into which they might be entering. For whom is it (un)safe? What is the likely impact of being an outsider or insider researcher or groupwork practitioner? How does this organisation value evidence? Is it possible to convene people to ask them what this research or groupwork is for, why it is being proposed now, who it might be what type of problem for, and what to do if particular eventualities arise?

These considerations focus on the importance of the researcher's (and groupworker's) curiosity. For example, how prominent are values and ethics in this organisation? Equally, how embedded are practice codes? Whether or not research participants are staff or service users, can they *really* actively consent or refuse to participate? Is there <u>really</u> a safe space in which research can take place or will the project be exposing either staff and/or service users to further stress? Will there be an opportunity to make use of the findings that emerge from the project? What these questions address is scrutiny of triangular relationships – between researchers, research participants and those in the surrounding organisational context, and equally between groupworkers, group members and the agency in which the group meets and works.

Disconcerting questions for groupwork

The registration of social workers, the creation of key performance indicators, and the opening up to challenge through the courts of the practice of organisations performing public functions (Human Rights Act 1998) demonstrate an increasing preoccupation with accountability. However, within this accountability mosaic, the place of social work and groupwork research evidence, at least in the UK, remains under-developed and under-resourced (JUCSWEC, 2006). Increased investment in research capacity, for instance through joint practitioner-researcher career paths, should target development of workforce skills in critically appraising and applying research findings, and integrating these signposts with practice wisdom and learning from service users. However, research budgets within social work service delivery organisations remain small, if not non-existent. Research funding available from central government departments, whether directly or through the Centre for Excellence and Outcomes and the Social Care Institute for Excellence, remains driven by policy-makers' priorities. A real need remains to address the problems arising from the lived experience of work in agencies.

Equally, groupwork's own evidence-base is thin (Preston-Shoot, 2004). Arguably, groupwork has yet to collate and disseminate the components of its evidence base. Long overdue is the task of presenting the evidence, perhaps initially through systematic reviews, and then exploring with practitioners the implications for further research and service delivery. This synthesis will need to capture insights from different types of knowledge for practice, including service user and practitioner perspectives (Humphreys *et al*, 2003; Pawson *et al*, 2003; Grey and McDonald, 2006; Macgowan, 2006).

Additionally, the proposition that a failure to incorporate evidence into practice is itself a violation of codes of ethics is far from secure. Evaluative evidence remains scarce and research skills under-developed on qualifying social work programmes in the UK. The post-qualifying social work framework does not extend to doctoral level, currently, and does not foreground the development of research skills. It is still possible to find practitioners, managers and groupwork researchers who say that assessing evidence of effectiveness is too challenging or, if attempted, has proved insufficiently rigorous and systematic.

Arguably, especially in statutory agencies, the dominant culture has become one of demonstrating institutional success and the achievement of targets (Green, 2009). Other values have become marginalised, undermining professional integrity. There is little evidence in specialist journals about how groupwork has responded to practitioner and organisational need for success, or the rising eligibility thresholds and the paucity of provision that have come to characterise statutory services. Research continues to draw attention to the impact of managerialism and procedural practice on staff and service users alike (Chard and Ayre, 2010). Have groupwork knowledge and skills been used to challenge the disconcerting organisational context sketched out herein? The evidence in child care (Sinclair and Bullock, 2002; Office for Standards in Education, 2009) is that policy-makers and managers in social services organisations have yet to learn the repeating lessons. These focus on the need for reflective space, particularly in supervision, the importance of time for building relationships, the confidence to express curiosity through asking challenging questions, and the centrality of transparent communication.

Focusing forward

This final section is about creating a future for social work, and in particular groupwork research. Hitherto the chapter has stressed the importance of an ethical and legal literacy when contemplating research into practice. In relation to ethical literacy it has identified the importance of a relational context for research projects, where responsibility is jointly owned and when the "health" of organisations (Social Work Taskforce, 2009) is scrutinised as much as the competence of groupwork researchers. It has stressed the importance of practitioners having ethical reasoning skills (Grey and McDonald, 2006), and the confidence that their employing organisations value their deployment. It has implied the value of having spaces in which to work through tricky "what if" situations, whether by means of formal reviews, periodic ethical audits of practice, or use of supervision and consultation. In relation to legal literacy, it requires groupwork practitioners and researchers to have considered, for instance, not just when they would highlight evidence of significant harm experienced by group members, but under what circumstances they would share information also about the organisational context.

This chapter invites a focus on where might the spaces be in which to think about when and how to challenge poor practice? How and when do researchers mediate between research participants and those surrounding them in the organisational context? How do researchers understand and manage the fact that research makes more public and observable what is often more private, secluded, or hidden from view? How do we manage the personal in the research interview – not just the impact on the researcher but what the participant discloses beyond the focus of the project?

In summary, the literacy on which practice and research depend revolves partly around the distillation of knowledge, understanding, skill and values that enables practitioners to connect relevant legal rules with professional priorities and objectives of ethical practice, and with the knowledge and skills of groupwork. Harnessed to this is the emotional resilience to comment, challenge, critique and resist. This requires the creation of spaces where individuals and their organisations can think through how to act care-fully. It also requires the recognition of what groupwork knowledge and skills can contribute to navigating these challenges. It holds out the hope that groupwork and research, together and individually, can enable organisations to improve the environment offered to employees and the provision offered to service users.

References

Adams, G. and Balfour, D. (1998). *Unmasking administrative evil.* London: Sage.

Association for the Advancement of Social Work with Groups (2006). *Standards for social work practice with groups* (2nd edn.). Akron, OH: AASWG.

Balloch, S., McLean, J. & Fisher, M. (1999). *Social services: Working under pressure.* Bristol: Policy Press.

Banks, S. & Williams, R. (2005) Accounting for ethical difficulties in social welfare work: issues, problems and dilemmas. *British Journal of Social Work, 35*(7), 1005-1022.

Bates, N., Immins, T., Parker, J., Keen, S., Rutter, L., Brown, K. & Zsigo, S. (2010). Baptism of fire: the first year in the life of a newly qualified social worker. *Social Work Education, 29*(2), 152-170.

Bellamy, J., Bledsoe, S. & Traube, D. (2006). The current state of evidence-based practice in social work: a review of the literature and qualitative analysis of expert interviews. *Journal of Evidence-Based Practice, 3*(1),

23-48.

Branch, W. (2000). Supporting the moral development of medical students. *J. Gen Intern Med, 15*, 503-508.

Braye, S., Preston-Shoot, M. & Thorpe, A. (2007). Beyond the classroom: learning social work law in practice. *Journal of Social Work, 7*(3), 322-340.

Carpenter, J. (2005). *Evaluating outcomes in social work education.* London: Social Care Institute for Excellence.

Chard, A. & Ayre, P. (2010). Managerialism – at the tipping point? In P. Ayre & M. Preston-Shoot (Eds.) *Children's services at the crossroads: A critical evaluation of contemporary policy for practice.* Lyme Regis: Russell House Publishing.

Economic and Social Research Council (2005). *Research ethics framework.* Swindon: ESRC.

Flynn, M. (2006). Joint investigation into the provision of services for people with learning disabilities at Cornwall Partnership NHS Trust. *Journal of Adult Protection, 8*(3), 28-32.

Green, J. (2009). The deformation of professional formation: managerial targets and the undermining of professional judgement. *Ethics and Social Welfare, 3*(2), 115-130.

Grey, M. & McDonald, C. (2006). Pursuing good practice? The limits of evidence-based practice. *Journal of Social Work, 6*(1), 7-20.

GSCC (2002). *Codes of practice for social care workers and employers.* London: General Social Care Council.

Horwath, J. (2000). Child care with gloves on: protecting children and young people in residential care. *British Journal of Social Work, 30*(2), 179-191.

Humphreys, C., Berridge, D., Butler, I. & Ruddick, R. (2003). Making research count: the development of 'knowledge-based practice'. *Research Policy and Planning, 21*(1), 11-19.

Hunt, G. (Ed.) (1998). *Whistleblowing in the social services. Public accountability and professional practice.* London: Arnold.

Janis, I. (1972). *Victims of groupthink: A psychological study of foreign policy decisions and fiascos.* Boston, MA: Houghton Mifflin.

JUCSWEC (2006). *A social work research strategy in higher education 2006-2020.* London: Social Care Workforce Research Unit, Kings College.

Karban, K. & Frost, N. (1998). Training for residential care: assessing the impact of the Residential Child Care Initiative. *Social Work Education, 17*(3), 287-300.

Kline R. & Preston-Shoot, M. (2012) *Professional accountability in social care and health: Challenging unacceptable practice and its management.* London: Sage/Learning Matters.

Kroll, L., Singleton, A., Collier, J. & Rees Jones, I. (2008). Learning not to take it seriously: Junior doctors' accounts of error. *Medical Education*, 42, 982-990.

Lonne, B., McDonald, C. & Fox, T. (2004). Ethical practice in the contemporary human services. *Journal of Social Work*, 4(3), 345-367.

Macgowan, M. (2006). Evidence-based group work: a framework for advancing best practice. *Journal of Evidence-Based Practice*, 3(1), 1-21.

Manthorpe, J., Cornes, M., Moriarty, J., Rapaport, J., Iliffe, S., Wilcock, J., Clough, R., Bright, L. & OPRSI (2007). An inspector calls: adult protection in the context of the NSFOP review. *Journal of Adult Protection*, 9(1), 4-14.

Marsh, P. & Fisher, M. (2005). *Developing the evidence base for social work and social care practice*. London: Social Care Institute for Excellence.

Marsh, P. & Triseliotis, J. (1996). *Ready to practise? Social workers and probation officers: Their training and first year in work*. Aldershot: Avebury.

Musil, L., Kubalčíková, K., Hubíková, O. & Nečasová, M. (2004). Do social workers avoid the dilemmas of work with clients? *European Journal of Social Work*, 7(3), 305-319.

NASW (1996). *Code of ethics*. Washington, DC: National Association of Social Workers.

Office for Standards in Education (2009). *Learning lessons from serious case reviews: Year 2*. Manchester: OFSTED.

Pawson, R., Boaz, A., Grayson, L., Long, A. & Barnes, C. (2003). *Types and quality of knowledge in social care*. London: Social Care Institute for Excellence.

Perkins, N., Penhale, B., Reid, D., Pinkney, L., Hussein, S. & Manthorpe, J. (2007). Partnership means protection? Perceptions of the effectiveness of multi-agency working and the regulatory framework within adult protection in England and Wales. *Journal of Adult Protection*, 9(3), 9-23.

Pinkney, L., Penhale, B., Manthorpe, J., Perkins, N., Reid, D. & Hussein, S. (2008). Voices from the frontline: social work practitioners' perceptions of multi-agency working in adult protection in England and Wales. *Journal of Adult Protection*, 10(4), 12-24.

Preston-Shoot, M. (2004). Evidence: the final frontier? Star Trek, groupwork and the mission of change. *Groupwork*, 14(3), 18-43.

Preston-Shoot, M. (2007). *Effective Groupwork* (2nd edn.). Basingstoke: Palgrave Macmillan.

Preston-Shoot, M. (2010). On the evidence for viruses in social work systems: law, ethics and practice. *European Journal of Social Work*, 13(4), 465-482.

Preston-Shoot, M. (2011). On administrative evil-doing within social work policy and services: law, ethics and practice. *European Journal of Social Work*, 14(2), 177-194.

Preston-Shoot, M. & Kline, R. (2009). Memorandum of written evidence . In House of Commons Children, Schools and Families Committee *Training of children and families social workers. Seventh report of session 2008-09* (vol. II). London: The Stationery Office.

Preston-Shoot, M. & McKimm, J. (2010). *Teaching, learning and assessment of law in medical education.* Coventry and Newcastle upon Tyne: The Higher Education Academy UK Centre for Legal Education and The Higher Education Academy Subject Centre for Medicine, Dentistry and Veterinary Medicine.

Preston-Shoot, M., Wigley, V., McMurray, I. & Connolly, H. (2008). Reflections on ethical research in action: working at the practice edge. *Ethics and Social Welfare, 2,* 150-171.

QAA (2008). *Subject benchmark statements: Social work.* Gloucester: Quality Assurance Agency for Higher Education.

Sheldon, B. & Chilvers, R. (2002). An empirical study of the obstacles to evidence-based practice. *Social Work and Social Sciences Review, 10*(1), 6-26.

Sinclair, R.& Bullock, R. (2002). *Learning from past experience – A review of serious case reviews.* London: Department of Health.

Social Work Task Force (2009). *Building a safe, confident future. The final report of the Social Work Task Force.* London: The Stationery Office.

Stephenson, A., Higgs, R. & Sugarman, J. (2001). Teaching professional development in medical schools. *The Lancet, 357,* 867-870.

Strom-Gottfried, K. (2000). Ensuring ethical practice: an examination of NASW Code Violations, 1986-97. *Social Work, 45*(3), 251-261.

Walter, I., Nutley, S., Percy-Smith, J., McNeish, D. & Frost, S. (2004). *Improving the use of research in social care practice.* London: Social Care Institute for Excellence.

Wardhaugh, J. & Wilding, P. (1993). Towards an explanation of the corruption of care. *Critical Social Policy, 37,* 4-31.

Weiss, C. (1979). The many meanings of research utilization. *Public Administration Review, 39,* 426-431.

Index

organisational dynamics 235
organisational excellence model 229
organisational lethargy 233–4
Osterman, J.E. 133
outcome measures 214–15
Outcome Questionnaire 214

Papell, C.B. 180
parent-buddy training group 120
parent education and support group 119–20
Parteleno-Barehmi, C. 136
partnership, research and practice 236
Parveen, S. 156
peace, basis of 1, 3–4
pedagogy 47–8
   banking system 56–7
peer consultation
   absence of authority figure 67
   abstract 61
   areas for development 71
   cohesion 68
   context and overview 61–2
   group members 68
   group process 69
   implications 70–1
   limitations 70–1
   literature 65–7
   model 68–70
   nature of 64
   preparation 68–9
   questions 70
   skills 69
   strengths 71
   structure and routine 70
   see also mutual aid
peer-helpers 180, 191, 192
peer relations 162–3
perinatal parent association, parent advisory committee (PAC) 120
personal agendas 98–9
Pinderhugues, R. 169
Plan d'action individualisé de rétablissement (PAIR) *see* Wellness Recovery
         Action Plan (WRAP)
polarization 10

www.ingramcontent.com/pod-product-compliance
Lightning Source LLC
Chambersburg PA
CBHW050408280326
41932CB00013BA/1778

* 9 7 8 1 8 6 1 7 7 1 2 6 1 *